The Judge's Book

National Conference of State Trial Judges

Produced under a grant from
the American Bar Association Fund for
Justice and Education and a gift from
Judge George H. Revelle

American Bar Association
Chicago

Printed in the United States of America.

Library of Congress Catalog Card Number:
88-83421
ISBN: 0-89707-410-6

94 93 92 91 90 5 4 3 2 1

A good judge must have an enormous concern with life, animate and inanimate, and a sense of its tempestuous and untamed streaming. Without such fire in his belly, as Holmes also called it, he will turn into a stuffed shirt the instant a robe is put around him. The first signs of judicial taxidermy are impatience with trivial matters, and the statement that his time is being wasted, for the secret of a judge's work is that ninety-nine percent of it is with trivial matters, and that none of them will shake the cosmos very much. But they are apt to shake the litigants gravely. It is only his power over people that makes them treat him as a demi-god, for government touches them more perceptibly in the courtroom than at any other point in their lives. The cosmos is made up of little quivers, and it is important that they be set in reasonable unison. Show me an impatient judge and I will call him a public nuisance to his face. Let him be quick, if he must be, but not unconcerned, ever. Worse than judicial error is it to mishandle impatiently the small affairs of momentarily helpless people, and judges should be impeached for it.

Curtis Bok, *I Too, Nicodemus*

CONTENTS

CONTENTS

THE AUTHORS

Hon. Donald R. Fretz, editor, has been on the California Superior Court since his election in 1962. He was President of the California Judges Association in 1970-71, and Chair of the National Conference of State Trial Judges in 1980-81. He was the founding Dean of the California College of Trial Judges (1967-68) and taught judicial ethics there for fifteen years. He is a graduate of the first session of the National Judicial College in 1964, was a faculty advisor in 1966, taught there in 1967 and from 1970 to 1986. He is the author of *Courts and the News Media, Courts and the Public*, and *Ethics for Judges*, all of which are used as textbooks at the National Judicial College. He has written numerous articles for the *American Bar Association Journal* and other legal publications. The father of three daughters, Judge Fretz enjoys fishing, golfing, and raising and showing camellias, and he is active in his church, in Boy Scouting (Silver Beaver and Silver Antelope Awards), and Masonry (33°). In addition to being this book's editor, Judge Fretz authored a number of chapters in this book, including "The Family Effect," "Alternative Dispute Resolution," "Pretrial and Settlement Proceedings," "Trial By Court," "Listening," "Note Taking," "Decision Making," "Judicial Discretion," "Ethics for Judges," "The Judge and the Communities," and "Judicial Education."

Ronald L. Ellis is a 1975 graduate of New York University Law School where he was a Root-Tilden Scholar and an Editor for the Moot Court Board. He has been an Assistant Counsel with the NAACP Legal Defense and Educational Fund since 1976

where he has been the Director of the Fund's Fair Employment Law Program. Mr. Ellis is an Adjunct Professor of Law at New York University and has taught courses in "Racism and American Law" and "Employment Discrimination." He has lectured widely on employment discrimination, affirmative action and litigation techniques. Ellis co-authored the gender bias section of the chapter entitled "Avoiding Race and Gender Bias in the Courtroom" in this book and contributed to its chapter on "Integration of Women and Minority Judges into the American Judiciary."

Hon. Hilda R. Gage has been on the Sixth Judicial Circuit Court of Michigan since 1978. Judge Gage is a past Chair of the National Conference of State Trial Judges, and past President of the Michigan Judges Association. She has also served as Chairperson of the National Conference of State Trial Judges Court Delay Reduction Committee, which promulgated the Court Delay Reduction Standards and is appointed to the National Judicial College Board of Directors, where she serves as faculty in Caseflow Management. Judge Gage has authored numerous articles, including "Delay: How to Reduce the Docket," in the *Judge's Journal*. In the present book, Judge Gage co-authored the chapter on "Court Management and Delay Reduction."

Hon. Kenneth L. Gillis has been a Judge of the Circuit Court of Cook County for ten years and is currently assigned to its Chancery Division. Judge Gillis is a 1961 graduate of the University of Chicago Law School. He serves on the faculty of the National Judicial College in Reno and also teaches Trial Advocacy at the Illinois Institute of Technology Chicago-Kent School of Law. He is a member of the Executive Committee of the National Conference of State Trial Judges of the American Bar Association, where he also serves as the editor of that conference's newsletter, the *Trial Judges News*. Judge Gillis is also Third Vice-President of the Illinois Judges Association. Judge Gillis contributed two chapters to this book: "Trial by Jury," and "Courtroom Control."

Stephen Goldspiel is Staff Director of the ABA National Conference of State Trial Judges. He also serves as Staff Director for the Judicial Administration Division Lawyers Conference, the Committee on the Traffic Court Program, and the ABA Standing Committee on Judicial Selection, Tenure, and Compensation. In addition, he represents the ABA on national organizations including the National Committee on Uniform Traffic Laws and Ordinances and the National Safety Council. He serves on the Executive Board of the Eleventh International Conference on Alcohol, Drugs and Traffic Safety. He has appeared on judicial education programs in numerous states, as well as various highway safety programs. He received his J.D. with honors from Rutgers University School of Law, and his LL.M. from New York University. He is the author of the "Satisfactions of Judging: A Judge's Legacy" and "The Judge of the Future" chapters in this book.

Hon. William A. Grimes is Chief Justice of New Hampshire (retired). He is Distinguished Visiting Professor to the University of Oklahoma College of Law, and has been Distinguished Visiting Professor to the California Western School of Law and the University of San Diego School of Law. Justice Grimes was a charter member of the Faculty of the National College of the State Judiciary, now the National Judicial College, where he continues to teach today. He is Past Chairman of the ABA Judicial Administration Division, Past Chairman of the Judicial Administration Division's Appellate Judges' Conference, and Past Chairman of the New Hampshire Governor's Committee on Crime and Delinquency. Justice Grimes currently serves as the Continuing Education Committee Chairman of the Appellate Judges' Conference. He contributed the chapter on "The Qualities of a Judge" to this book.

Hon. Laurance M. Hyde, Jr. has served as Associate Dean of the National Judicial College since 1987. Born in Princeton, Missouri, in 1927, Judge Hyde received his A.B. and LLB from the University of Missouri–Columbia, and practiced law in St. Louis

from 1952 until he was appointed to the circuit court in 1962. He was a member of the 1964 charter class of the National Judicial College, a faculty advisor in 1965, and dean from 1965 to 1974. He was professor of law at Nova University Law School (Dean from 1975 to 1978) until 1987. He has written and lectured on family law, criminal law, and administration of justice subjects, and was the editor of the second edition of *The State Trial Judges Book*, published in 1969 by the West Publishing Company. Judge Hyde wrote the chapter on "The Unique Role of the Trial Judge" for this book.

Hon. Gladys Kessler has served as a trial judge on the D.C. Superior Court since 1977. During that time she has been Presiding Judge of the Family Division, has handled complex civil cases, and is now handling a felony calendar. She is also Supervising Judge of the D.C. Multi-Door Dispute Resolution Program and is a member of the ABA Standing Committee on Dispute Resolution. Judge Kessler graduated from Cornell University with a B.A. in Government, and received her LL.B. from Harvard Law School. She was Founding President of the Women's Legal Defense Fund, was President in 1982-83 of the National Association of Women Judges and has been president or a member of the Board of Directors of the Women Judges' Fund for Justice since its establishment in 1980. She has served on the Board of Directors of the National Center for State Courts and is currently serving a second term on the Board of Directors of the American Judicature Society. Judge Kessler co-authored the chapter on "Integration of Women and Minority Judges into the American Judiciary" in this book.

Hon. James A. Noe has served as a judge on the King County Superior Court since 1971, and as a judge on the Seattle Municipal Court from 1967 to 1971. Judge Noe is the current Chair of the ABA Judicial Administration Division, and has served as the Chair of that Division's National Conference of State Trial Judges in 1981-82. His other ABA involvements include terms as a delegate to the

House of Delegates, and a member of the Judicial Code Subcommittee, the Special Committee on Evaluation of Judicial Performance, and the Jury Standards Task Force. He is a current member of the National Judicial College Board of Directors. He is a past President-Judge of the Washington State Superior Court Judges' Association. Judge Noe received his Bachelor of Arts in Political Science and his Juris Doctor from the University of Washington. He also was granted an honorary Doctor of Letters from Christian Theological Seminary in Indianapolis. Judge Noe wrote the chapters entitled "The Unique Environment of a Judge" and "Stress Management and Health" for this book.

Hon. Romae T. Powell received her B.A. and Honorary Doctor of Laws degree from Spelman College, Atlanta, Georgia, and LL.B. and J.D. degrees from Howard University, Washington, D.C. She practiced law in Atlanta, Georgia, from 1951 to January 1973, when she was sworn in as Judge of Juvenile Court of Fulton County, and became the first black judge of a court of record in Georgia. She has served on numerous boards and committees. She has held position as President of the Gate City Bar Association and Georgia Council of Juvenile Court Judges. She presently serves on the Board of Directors of SEARCH Group, Inc. She is a member of Judicial Nominations Commission for Georgia and is President of the National Council of Juvenile and Family Court Judges. Judge Powell contributed to the chapter on "Integration of Women and Minority Judges into the American Judiciary" for this book.

Lynn Hecht Schafran is an attorney and Director of the National Judicial Education Program to Promote Equality for Women and Men in the Courts, a project of the NOW Legal Defense and Education Fund in cooperation with the National Association of Women Judges. She is Special Counsel to the New York City Commission on the Status of Women, immediate past chair of the Committee on Sex and the Law of the Association of the Bar of the City of New York, and a member of the

American Bar Association Commission on Women in the Profession. Schafran co-authored two of this book's chapters: "Integration of Women and Minority Judges into the American Judiciary" and "Avoiding Race and Gender Bias in the Courtroom."

Saundra L. Smith was appointed Regional Administrator for the Region III division of the Michigan State Court Administrative Office in January 1988. Ms. Smith was formerly the Lead Court Analyst and Director of Trial Court Delay Reduction Project for the Michigan State Court Administrative Office. Prior to moving to Michigan, Ms. Smith was Assistant Staff Director of the American Bar Association Action Commission to Reduce Court Costs and Delay in Washington, D.C. Ms. Smith has a Bachelor of Science degree from Michigan State University and the degree of Master of Judicial Administration from the American University, Washington, D.C. She collaborated with Hilda R. Gage on this book's chapter entitled "Court Management and Delay Reduction."

ACKNOWLEDGEMENTS

Development and production of The Judge's Book was a four-year team effort that drew widely on the membership of the National Conference of State Trial Judges.

The project began by asking members to contribute ideas that were important to them as judges, as well as suggestions for the contents of the all new book. Their extensive response was very helpful to the Publications Task Force, which relied upon those suggestions in developing the book's outline and the chapter objectives which guided the authors.

The members of the Task Force shared the responsibility for determining the direction and content of the book. Several of them are also authors. Task Force members include Judge James A. Noe, Judge Kenneth L. Gillis, Dean Felix Stumpf, Dean and former Judge Jack Etheridge and Staff Director Stephen Goldspiel.

The several Chairpeople of NCSTJ during whose terms the work was in gestation gave real help and showed understanding and patience. They provided necessary encouragement and resources. We thank Judge Rodney Peeples, Judge Hilda Gage, Judge Warren Chan and Judge B. B. Schraub.

We acknowledge with thanks the work of Stephen Goldspiel, NCSTJ Staff Director, who was a member of the Publications Task Force, wrote several chapters, and was a continuing source of information concerning the content and process of publication. Without his aid and guidance the work would not have been completed.

He was most ably assisted by Michael Winkler, who put the manuscript in format for computer typesetting, obtained permissions to reprint copyrighted excerpts, checked our citations and worked closely with Brian Sullivan and the ABA Press editorial and production staff.

Karen Schenkenfelder, our editorial consultant, harmonized the disparate styles of the authors and organized the manuscript into a cohesive whole.

Among the secretaries who deserve particular thanks are Margaret Lawrance, Gloria Calistro and Nancy Chiesa.

A special statement of appreciation goes to Judge George H. Revelle whose generous gift started the project on its way.

There are others whose efforts for this book have made it possible. To all these people we say, THANK YOU!

Hon. DONALD R. FRETZ
Editor and Chair, Publications Task Force

Merced, California
June 1989

PREFACE

This book is by judges and for judges. It is a product of the National Conference of State Trial Judges. The National Conference of State Trial Judges was the moving force in the creation of the National College of State Trial Judges, now called the National Judicial College.

In 1964 the conference, with the assistance of West Publishing Company, published a paperback volume entitled *The State Trial Judge's Book*. That book was used at the first session of the college. The hardback first edition was published in 1965. A second edition was published in 1969. *The Judge's Book* is a new format with a new title.

The exchange of information among judges takes many forms—printed, oral, formal, informal, bench books, desk books, textbooks. Each plays a role in furnishing knowledge about the philosophy and technique of judging.

This book is not a substitute for formal judicial education at the state or national level. Such educational efforts offer greater breadth of subject matter in greater depth.

We offer this book with the hope that wherever you are in your judicial career, you will be a better judge for having read it.

Hon. DONALD R. FRETZ

INTRODUCTION

The National Conference of State Trial Judges is pleased to present The Judge's Book. This book is intended to provide both a rapid orientation for the new trial judge and refreshment and renewal for the experienced jurist.

The book avoids discussion of technical points of law. There are many fine publications that provide guidance on state and national jurisprudence. Rather, the focus is upon the unique role of the judge in society, and the need for continuing adjustments he or she encounters during a judicial career.

We offer thoughts on the life of a judge, the judge's work, techniques of judging and the nature of the judicial profession to support each other in our demanding but rewarding work. Our special thanks go to Judge Donald R. Fretz, our editor and principal author, for his many contributions in bringing this book into being.

Hon. B. B. SCHRAUB
Chair, National Conference of State Trial Judges

Seguin, Texas
June 19, 1989

I

The Life of a Judge

1

THE UNIQUE ROLE OF THE TRIAL JUDGE

In spite of lawyers' frequent criticism of individual judges, their decisions, their opinions, and even their sanity, the legal profession traditionally views the judiciary with respect and perhaps reverence. Even in this day of cynicism about our leaders at all levels and about all three branches of our government, the traditional view remains—the bench is the pinnacle of our profession. So much so that it will be rare to find a lawyer, especially one who practices in the courts, who has not, from time to time, imagined how it would be to don those black robes, leave the fray of the advocates' arena, and ascend to that symbolically and physically high position on the bench.

If lawyers are close observers of the judiciary, it would seem that they should have a good idea of the nature of the career change from lawyer to judge. However, the extent of the change can never be fully appreciated except by those who have actually experienced it.

The Similarities between the Lawyer Advocate and the Judge

The practice of law is, of course, excellent training for the judicial role. To be a good lawyer and to be a good judge, one must meet the same basic requirements:

- Knowledge of how to find and apply the law—There is no other way to become skilled in the use of this vital tool but to study and practice it.
- The habits of hard and disciplined work.
- Experience in facing and overcoming temptations to shirk the difficult task and the unpopular cause—Courage is expected of judges and lawyers, who protect our rights, liberties, and system of justice.
- Understanding of the relationship of the trial to the law—The more exposure the new judge has had to the drama and the dy-

namics of the courtroom, the better. This is true for trial lawyers as well, though they differently handle the rapid-fire application of the rules of evidence and procedure, and the complex psychology of the trial.

- Acceptance of the dilemma of conflicting obligations—Although judges find the number and importance of conflicting obligations to be a particularly great problem, the lawyer also encounters them. The lawyer has the sacred duty to represent the client "zealously within the bounds of the law" and at the same time has potentially conflicting obligations to be candid to the court; to support the system of justice, the legal profession, and the welfare of the community; and to live up to personal ethical ideals. The lawyer also has economic needs, which can be harmed by complying with the other duties, and an obligation to see that persons who need counsel are not deprived of it. But while the lawyer is not ethically obligated to accept every case offered, the judge is more often required to take on the unpopular, difficult, or controversial case.

The Dilemma of the Judge

Contemporary American society places justice as one of the highest, if not the highest, of our aspirations. Daniel Webster said, "Justice, Sir, is the great interest of man on earth. It is the ligament which holds civilized beings and civilized nations together. Wherever her temple stands, and so long as it is duly honored, there is a foundation for social security, general happiness, and the improvement and progress of our race."[1] The English lords wrested by force of arms from King John the promise that "To no one will we sell, to no one will we refuse or delay, right or justice."[2] Inscribed over the entrances to the U.S. Supreme Court Building are two phrases: "Equal Justice under Law" on the west portico and "Justice the Guardian of Liberty" on the east portico.

If these and many other similar statements reflect our commitment to justice, how have we sought to achieve it? In large part by placing great power, trust, and responsibility in our judiciary.

Visiting judges from many other nations, knowledgeable and well educated, have the greatest difficulty understanding our concept of separation of powers which entrusts to the judiciary the authority to overturn acts of the legislature. This power is enhanced by the English common-

1. WEBSTER, *Funeral Oration on Mr. Justice Story,* WRITINGS AND SPEECHES OF DANIEL WEBSTER (1909).

2. Magna Carta, Ch. 40, *as found in* W. S. MCKECHNIE, MAGNA CARTA: A COMMENTARY ON THE GREAT CHARTER OF KING JOHN 395 (1958).

law tradition of evolution of the law through judicial decisions and the broad, though uneven, recognition of the need for judicial independence.

This empowerment of American judges and its concomitant obligations create the dilemmas of the judicial role. Judges are expected to be experienced; wise and worldly; involved in the leadership of the community; sensitive to the problems in the society, including the economic and political issues; conversant with the cutting edge of knowledge of scientific and medical issues; active in the critical examination and reform of the law and the agencies of the law; warmly concerned for the tribulations of those who are troubled; and certainly possessing the humanizing benefit of a sense of humor, as well as the modesty and humility to recognize that they cannot have all of those things.

At the same time, judges are supposed to be unbiased, which might mean without prior knowledge of the issues that may come before them. They are warned that they should not take public positions on matters of controversy, and that they are to be detached, which can be interpreted to mean that they are unconcerned, aloof, and nonparticipative.

The judge's private life is potentially affected, though less so today than in times past. When nearly all judges were male and nearly all of their wives were full-time helpmates, homemakers, and mothers, it was easier to say that the judge's career was the family's career, and to seek to control any activities, political or social, of the wife that might interfere with the goal of the appearance of neutrality, recalling Ceasar's need for his wife to be above suspicion.[3]

Today, when the number of women judges has greatly increased and most judges' spouses have their own careers, the effort to restrict the activities of judges' spouses has nearly ended. Nevertheless, many of the pressures remain. The judge, whose friends were colleagues at the bar, may feel the need to be circumspect about social contacts to preserve the appearance of neutrality. The judge will find that many lawyers are less comfortable than previously about social contact, probably because they are sensitive to the judge's concern or perceived concern about neutrality.

Must the judge change his or her personality? Surely not, but Sir Francis Bacon said, "Judges should be more learned than witty, more reverend than plausible, and more advised than confident . . . Patience and gravity of bearing is an essential part of justice; and an over-speaking judge is no well-tuned cymbal."[4] Robert Satter, a Connecticut Superior Court judge, has written an excellent article discussing the forces of

3. PLUTARCH'S LIVES; LIFE OF CAESAR, A.H. Clough revision, 1864 (Modern Library reprint edition), 860.

4. Bacon, *Essay: Of Judicature, as found in* AMERICAN JUDICATURE SOCIETY, HANDBOOK FOR JUDGES 25-26 (1961).

isolation, status, caution, and detachment which combine to pull judges toward becoming colorless and ponderous, both on the bench and in their private lives.[5]

Judges are public officials, and most state trial judges must periodically run for reelection or retention. Herein lies another dilemma. Bacon said, "A popular judge is a deformed thing: and *plaudite's* are fitter for players than magistrates."[6]

Judicial independence is our polestar. John Marshall said, "I have always thought, from my earliest youth till now, that the greatest scourge an angry Heaven ever inflicted upon an ungrateful and a sinning people, was an ignorant, a corrupt, or a dependent Judiciary."[7] To give the greatest possible opportunity for independence, our founders adopted the life tenure of the federal judiciary, so that judges would rule only according to the law, living up to the words of Sir Thomas More: "If the parties will at my hand call for justice, then all were it my father stood on the one side, and the devil on the tother, his cause being good, the devil should have right!"[8]

Can judges be expected to meet these high aspirations in the real and rough world of judicial elections? Many do. Probably by far most do, but the pressures can be enormous, and they must be recognized. What is a judge to do in a contested election, whether against an opponent or in a retention election running without an opposing candidate but with an organized challenge to retention? During the 1986 retention election for the California Supreme Court (in which the chief justice and two associate justices were defeated), former Justice Otto Kaus, who had previously retired, observed that when he cast his vote with the 4-3 majority in a controversial case in June 1982, he tried not to be influenced by the fact that his retention election would be held just five months later. Justice Kaus said, "I decided the case the way I saw it. But to this day, I don't know to what extent I was subliminally motivated by the thing you could not forget—that it might do you some good politically to vote one way or the other."[9]

Perhaps that is all that any of us can do. Recognize the pressures, face them with courage, and do our best, as did Justice Kaus, to follow the law, the evidence, and the oath of office.

---

5. *See* Satter, *The Quality of a Judge's Experience,* 65 ABA JOURNAL 933-35 (1979). *See also*, Mosk & Fortier, *Should Judges Speak Out?* 24 JUDGES' JOURNAL 42 (1985).

6. F. BACON, *Speech to the Star Chamber*, 1617, to judges before the summer circuit.

7. J. Marshall, Virginia Constitutional Convention, 1829-30, *Debates* 619.

8. W. ROPER, THE LYFE OF SIR THOMAS MOORE, KNIGHTE, J. M. Cline ed. 42 (1950).

9. Los Angeles Times, Sept. 28, 1986 at 1:3. *See* Wold & Culver, "The Defeat of the California Justices: The campaign, the electorate, and the issue of judicial accountability" 70 JUDICATURE 348, 351 (1987).

The dilemma is one of independence versus accountability. Judges should be accountable for misconduct in office, lack of diligence, or lack of attention to duty. Removal from office for unpopular decisions, or because of the vagaries of the political winds, is inconsistent with judicial independence, but it happens in our states and is one of the difficulties in the role of the trial judge.

A further difficulty in the judge's struggle to act without fear or favor is the erosion of the doctrine of judicial immunity. The results are yet to be seen, but there can be little doubt this development adds to the pressures faced by our nation's judges.[10]

The Transition from Bar to Bench

The dilemmas of the judicial role provide the backdrop to the issue of the individual's transition from lawyer to judge. This transition will, for most, take more than months, more than a year to complete. It is a quite different career, and is thus a major change.

The new judge will find that the network of lawyer friends developed over years of law practice, who were once a ready source of advice or help of all sorts, is no longer available. A new network, probably largely composed of judicial colleagues, must be painstakingly created.

However, it is much more than that. The new role greatly changes the perspective from which one views the trial, the law, the profession of law, justice, and, in turn, our entire society, in which justice is such a vital part.

Of those who have had personal judicial experience, as well as an opportunity to interact with large numbers of judges and to sift the ideas on the subject, most have strong impressions as to the process of socialization of new judges. However, these impressions are selective and are colored by the views of the observer. For a scientific study of this socialization process, see Alpert, Atkins and Ziller, "Becoming a Judge: The Transition from Advocate to Arbiter."[11] This study finds that there are four steps to the socialization of a judge, and that moving through all the steps takes at least 15 years of judicial service. The first of these steps, Professional Socialization, occurs in the period before a person becomes a judge, and includes law school, legal experiences, and other career-related experiences. The second step, Initiation and Resolution, includes the first five years on the bench. During this period the judge

10. *See* Weisberger, *The Twilight of Judicial Independence—Pulliam v. Allen,* 19 SUFFOLK UNIVERSITY LAW REVIEW 537-560 (1985); and Reynoldson, *The Erosion of Judicial Immunity,* 69 JUDICATURE 114 (1985).

11. Alpert, Atkins & Ziller, *Becoming a Judge: The Transition from Advocate to Arbiter,* 62 JUDICATURE 325-35 (1979).

undergoes an initial adjustment and self-concept change as he or she tries to define his or her role as a judge. Toward the end of this stage there is a resolution of role conflicts, and a transition to the decision to remain on the bench. The third step, Establishment, covers years six through 15 on the bench. During this stage the role of the judge changes from that of altruist and legalist to guardian of the law, as another role redefinition and resolution of conflict occurs within the judge. The final step, Commitment, begins when the judge has served on the bench 15 or more years. During this final stage, there is an increased commitment to the bench, marked by a satisfaction with judicial life. The new judge would do well to consider these findings and thereby be forewarned of what lies ahead.

The lawyer's profession imposes relatively few ethical constraints that are personal and outside of the law practice. The new judge will discover that activities which are honorable and open to lawyers may be proscribed by the Code of Judicial Conduct, which is in effect in nearly every state.[12] This means that the new judge must be aware that there are restrictions on a judge's personal, social, political, business, religious, charitable, and civic activities, and even on the right of free speech.

The appearance of impropriety is a slippery concept. Fortunately, readable articles are available.[13]

Conclusion

This discussion of the role of the trial judge has focused in large part on the problems with that role. However, there are many positives to the role of judges and they far outweigh the negatives.

Most of those who would be judges and who are judges are attracted to the office by the opportunity to be of service to the law, to society, and to the concept of justice. The rewards are in the challenges provided by those opportunities, by the intellectual stimulation of the vast variety of legal issues which are brought to the courts, and by pursuit and occasional attainment of innovative solutions to a problem presented by a specific case and to administrative burdens of the case load of the court system, including the individual department or division in that system.

---

12. Lubet, *Judicial Ethics and Private Lives,* 79 NORTHWESTERN UNIVERSITY LAW REVIEW 983 (1985).

13. *See,* Lubet, *The Search for Analysis in Judicial Ethics or Easy Cases Don't Make Much Law,* 66 NEBRASKA LAW REVIEW 430 (1987); Lubet, *Judicial Impropriety: Love, Friendship, Free Speech, and Other Intemperate Conduct,* 1986 ARIZONA STATE LAW JOURNAL 379 (1986); and Lubet, *Regulation of Judges' Business and Financial Activities,* 37 EMORY LAW JOURNAL 1 (1988).

2

THE UNIQUE ENVIRONMENT OF A JUDGE

Justice does not depend upon legal dialectics so much as upon the atmosphere of the court room, and that in the end depends primarily upon the judge.

—Judge Learned Hand[1]

The transition from lawyer to judge is a significant life-changing experience. The excitement accompanying this change in careers may delay the realization, but sooner or later the new judge appreciates that he or she has taken on an awesome responsibility.

In making this transition, the lawyer enters the unique environment of the judge—an environment of structured power, symbols, rituals, and human drama in which the judge will carry out the traditional judicial responsibilities.

The judge's environment has three major components: the facilities (the courtroom itself), courtroom conduct and atmosphere (the behavior of those affecting court proceedings), and the judicial role (wisely managing the first two components). The quality of this environment depends not only on the judge's legal knowledge and training, but also on the judge's willingness to learn and ability to manage the new environment with wisdom and understanding.

The Facilities

Brought up as I was to looking at Gothic architecture with contempt, I despised it; but when I went inside I was struck with wonder and I felt the attraction of its beauty.

—Johann Wolfgang von Goethe[2]

1. Brown v. Walter, 62 F.2d 798, 800 (1933).
2. W. Durant, The Age of Faith 882 (1950).

The judge's workplace is truly unique. No other job site, save perhaps the operating room, involves such significant matters in the lives of individuals. It therefore should be a site equal to its noble purpose, a place where the physical appearance and psychological ambience form an appropriate environment for the administration of justice. In this place, a judge must carry out the systematic responsibilities of the judicial office while nurturing the delicate fruit of the court system: justice.

The courthouse and courtroom will not be strange to the new judge, but the judge will want to evaluate this working arena with a fresh perspective. The judge should begin by evaluating the physical surroundings. Justice can be administered best in an attractive, well-designed courtroom that enhances the respect, comfort, and productivity of all participants in court proceedings.

Many judges, however, inherit chambers and courtrooms that leave much to be desired. If that is the case, the judge should determine whether remodeling can improve the efficient and effective administration of court business. Often a judge can persuade the local legislative or executive branch of government to provide improvements. This is especially true if the judge can show that the courtroom lacks adequate security or that the current design, furnishings, or environmental systems are seriously hindering the effective operation of the court.

It is wise to have a licensed architect assist in the design of a new or remodeled courtroom. To be effective, however, the architect should fully understand the court's needs:

> The architect, then, must have a firm understanding of the objectives and operations of the judicial system if he is to design a physical environment that will enhance the system's performance and the effectiveness of the people who operate it.[3]

One study shows six basic criteria that can be used to test how the courtroom is functioning:[4]

1. Function and organization
2. Symbolic values
3. Environmental factors
4. Construction, materials, and furniture
5. Provisions for audiovisual displays
6. Security

---

3. American Bar Association and American Institute of Architects Joint Committee on the Design of Courtrooms and Court Facilities, The American Courthouse (1973).

4. Burns, *Designing the Good Courtroom*, Popular Government (Fall 1984).

Function and Organization

The courtroom's space should be designed in light of how it is used. Is the courtroom used primarily for jury trials? Is it a special courtroom for juvenile cases, mental illness hearings, appeals, arraignments, special calendars, probate or ex parte matters? Of course, an evaluation of one courtroom must take into consideration the uses of the other courtrooms in the courthouse.

The use determines how the space should be organized. For example, it may be appropriate to have more space for court staff, lawyers, and litigants than for spectators. Perhaps more space should be allocated for displaying demonstrative evidence.

The judge's bench should be elevated and prominent to symbolize the central nature and importance of the judge. The witness stand should be placed so that the jury can see and hear witnesses clearly. Some courtrooms have been designed with a movable witness stand to allow for a change in position when the trial is to the judge without a jury. This is an alternative to a design that gives the judge, jury, and lawyers all front views of a witness. The design should also provide adequate working space for the clerk, reporter, bailiff, lawyers, and litigants.

Many courts now select one or more alternate jurors to serve if a regular juror is unable to complete the case. A jury box should include chairs for these extra jurors.

It is fundamental that an institution created for the purpose of providing justice for the community should make every reasonable effort to accommodate handicapped persons. Therefore, any new construction or remodeling of a courtroom or courthouse should include access for the handicapped.

The comfort and use of the jury should be given high priority. Juror chairs should be comfortable and spaced to allow freedom of movement and to prevent a feeling of overcrowding. The jury room should be large enough to comfortably accommodate the jurors, with appropriate furniture. Restrooms should be near the entrance.[5]

Symbolic Values

The design, furnishings, and construction materials of the courtroom reflect the social and cultural values of the community and announce the importance of the administration of justice. So that the law can be properly administered, the courtroom should never be just another governmental work space, void of symbolic and psychological enhancements:

5. *See* American Bar Association, Standards Relating to Juror Use and Management, Standard 14 (1983).

> Once law is understood as an active, living human process, then it is seen to involve—just as religion involves—man's whole being, including his dreams, his passions, his ultimate concerns.
>
> The principal ways in which law channels and communicates [these] transrational values are fourfold: first, through *ritual*, that is, ceremonial procedures which symbolize the objectivity of law; second, through *tradition*, that is, language and practices handed down from the past which symbolize the ongoingness of law; third, through *authority*, that is, the reliance upon written or spoken sources of law which are considered to be decisive in themselves and which symbolize the binding power of law; and fourth, through *universality*, that is, the claim to embody universally valid concepts or insights which symbolize the law's connection with all embracing truth. These four elements—ritual, tradition, authority, and universality—are present in all legal systems, just as they are present in all religions.[6]

Rituals, symbols, and formality have their place in the judicial environment as significant legacies of Western civilization. Through the centuries, structures, trappings, artifacts, and other aids have given human events special meaning by arranging the physical environment to enhance the event itself—to add a psychological dimension and often to evoke mystery and awe. Kings have worn crowns and held scepters, both symbols of sovereignty and power. The medieval cathedrals were built with high ceilings and spaciousness. One who entered the dimly lit sanctuary was swallowed up in a sense of insignificance—an appropriate feeling for approaching the presence of God. In fact, religions are replete with rich symbols of faith. The cross, chalice, and dove are significant symbols for Christians. The Star of David, the menorah, and the yarmulke are symbols of great meaning for Jews.

In one sense, what Alvin Toffler called "future shock"—the dizzying disorientation brought on by the rapidly changing world around us—has been a threat to tradition, ritual, and symbols. Life now changes at such an accelerated pace that much of the past is forgotten or ignored, ridding us of unwanted baggage but also depriving society of many rich traditions.

Justice is an enduring value and as such benefits from connections to the past. Specifically, the centrality and elevation of the judge to the highest position in the room, even while sitting, is a symbolic acknowledgment of the power entrusted to the judge. It also is a clear psychological advantage for the manager of the courtroom.

Other elements of the courtroom have symbolic value as well. The flag symbolizes the authority of the government. The materials, construction, and colors usually convey strength, quality, and importance. Often in-

6. H. Berman, The Interaction of Law and Religion 31 (1974).

dependent art objects symbolize the underlying principles of the court's business: justice, mercy, law, tradition and history.

Although some older symbols may today strike us as archaic and a bit naive, there is a great potential for contemporary designers and artists to create meaningful symbolic expressions of the values that underlie the administration of justice.

Environmental Factors

A well-functioning courtroom should also meet more pragmatic criteria:

> It is absolutely essential that participants in trials, and in fact everyone in the courtroom, be able to see and hear everything that transpires. It is nearly as important that courtrooms be comfortably heated and air-conditioned. Courtrooms both old and new are most criticized for failures in one of these essentials. Whether people can see and hear and whether the temperature and humidity are comfortable are crucially significant in the design of courtrooms.[7]

The courtroom should be designed to enhance sight and sound. Materials should be used that contribute to acoustical excellence. Public address systems should be of high quality and designed to enhance amplification with static-free, good quality transmissions.

Lighting should not rely on undependable natural light. Instead, professionally designed artificial lighting should be provided to enable judge and jury to clearly see all evidence and witnesses presented.

Courtroom temperature-control and ventilation systems should be efficient, effective, and quiet. The participants should be able to perform within the courtroom year-round without distractions or discomfort. Uncomfortable temperature should never deter the search for justice.

Construction, Materials, and Furnishings

The quality of construction and the decor directly affect the dignity, durability and effectiveness of the courtroom. The courtroom design, construction, and furnishings reflect the community's value of the function of the court. The atmosphere created by the physical surroundings nurtures the ideal that what occurs here is of high importance to the community. A high-quality environment enhances confidence, respect, and deference.

Even though the court must compete for public funds with other important and necessary governmental functions, it is shortsighted to cut corners in courtroom remodeling or construction. Local officials should recognize that "the appearance and quality of courtrooms represent the value their citizens place on a central cultural ideal."[8] Furthermore,

---

7. Burns, *supra* note 4, at 8.
8. *Id.* at 9.

courtrooms will be used for many years, and construction of quality and durability makes economic sense.

The appearance of the courtroom also involves an element of morale. Those who participate in court proceedings may be encouraged to perform with more dedication and attention if the evirons are suitable. High-quality surroundings should encourage high-quality performance.

Audiovisual Displays

Traditionally the trial consisted of oral presentations with a few supporting documents or other items of physical evidence. Today, however, the trial lawyer relies heavily on the psychological advantage of visual aids to enhance the spoken word. Audio- and videocassettes are used in addition to movies and slides. These developments require space, appropriate power outlets, equipment, and ability to darken the room.

Also relevant is the trend toward allowing cameras in the courtroom. (The pros and cons of this issue are discussed in Chapter 19.) The judge contemplating a new courtroom or remodeling should consider a design that will accommodate still and television cameras. For example, access can be provided by a window view from outside or in the back of the courtroom.

The court may benefit from providing access for TV cameras. The court could use TV cameras to transmit the trial to another room for students, reporters, spectators, or even an unruly defendant banned from the courtroom by appropriate findings and rulings of the court. Televising a trial to another room for viewing could also serve as part of a security plan.

Security

Perhaps the most troubling issue in courtroom design is security. Most courthouses were constructed before the rash of disruptive and violent outbursts in the courtroom. Such episodes are myriad and appear to be a permanent part of the risk of the administration of justice in a free society. Overreaction would make the courthouse an armed fortress, which could seriously damage the image and ability of the court to reaffirm that we live in a free society. Security, and the design of the court facility, must serve the objectives of the judicial process, not dominate them.[9]

Yet, for the protection of all, an overall plan should be worked out with law enforcement and other affected agencies. The organizational

9. American Bar Association and American Institute of Architects Joint Committee on the Design of Courtrooms and Court Facilities, *supra* note 3, at 219.

part of the security plan is paramount, and judges should be thoroughly familiar with it. Perfect security is impossible, but flexibility in design, commitment to the plan, alertness, and commonsense application will provide competent security without significantly preventing the court from achieving its other goals.

A report by the Illinois Sheriffs' Association and the Illinois Judges Association outlines a comprehensive security plan calling for such procedures as identification cards for all personnel, systematic searches of courtrooms and chambers, training for court personnel concerning whom to observe and how to observe courtroom attendees, operation of a system of intelligence about security problems and an effective communication relay system. The report recommends the following physical equipment and construction:

- An overall lock system to secure court and chambers when not in use
- Bulletproof materials around the bench, witness and jury areas
- A silent alarm system to be activated by the judge
- Entry screening devices to allow nonintrusive searches for metal objects
- Bulletproof vests for judges when appropriate

The full plan can be obtained from the Illinois Judges Association, the National Conference of State Trial Judges, or the National Center for State Courts.

Finally, the judge must remember that he or she is responsible for the proceedings in the courtroom. Security is an integral part of those responsibilities.

Courtroom Conduct and Atmosphere

Justice Benjamin N. Cardozo asserted, "The final cause of law is the welfare of society." "Justice," declared Daniel Webster, "is the greatest interest of man on earth." But, perhaps a common-law maxim says it best: *Jus est ars boni et aequi*—the law is the science of what is good and just.

Law and justice are not self-executing. The great principles underlying both must be brought to life in specific cases and specific places and with specific individuals, most often in a courtroom before a judge. Therefore the courtroom should reflect the high purposes for which it exists. Those entering the courtroom should be impressed by the overall dignity, fairness and orderliness of the proceedings. They should expect to preserve that atmosphere, not detract from it. The courtroom that appears informal, disorderly, or unkempt belittles the role of law and justice in a free society and undermines the confidence of those appearing in such a courtroom.

General Court Demeanor

Ringing telephones and one-sided conversations are substantial distractions in the courtroom. Files, stacks of paper, and clutter should not be allowed to accumulate. Persons moving about without a purpose directly related to the court proceeding can detract from the formal atmosphere.

All in the courtroom should attend to the main proceedings. Activities that subtly show disrespect for the court or the proceedings should be disallowed. Examples of inappropriate activities include newspaper reading, eating or drinking (other than water by the participants), talking other than in the proceedings before the judge, failure to remove a hat, appearing at the bar or the witness stand without removing an overcoat or outdoor jacket, and any other activity that detracts from the dignity of the proceedings or otherwise violates a community standard for courtesy and respect. For a discussion of enforcing appropriate courtroom behavior, see Chapter 17.

Staff

The judge is responsible for the conduct of staff, not only while in the courtroom but also while in chambers. Clerks, reporters, and bailiffs are ambassadors for the administration of justice and more particularly are representatives of the judge.

Since the judge while in chambers does not know what is occurring in the courtroom, the judge should make a special effort to train staff to be courteous, accessible, and helpful. The formality of the courtroom can be relaxed to some degree when the judge is not present, but staff should encourage an atmosphere that is appropriate. Loud and boisterous conduct should be curtailed, and although a certain amount of friendly conversation may be appropriate, staff at all times should recognize that persons observing proceedings, including litigants, may not understand the staff's interaction with each other and with the lawyers.

The matters before the court are serious to all participants, even during recesses and before and after court sessions. Conduct that communicates to observers that the staff members do not take the proceedings seriously damages the image of the court system and, specifically, the image of the judge. Such damage undermines confidence and promotes disrespect.

Jurors

Jurors' conduct, comfort, and time should be a continuing concern of the judge. These people are special participants in the administration of justice, and their services are indispensable. Jurors should be clearly instructed on their duties and responsibilities while serving on a case. Their conduct should be monitored by the bailiff, and any variance from court instruction should be immediately reported to the judge.

Jurors should be treated with due consideration and thoughtfulness. The judge can do this, in part, by keeping the jury fully informed as to the progress of the trial, explaining delays and procedures. Keeping the jury informed not only satisfies a natural curiosity, but also corrects misunderstandings and reassures the jurors that they really are an integral part of the administration of justice. They are not just outsiders being "used."

A juror's experience may be the single most important role a citizen will ever play in the governmental affairs of the community. That experience should fulfill the citizen's best expectations and enhance confidence in the administration of justice. Jurors are special observers of the system of justice and therefore special public relations agents. What they observe they will report to the community; what they experience will serve as the basis for evaluating the ongoing business of the court.[10]

Witnesses

Witnesses also have a special, indispensable role. Their conduct and the conduct of those who deal with them will substantially affect the trial.

The judge must be careful not to imply to the jury that a witness has special standing in the eyes of the court. With that thought in mind, however, the judge should do whatever is reasonable to make witnesses feel comfortable. They are often upset and frightened by the experience. Kindness to witnesses, evenly administered, is a quality appreciated by all in the courtroom.

The judge should be ready to protect the witness from intimidation and harassment, but the judge should also be prepared to deal appropriately with a witness who is evasive, unresponsive to questions, or in any way detrimental to the dignity of the proceedings. There is an art to treating each witness with a warm, friendly manner while at the same time communicating to the witness that responsive, truthful, and courteous answers are expected.

Dealing with special witnesses, such as children, sex case victims, and the handicapped is beyond the scope of this section. However, special accommodations may be appropriate, indeed, required in circumstances involving witnesses with special needs. The developing body of law in this field is different from jurisdiction to jurisdiction, and judges should be fully informed concerning the applicable law.

10. American Bar Association, *supra* note 5, Standard 16.

The Oath

It is the judge's responsibility to ensure that an appropriate oath is administered to the jury and to all witnesses called to testify.

Jurors must take two oaths: one requiring them to answer all voir dire questions truthfully and, for those selected as the jury panel, a second oath requiring generally that they, as a group and individually, will try the matter at issue between the parties and render a true verdict according to the law and evidence given them during the trial.

Witnesses must subscribe to an oath that requires them to swear or affirm that the testimony they give in the matter pending before the court will be "the truth, the whole truth, and nothing but the truth, so help you God."

Some witnesses or jurors may object to the traditional oath of swearing to tell the truth, even if the words "so help you God" are deleted. Conscience or religious scruples usually provide the basis for the objection. The requirement of an oath is to commit the taker to a known unequivocal obligation to tell the truth. The unequivocal act is more important than any ritual or formality.

It is, therefore, generally unnecessary for the judge to insist on a sworn oath to make the oath valid for purposes of a perjury charge. If the witness or juror is willing to affirm that he or she will accept the obligation of the oath, the oath is valid and can be used as a basis for a subsequent charge.[11]

Some jurisdictions, however, may have a specific statute or rule that permits affirmation only if religious scruples against swearing are shown. In those cases, such scruples must be shown on the record.[12]

Some special problems are associated with administering oaths. Some persons speak no English or have communication impairments. A qualified interpreter will be necessary to ensure that the impaired or non-English-speaking person understands the court proceedings. Before beginning to interpret, the interpreter must take an oath that he or she will make a true interpretation of all proceedings in a language or in a manner that the person understands, and will repeat the statements of that person to the court in the English language, to the best of the interpreter's skill and judgment. Once the interpreter has sworn or affirmed to such an oath, then the judge can proceed to place the witness or juror under the appropriate oath.

Who administers an oath varies from jurisdiction to jurisdiction. Some judges may do it all; others do none or split the assignment with a clerk

---

11. United States v. Rabb, 394 F.2d 230 (1968).
12. 67 *Corpus Juris Secundum* 11.

or bailiff. In any event, the content and method of administering the oath are under the supervision of the judge.

All oaths should be administered solemnly, not merely perfunctorily. The speaker should look directly at the person or persons being sworn or affirmed and speak loudly, clearly, and slowly enough to be understood. The person or persons taking the oath should be impressed with the serious obligations attendant to the oath.

Conduct During Sentencing

In many sentencings, there is a delicate balance between showing disapproval of the conduct and impugning the personhood of the defendant. Sentencing is part of a ritual that reflects the community's formal condemnation for unlawful acts committed without substantially undermining the hopes and aspirations of an individual who must continue to live out the life ahead. Too much empathy and informality deprive the defendant of the experience intended. Too much condemnation and condescension will reap no benefit to the defendant or the community. The judge must select the words and set the tone for the sentencing process. Indignation and harsh words, if appropriate, must be measured by the goals of the administration of justice and community values; the judge dare not be self-indulgent to satisfy a personal need.

The Robe

The wearing of a robe is a separate issue of judicial conduct and deserves special attention:

> The trial judge's appearance and demeanor should reflect the dignity of the judicial office and enhance public confidence in the administration of justice. The wearing of the judicial robe in the courtroom will contribute to these goals.[13]

Most trial judges in the United States wear black judicial robes, but some states have been reluctant to require or even allow the robe.

Historically, the judicial robe is a product of English tradition evolving from ecclesiastical origins. Colors and fashions of the English judicial robes have varied during the past seven centuries. Currently, every member of the High Court of Justice must own three sets of robes. The scarlet robes are worn during criminal trials and on ceremonial occasions. Violet robes are reserved for all other trials and a black robe is worn by judges providing judicial services other than trials.[14]

After the American Revolution, the common law was retained, but the judicial robes and wigs were discarded as symbols of an unsympathetic system of justice. As the passions of the Revolution mellowed, the

13. American Bar Association Standards for Criminal Justice 6-1.3 (2d Ed. 1980).
14. Ferguson, *To Robe or Not to Robe*, 39 Judicature (April 1956).

judiciary again considered the robe as making a meaningful contribution to the administration of justice. Since the beginning of the twentieth century, judicial robes have appeared more and more frequently until at the present most judges wear black robes on the bench. The forsaking of the red and violet for the conservative black is probably a compromise; those colors were more closely associated with aristocracy and pomp.

Attire is often used for symbolic purposes to identify position or status. Police officers and military personnel use uniforms for identification and as symbols of power. The primary actors use robes in religious, academic, and fraternal events to enrich the proceedings and set apart those with special roles.

Many experienced judges insist that the robe is an important symbol of the judicial office, evidencing the judge's commitment to impartiality. "If the trial judge is to maintain the dignity of the courtroom and to convince the participants of his universal role, an overt symbol stressing his dedication to justice will place the judicial function in the proper perspective."[15]

Courtroom Dress

Twenty-five years ago, it was the norm to require all men who appeared in a courtroom to wear a coat and tie. Women were seldom seen in court in anything but dresses or suits. Slowly over the years, dress codes have become less strict. Formal dress codes have all but disappeared, and those that remain are usually general. In Louisiana a rule states, "All persons in the courtroom or on the court floor shall be decently attired." A North Carolina rule on courtroom decorum contains the following statement: "Business attire shall be appropriate dress for counsel while in the courtroom."

It apparently is still the norm in most every jurisdiction that male lawyers must wear ties and coat, while female lawyers wear comparable business attire. The dress of counsel may vary depending on the weather, the local legal culture, and community standards.

Dress codes have occasionally become a matter of dispute. Several court orders requiring female attorneys to wear "traditional courtroom attire" have been struck down on appeal.[16]

The matter of appropriate attire, however, is usually settled by custom within a particular jurisdiction. The underlying principle is the dignity and decorum of the courtroom and the court's authority and responsibility to protect the court and the proceedings from being demeaned by inappropriate dress.

15. *Id.*, at 171.

16. *See* Peck v. Stone, 304 N.Y.S.2d 881 (App. Div. 1969); *also In re* DeCarlo, 357 A.2d 273 (N.J. Super. Ct. App. Div. 1976).

Conduct of Lawyers, Litigants, and Observers

> *A judge should maintain order and decorum in the proceedings before him or her.*
>
> —*Code of Judicial Conduct 3A(II)*

Within the scope of the judge's duties in the courtroom is the responsibility to set limits on conduct and provide a certain tone for treatment of all who participate in court proceedings. In addition to staff, jurors, and witnesses, already discussed, the judge must pay close attention to the conduct of lawyers, litigants, and court observers.

If all the world's a stage, the courtroom is a primary theater of human drama—an arena of human events and circumstances. Like a theater, it is a stage on which actors develop a plot and act out tragedy, high and low drama, satire, and even comedy. The law, court rules, and facts provide a script. And, as in all plays, there are stars, supporting actors, directors, stage hands, various supporting staff, and even special attire. The roles are further defined by procedures and process.

As on the stage or screen, emotion is no stranger to the courtroom. Bizarre scenes are created by the mentally ill, the emotionally devastated, and those torn by anger or resentment. There is the pathos of tragedy and suffering. Outbursts of frustration exhibit the feelings of those unable to understand "the system" or express themselves clearly. Cross-motives and undercurrents of distrust and suspicion complicate and distract from orderly processes. The maelstrom potential of every courtroom is part of the human condition. Every judge must be aware of the possibilities and be prepared to deal with the unorthodox, the uncomfortable, and the bizarre caused by those caught up in what they often perceive as an uncaring and ineffectual system.

As stated earlier, the judge is responsible for the demeanor in the courtroom. The judge may prevent inappropriate behavior if he or she understands the cause of the disturbance or is aware of the potential for hostile or explosive conduct. In fact, the judge may be able to prevent an outburst by not adding to the tensions of the moment. There is a thin line between a necessary response by the judge to preserve the order of the courtroom and overreaction contributing to the disturbance. A judge should be slow to anger and ever aware that his or her reactions should be objective and reasonable.

To control the courtroom, a judge must control his or her own feelings first. Edmund Burke, eighteenth century political philosopher, stated, "It is ordained in the eternal constitution of things that men of intemperate minds cannot be free—their passions forge their fetters." The poet Kahlil Gibran puts it this way: "For reason, ruling alone, is a force confining; and passion, unattended, is a flame that burns to its own destruction."

One judge reported that early in his career he was attempting to arraign a defendant on disturbance charges. The defendant refused to listen to the admonishment of his rights, paced back and forth, and finally tore up the criminal complaint and threw it on the prosecutor's desk. The judge became angry and even embarrassed by the threat to his ability to manage the courtroom. He promptly declared the defendant in contempt and sentenced him to a term in jail. Later that afternoon, his bailiff advised him that the defendant had walked away from a state mental hospital, and the reports from the hospital indicated he was acutely psychotic. The judge confessed that he was so caught up with his own emotions that he was unable to decipher the bizarre antics of a patently psychotic person.

Since the judge is responsible for the orderly process of justice within the courtroom, the judge should create a distance between personal feelings and the human drama in the courtroom. That distance should not be so far as to make the judge indifferent and uncaring, but sufficient to allow the judge to remain objective and detached enough to carry out the responsibility of maintaining order, decorum, and fairness. The judge should not indulge in petty feelings or feelings that would dissipate or detract from the necessary ability to be objective and reasonable. Displays of emotion can be contagious, and the judge should strive at all times to be not unaware or unempathetic, but immune from the symptoms of emotionalism.

The American Bar Association Standards for Criminal Justice provides the following caution on exercising self-restraint:

> The trial judge should be the exemplar of dignity and impartiality. The judge should exercise restraint over his or her conduct and utterances. The judge should suppress personal predilections, and control his or her temper and emotions. The judge should not permit any person in the courtroom to embroil him or her in conflict, and should otherwise avoid personal conduct which tends to demean the proceedings or to undermine judicial authority in the courtroom. When it becomes necessary during the trial for the judge to comment upon the conduct of witnesses, spectators, counsel, or others, or upon the testimony, the judge should do so in a firm, dignified, and restrained manner, avoiding repartee, limiting his or her comments and rulings to what is reasonably required for the orderly progress of the trial, and refraining from unnecessary disparagement of persons or issues."[17]

Disorder in the Courtroom

Disorder in the courtroom has been a part of judicial systems for centuries. It is perhaps an unavoidable element of a system that wields so much power over the lives and fortunes of individuals. The risks include not only the obstreperous, angry, or mentally unbalanced party

17. American Bar Association, *supra* note 13.

or lawyer, but also those who intentionally disrupt court proceedings.

In recent times, instances of intentional disruption include the Sedition Trial in 1942 and the Communist Smith Act Trials before Judge Harold M. Medina in 1949. During the ten-month Medina trial, constant tension, frequent insults, and disruptive conduct resulted in five lawyers and one defendant being held in contempt at the conclusion of the trial. Referring to the Communist Trial, a 1973 report by the Association of the Bar of the City of New York observed:

> At this point it is difficult to decide whether the obstructive behavior at the trial arose out of the lawyers' individual, vigorous assertion of their clients' cause or was planned beforehand to duplicate the events of the Sedition Trial, or whether their conduct was the result of a self-fulfilling prophecy, a consequence of Judge Medina's own behavior. Certainly, . . . there was extensive contention between the judge and the lawyers. The lawyers reacted and overreacted to what the judge said about them, which soon became the main point of conflict.[18]

The Chicago Seven conspiracy trial of 1969-1970 before Federal District Judge Julius Hoffman is a clear example of intentional disruption. The defendants were charged with conspiracy to incite riots at the 1968 Democratic National Convention in Chicago. The trial was a bizarre combination of contemptuous conduct, political radicalism, and overreaction by all participants, including the judge.

The convictions and the contempt citations were reversed, and the court of appeals criticized the judge's handling of the case. It is clear that much of the conduct was contemptuous, but it is also clear that the judge aggravated the situation by his own conduct.

In the judge's defense, it can be said that the physical and psychological demands of the trial were overwhelming and took their toll on the seventy-five-year-old judge. Early in the proceedings, the judge was drawn into a web of chaos and was unable to remain detached, objective, and reasonable.

Few judges will be tested by the likes of the communist trial, the Chicago conspiracy trial, or other such lengthy, notorious trials. However, judges should be aware that intentional—even preplanned—disruption is a serious possibility in any courtroom. Many judges have been challenged by the courtroom antics of individual members of fringe groups holding fanatical religious or political beliefs that are radically opposed to accepted interpretations of law or constitutional rights. Some groups will not recognize the jurisdiction of the court to hear the cases against their members.

---

18. N. DORSEN & L. FRIEDMAN, DISORDER IN THE COURT: REPORT OF THE ASSOCIATION OF THE BAR OF THE CITY OF NEW YORK 50 (1973).

Among ways of showing disrespect for the system, the litigant may attempt to have a nonlawyer represent him or her, will remain seated when the judge enters, refuse to take an oath before testifying, urge the jury to disregard the judge's instructions on the law, and generally show contempt for the court's authority and procedures. Most often the conduct is intended to make a statement on behalf of the litigant's beliefs and to provoke the judge into some precipitous reaction.

Often the litigant's group will have compiled a multipage "brief" setting forth the case against the "unlawful" conduct of the opposing party, the court, and the whole administration of justice. Interspersed with the fanatical rhetoric are seeds of appropriate constitutional rights, and the underlying claims cannot be dismissed out of hand. As irrational as the litigant may appear, he or she typically believes the party line deeply and, for whatever reason, has chosen to rebel in an unorthodox manner. The judge must exercise great patience and objectivity and should not allow the litigant, or others in the courtroom, to draw him or her into the quagmire of fanaticism.

But what does the judge do when there is intentional disorder in the courtroom? There is no single answer nor a fail-safe formula. There are some guidelines, however, that may assist.

First, the judge must display patience and objectivity and attempt to discover the underlying causes for the disorder. Ignoring borderline conduct is a judge's option. The judge also must be confident that the court system, no matter how uncomfortable its process, will eventually prevail.

A recess or brief continuance may allow a disruptive situation to calm down. The extra time will also allow the judge to give further thought to the problem. Often, discussions with colleagues will provide new ideas and options. The recess allows the judge to rejuvenate—physically, mentally, and spiritually.

The judge can lay down specific ground rules for conduct. All participants and observers should be clear about the conduct required by the judge. This may serve to get unknown issues resolved early, so that the judge can avoid dealing with each issue separately as it arises. It also may allow the litigant to let off steam.

The judge also has the contempt power. Although a judge is under a good deal of stress during such an ordeal, the judge must be slow to react. Control of the courtroom and the proceedings must, however, be maintained. Unusual accommodations to the litigant may be appropriate under certain circumstances. Avoiding the collateral issues that can develop in contempt proceedings often can result in a speedy disposition of the primary case. Judges who have weathered the storm of such a trial find juries unsympathetic to the conduct of the dissidents and further discover that most often the last thing the litigant wants is a speedy and reasonable conclusion to the trial. The judge, at all times, must watch the line separating tolerable disruptive tactics and contemptuous conduct. Contemptuous conduct must be addressed, but moving the trial to a speedy conclusion may be the judge's best counterweapon.

When all else fails, the judge can have a criminal defendant removed from the courtroom while the trial continues. An obstreperous criminal defendant may be nearly uncontrollable in any setting and least of all in a trial based on rules and procedures. Many such individuals have significant psychological or emotional problems and will not respond to judicial advice or admonitions. The ruling in *Illinois v. Allen*[19] allows the judge to remove a defendant from his or her own trial if the disruptive behavior cannot be curbed by in-court procedures. In the *Allen* case, the U.S. Supreme Court held:

> Although mindful that courts must indulge every reasonable presumption against the loss of constitutional rights . . . we explicitly hold today that a defendant can lose his right to be present at trial if, after he has been warned by the judge that he will be removed if he continues his disruptive behavior, he nevertheless insists on conducting himself in a manner so disorderly, disruptive and disrespectful of the court that his trial cannot be carried on with him in the courtroom. Once lost, the right to be present can, of course, be reclaimed as soon as the defendant is willing to conduct himself consistently with the decorum and respect inherent in the concept of courts and judicial proceedings.[20]

The American Bar Association Standards Relating to the Administration of Criminal Justice provide guidelines and helpful suggestions on the role of the judge in a criminal trial. In addition to a standard dealing with a disruptive defendant,[21] the standards provide assistance in dealing with lawyer misconduct[22] and spectator misconduct.[23]

Pro Se Litigants—Criminal

Defendants acting as their own attorney present another issue of courtroom conduct—conflicting fundamental rights. In *Faretta v. California*,[24] the U.S. Supreme Court recognized a defendant's fundamental right to self-representation. The right is not absolute. The sixth amendment right of the assistance of counsel cannot be waived unless the waiver is a knowing, intelligent, and voluntary one.

Once a defendant clearly and unequivocally asserts the right to act as attorney pro se, the trial judge is faced with multiple and continuing problems. Not only must the judge conduct a thorough hearing where the defendant is advised of the peril, but the judge must demonstrate on

---

19. 397 U.S. 337 (1970).
20. *Id.*
21. American Bar Association, *supra* note 13, Standard 6-3.8.
22. *Id.*, Standard 6-3.5.
23. *Id.*, Standard 6-3.10.
24. 422 U.S. 806 (1975).

the record that the defendant is capable of understanding what is being waived and that in fact the waiver is knowing, intelligent, and voluntary. The record must further reflect that the defendant has consulted with a lawyer and that the defendant possesses the mental capacity to understand the pitfalls of self-representation before finalizing any waiver.[25] The hearing should not be perfunctory. The facts must be weighed and, if the judge finds that the defendant would be clearly ineffective and unable to deal with the issues likely to be raised at trial or would likely significantly impede or disrupt the trial, the judge may decide to deny the right to appear pro se.[26]

In all pro se cases, a standby counsel must be appointed to assist the defendant during the trial. Standby counsel must be available to the defendant in the courtroom and should also be instructed by the judge to bring to the judge's attention matters favorable to the accused upon which the judge should rule on his or her own motion.[27] Standby counsel must, however, be careful not to undermine the defendant's control of the trial and thereby lay the foundation for a posttrial motion or a successful appeal.[28]

The jury should be advised that the defendant will act as his or her own attorney. Further, the judge must tell the jury that the accused has been offered the opportunity to be represented by a retained lawyer or one appointed by the court at no expense to the defendant and the defendant has declined lawyer representation.[29]

During a trial, the judge must be cognizant of the defendant's rights but also must require the defendant to act with appropriate decorum and respect. The defendant should not be allowed to harass witnesses and should be confined to the counsel table unless given permission to move about for legitimate purposes of the trial.

Pro Se Litigants—Civil

More and more courts are faced with civil litigants appearing pro se. Most such appearances are for financial reasons. Also there are a number of how-to books on the market dealing with fields such as divorce and probate. Citizens expect that the judge, being a public officer, should help a citizen attempting to obtain justice without the assistance of a lawyer.

A pro se appearance is usually a problem for the judge and may present questions of law and propriety that would not be present if the litigant

25. United States *ex. rel.* Martinez v. Thomas, 526 F.2d 750 (1975).
26. *Id.*
27. *See* American Bar Association, *supra* note 13, Standard 6-3.7.
28. McKaskle v. Wiggins, 465 U.S. 168 (1984).
29. *See* American Bar Association, *supra* note 13, Standard 6-3.6.

was represented by a lawyer. Questions arise: How much can the judge help? Where is the line between assisting a citizen in the lawful pursuit of justice and giving legal advice? In such a case, is the opposing party, represented by a lawyer, at a disadvantage? What fundamental constitutional rights are involved? A trial with a pro se litigant will often take more time. How much extra time can be justified?

Faced with the reality of pro se litigants and the many related problems, some courts have special out-of-court programs to assist persons acting as their own lawyer. Information supplied to a pro se litigant before she or he enters the courtroom may deter unnecessary pro se appearances. Most local bar associations have pro bono legal services and other programs to assist the poor or financially stretched litigant. Directing persons to those services may solve the problem.

One court has proposed a pro se handbook filled with information about where to get assistance, what will be expected in court, a description of pitfalls, an outline of in-court procedures, and other information designed to make the pro se experience as comfortable as possible for all concerned: the litigants, opposing lawyer, court staff, and, of course, the judge.[30]

Once the pro se case is in court, however, the judge still must address the myriad of issues that will arise, attempting to meet the legitimate needs of the pro se litigant while not compromising the rights of a party represented by a lawyer. Experienced judges report that most pro se litigants will be satisfied with the result if the judge is courteous, appears to take their cause seriously, and will take the time to explain the reasons for the ruling or verdict.

Ours is an open court system, and justice must be available to all who seek it, regardless of socioeconomic status. The efficient use of court time is a valid standard, but must be tempered with the overall goal of the court: equal justice under law.

Communication Conduct

Communication is the soul of the courtroom, the life of every trial. It is the midwife of justice.

All that occurs in the courtroom depends on communication, by words, written and oral, and by other visual or auditory means such as photos, diagrams, figures, sounds, and symbols.

One of the danger areas of communication involves the use of body language. Body language can include any nonreflexive or reflexive movement of a part or all of the body, used by a person to communicate an emotional message to the outside world.[31] Head nods, lifting of an eye-

30. King County Superior Court, Seattle, Washington.
31. J. Fast, Body Language (1970).

brow, and facial expressions all are tools of communication.

It is a danger area because such expressions are not "on the record" but may be very influential in deciding the outcome of a trial. Clinical studies have revealed the extent to which body language can actually contradict verbal communication.[32] Further, body language by one party when the other party is making a presentation is distracting, discourteous, and an unfair tactic.

The judge must not engage in body language that inappropriately discloses the judge's feelings or conveys a belief as to the weight of evidence. A judicial sneer during the testimony of a witness would most likely convey to the jury a comment on the credibility of the witness. Such a comment is disallowed in almost every jurisdiction.

Even the judge's posture or lack of attentiveness can communicate feelings and attitudes. The words on the record do not always describe the proceedings accurately. For example, they may not disclose the impatience displayed by the judge when the words were spoken.

Controlling intentional and unintentional body language in the courtroom is the responsibility of the judge. Much of the courtroom communication falls within the scope of the lawyer's responsibilities and in large part depends on the lawyer's skill, experience, and knowledge of communication mechanics. The judge, however, is very much a part of the communication system. The judge is a receiver of much of the communication and also has the authority to seek clarification, or even to require more information or data from the litigants and their lawyers.

Others in the process are at the mercy of the communicators. Jurors seldom, if ever, can ask questions. Witnesses are also at a disadvantage. They must respond to questions from a lawyer, with little opportunity to express what they know in a manner of their choosing. The judge should be sensitive to the communication needs of jurors and witnesses.

There are also those who are afflicted with communication barriers, such as hearing, sight, or speech handicaps. It is the judge's responsibility to aid those needing communication assistance.

Indeed, if the defendant in a criminal case cannot understand the testimony or other critical parts of the trial, his or her rights are in jeopardy. In such cases, the court must supply interpreters, signers, or specialized equipment as the situation dictates.

Persons who do not understand the English language present a special problem. It may be necessary to provide, or at least accommodate, interpreters. The court plan should include procedures for swearing in the interpreter and providing access to the non-English-speaking person to allow communication to flow with the least amount of distraction.

---

32. *Id.*

Even instructions to the jury involve important communication dynamics. Both written and oral instructions should be clear, concise, and couched in understandable language, free wherever possible of legal jargon.[33]

Collegiality as Conduct

Collegiality is a special category of judicial conduct. Because of the role of judges in society, they are set apart from the community in significant ways. The Code of Judicial Conduct requires a higher standard of conduct for judges than citizens, other professionals, or public officials, and in many respects isolates the judge from the community. It is a natural response for judges to join together in a special collegiality. This new relationship with other judges can provide support, camaraderie, education, and problem solving.

Experienced judges are willing to help new members of the bench make the transition from lawyer to judge. Many court systems or judges' associations have formalized plans to provide the new judge with helpful and efficient orientation to the new role. The new judge should take advantage of such opportunities. Sometimes an experienced lawyer assumes he or she needs no assistance or orientation. The roles and responsibilities are different, however, and experienced lawyers do not automatically become experienced judges.

Collegiality expresses itself in a variety of ways. A discussion with a single member of the bench about a unilateral or common problem is an expression of collegiality. Judges acting on a committee or task force for the improvement of the court are displaying collegiality. State judges' associations provide a myriad of opportunities for collegial involvement. On a national level, the National Judicial College at Reno, Nevada, provides a collegial education experience (judges teaching judges), and the National Conference of State Trial Judges offers an opportunity to participate in collegial activities on a national scale.[34]

The judge who believes that the only important activity of a judge occurs in the courtroom is misinterpreting the total role of a judge, encouraging isolation, and missing the opportunity to grow in skill and wisdom through the collegial experience.

Conclusion

This chapter has introduced the unique environment of a judge: the facilities, courtroom conduct, and appearance and role of the judge within

33. *See* American Bar Association, *supra* note 5, Standard 16.

34. Information about membership in the National Conference of State Trial Judges may be obtained by contacting the conference office, American Bar Association Center, 750 N. Lake Shore Drive, Chicago, Illinois 60611; 312/988-5691.

this environment. The chapter's purpose has been to help lawyers make the transition into a new working arena, to help new judges understand the dynamics of the courtroom from the judge's perspective, to provide some new insights, and to assure a new judge that other judges from across the nation care about him or her and further care about the quality of justice in every jurisdiction.

3

THE QUALITIES OF A JUDGE

If thou be a leader, be gracious when thou hearkenest unto the speech of a suppliant. Let him not hesitate to deliver himself of that which he hath thought to tell thee but be desirous of removing his injury. Let him speak freely that the thing for which he hath come may be done.

—*The Instructions of Ptah Hotep*
c. 3550 B.C.

Twenty years ago, our friend Professor Maurice Rosenberg wrote a piece entitled "The Qualities of a Justice—Are They Strainable?"[1] Professor Rosenberg aimed in part at identifying qualities to look for in picking a judge. Here we are examining only the qualities a judge should strive to acquire if he or she does not already possess them. Nothing can be done about one's past, such as preparatory education, professional attainment, and political affiliations. There are, however, qualities the judge can acquire through some effort. Most of them are not new but have been recognized for centuries as essential qualities of a good judge.

Graciousness

Ptah Hotep was an official during the old kingdom of Egypt over 5,500 years ago. One of his duties was to serve as a judge. Like Polonius, he gave instructions to his son. The quotation opening this chapter is part of those instructions. He also said, "Listen attentively to the petitioner, for a good hearing is a soothing to the soul." These words of Ptah Hotep come to us, a voice out of the past, over a great time span from an ancient civilization. They are, however, as true today as they were in

1. American Judicature Society, Handbook for Judges (1984).

those days of the first pharaohs. Now, as then, one of the important qualities of a trial judge is the ability to be gracious and to listen attentively to the parties and their cases.

No case is unimportant to the parties. Whether it is a civil or criminal case, the parties have come to court for justice. One of the marks of a civilized society is that its citizens have given up the right to settle their disputes by private strife and have agreed to submit the disputes to an impartial decision maker. Crimes are against the state which prosecutes and metes out punishment to the guilty party. It is important that people have faith in this system.

Judges at best can please only half the litigants who come before them. Someone has to lose. But if, in addition to losing, a party leaves with the feeling that the judge did not pay full attention to the case, the system is not respected. As in ancient times, a good hearing is still soothing to the soul. So the judge should make it a point to show interest in every case, no matter how unimportant it seems to be.

As Ptah Hotep said, it is important for a judge to be gracious to the parties and their witnesses so that they may tell their stories without hesitation. These people are under great stress. If the judge treats them in a gruff manner, they will be inhibited in their testimony, and the real truth may not emerge. A gracious judge will put them at ease so that they may freely relate their side of the case.

Moral Courage

According to Professor Rosenberg's survey of judges, moral courage is high on the list of required qualities. A judge should not expect to be popular. The great constitutional principles a judge is called upon to follow are in large measure restraints upon the majority to protect the rights of individuals and minorities. When a judge does his or her best work in upholding these principles, the judge is bound to be unpopular.

The trial judge is the closest to the people and the closest to the police. That closeness makes it all the more difficult to uphold the constitutional safeguards, and this is especially so in the case of judges facing election or reappointment.

Judges must remember why they are on the bench. They are not a part of the police department, the prosecutor's or the public defender's office. They are there to do justice according to settled principles, not according to what is popular at the moment. They must think that they are doing the most important job there is, because they are. Nothing is more important than justice, and for those who come to court, justice depends upon the judge. Judges should therefore develop the courage to do justice whatever the consequences, and they will truly be great judges.

Reputation for Fairness

High on any list is a reputation for fairness. This is something one can develop only by actually being fair. But being fair is not enough. A judge must give the impression of being fair. How a judge conducts his or her private life as well as the judge's manner in the courtroom can give the appearance of unfairness even in a judge who is, in fact, fair.

A judge who has taken a stand on an issue or engages in conduct before ascending the bench and then refuses to recuse when that same conduct or issue comes before him or her does not give the impression of fairness. A judge can give the impression of not being completely unbiased by associating too closely and openly with any one group or organization. A judge who decides a case against a litigant who is not a member of that group in favor of one who is will not give the impression of fairness. Even when it seems possible to be fair, the judge should consider whether others will think so.

A judge need not live like a monk, but he or she should avoid conduct and associations that may raise questions about his or her impartiality. This is especially important in smaller communities, where a judge's activities are more likely to be noticed.

Mercy

The quality of mercy, whether it is strained or unstrained, is also important to a trial judge. This does not mean that a judge should be "soft on criminals." Some deserve the severest of punishments and should receive mercy, if at all, only from God. But many defendants who come before the court have become entangled in a web of circumstances that has led them before the bench. They deserve a degree of mercy. The neat trick is to tell which type of defendant is which. A good judge will have the mercy to apply when appropriate.

Patience

Patience is a must for a trial judge. Judges need patience with the lawyers, patience with litigants, patience with the cases, patience with the witnesses, patience with the jurors, and patience with the staff. It may seem to be a waste of time to listen to extensive arguments on a point on which the judge has made up his or her mind. But judges owe it to the lawyers to listen to their arguments. One object of the adversary system is to afford an opportunity to correct premature judgments which all human minds are prone to form.

The judge should be especially patient with young lawyers. They are doing their best, and they will do better with a patient judge than in the atmosphere created by an impatient one.

Close to impatience is tyranny or despotism. Given the limits on appellate review, a trial judge wields enormous power over the lawyers, litigants, witnesses, jurors, and court staff. These people know it; they don't need to have it shoved down their throats. There is no more sorry spectacle than a trial judge throwing his or her weight around. A judge should be dignified and firm but should not be mean. Power can be exercised gently and with restraint even more effectively than in a high-handed and gruff manner.

The confident and enlightened judge frames commands in the form of requests, makes them in a pleasant way, and is respected. The insecure judge shouts orders, which are obeyed but without respect. If the judge ever comes to a time when his or her "requests" are not followed, that is time enough to give direct orders. Even then a wise judge will do so in a calm, albeit forceful, manner.

Witnesses are essential to a lawsuit. Most of them are in court for the first time and would probably rather be somewhere else. The judge should be patient with them. If the judge needs to instruct or admonish them, he or she should do so in a kind and understanding way. The story is told about the witness who hesitated after a question was asked and was gruffly admonished by the judge to "come on, answer the question." The witness replied, "I ain't no lawyer and I ain't no judge. I have to think before I speak."

Jurors are another group who would usually rather be somewhere else. They are performing a duty of the highest order. There are only two instances when our government demands personal service of its citizens. One is to serve on juries, and the other is to serve their country in time of war. This ought to impress the trial judge with the importance of the function jurors serve and to lead the judge to treat them with respect and patience. They, like the witnesses, are in an unfamiliar atmosphere. The impression they get of the entire court system depends a great deal on how they are treated by the judge. If they must be kept waiting for long periods for one reason or another, the judge should let them know what is causing the delay, and that they also serve who only sit and wait.

Ability to Communicate

The ability to communicate with jurors and witnesses is also essential to a good trial judge. A trial judge is a teacher. When judges instruct jurors, the aim is to teach them enough about the law applicable to the case so they can render a proper verdict. This cannot be done properly by using lawyer language. The judge must learn to transform legal phrases into plain English that can be understood by lay people without jeopardizing the legal soundness of the instruction. The judge might practice communicating by trying out instructions on his or her spouse or on a nonlawyer friend. If this person does not understand the instructions, the judge should determine why not. That an instruction has been upheld by an appellate court is not proof the jury understood it.

Certain parts of a charge to the jury, such as the burden of proof, will be given in every case. The judge should boil these down to simple language and learn them so the judge can look the jurors in the eyes while giving them. Instead of telling jurors about the "preponderance of the evidence" in a civil case, the judge should tell them about deciding what is more probable than not. Instead of telling jurors they are to be "sequestered," the judge should tell them they will be kept apart without outside contact and will not be allowed to go home until the case is over. The judge must remember he or she is not dealing with lawyers, and that even college graduates are unfamiliar with some of the most basic principles of the law and terms used by lawyers.

Decisiveness

Decisiveness is an indispensable quality in a trial judge. A judge who does not possess it should acquire it. The cases come upon the judge relentlessly. A judge is never in a better position to decide a case than soon after it has been submitted. The longer the period between submission and decision, the dimmer the case is in the mind of the judge. By then several other cases have been tried and are awaiting decision. Their facts and problems will further dim the recollection of the earlier undecided cases.

Thoughtful consideration is essential, but indecisiveness is inconsistent with judicial responsibility. When deciding factual issues, the judge should remember what he or she tells jurors about the burden of proof. A judge who cannot make up his or her mind one way or the other in a civil matter has decided the case. The one having the burden of proof must lose. The same applies in criminal cases. If there is a reasonable doubt, the judge should acquit and be done with it. If not, the judge should convict.

Judges should be well acquainted with the rules of evidence so as to rule on most questions without much deliberation. If an unusual evidentiary question arises, it may be necessary to hear arguments and check the books, but the judge should not dillydally. And having decided, the judge should announce the decision with a show of confidence that it is right. A judge should never announce a decision in a manner that in any way indicates doubtfulness.

Judges should not fear reversal. One who shoots from the hip day in and day out is bound sooner or later to shoot himself in the foot. It is all part of being a trial judge. A trial judge who takes the time appellate judges do to decide issues would have trials that never end. This is not to suggest hasty decisions, but rather reasonably prompt ones.

Innovation

A quality seldom mentioned is the quality of innovation. A trial judge should not, of course, adopt harebrained methods, but on the other hand, a trial judge should not accept a method of doing things just because it has always been done that way. One of the problems in some courts is that those involved are still doing things the same way they were done 100 years ago. One of the great values of national judicial education is that it makes judges aware that there are different ways of doing things.

For example, until just a few years ago, very few trial judges gave basic instructions to the jury at the beginning about the case to be tried. Most judges left that to the end of the trial which is akin to giving a person a road map after reaching a destination. A few brief instructions on what issues the jury will be called upon to decide are very helpful to a jury before the evidence is introduced. This all started because some trial judges were innovative.

We operate under the adversary system, but what that means differs from person to person and from time to time. The basic premise of the system is that a decision maker is more likely to reach a correct result if both sides of an issue are fully presented, and that both sides are more likely to be fully presented if they are presented by partisan advocates, i.e., people with something to gain or lose. The desire to win is thought to compel a person to dig deeper and work harder to present that person's side of the issue, thus making more evidence available to decision makers. This desire to win, however, may also induce a party to withhold evidence favorable to the other side, thus hindering the ascertainment of the truth.

Trial by trick and ambush used to be the order of the day. It was not until the last quarter of a century that judges began to realize that the old view of the adversary system did not produce justice, and rules of discovery began to develop. Today full discovery is recognized as an essential part of the adversary system in both civil and criminal cases. So the system has evolved with time, but it took innovation.

One of the remaining misconceptions is that the trial judge is a mere umpire who should not speak unless spoken to. This conflicts with the purpose of a trial. The judge should, of course, rely on the adversaries for all that they can provide us, but the judge should not depend entirely upon them. A trial is not a game, and when a judge observes that justice may suffer because one lawyer or the other has failed in some way, the judge has the right and obligation to step in. This is not to suggest that the judge become an advocate, but at times, justice requires some action by the judge.

Just one example—if in an alcohol-impaired driving case requiring proof that the driver was on a public highway, the prosecutor forgets to put in such evidence, the judge should not dismiss the charges but should give the prosecution an opportunity to prove the point. To do otherwise is to frustrate the whole purpose of a trial.

The lawyers in a particular case may not like it, but lawyers, when they are considering what is generally good for the system, have come down in favor of action by the trial judge. Both the ABA Criminal Justice Standards on the Function of the Trial Judge and the Federal Rules of Evidence recognize the need for intervention by the judge under certain circumstances. Only recently, the ABA Commission on Professionalism has stated that the trial judge should take a much more active role in the conduct of litigation.

The judge must use care, especially in a jury case, not to cause prejudice, and it may be wise to make suggestions in the absence of the jury. The times when intervention is called for may be rare, but when and if the time comes, the trial judge should not hesitate to act.

Open-mindedness

Open-mindedness is an achievable quality in a judge, and every judge should strive to possess it. Individuals have control of their own minds. The judge should make an effort not to prejudge a case. Jumping to premature judgment is not uncommon, and the adversary system is designed to correct those prejudgments. But it is better if they do not form in the first place. A good judge's mind should be disciplined to remain open until all the evidence is in and all arguments have been heard.

Brevity

Not the least of the essential qualities of a good judge is brevity. Clear but concise instructions to the jury accomplish more than long ramblings filled with words that are meaningless to the jurors. As in writing, length can obscure meaning. Trial judges as well as appellate judges should stop writing law review articles instead of judicial opinions. Many reported cases are filled with needless verbiage. One notable gem runs 200 pages on the question of whether a party was entitled to a trial by jury. This kind of nonsense does not reflect a desirable quality in any judge, let alone a trial judge.

Trial judges should, on proper occasion, make findings and write opinions. This is necessary in order to inform the parties as to how the case has been decided and why. Findings and opinions are also invaluable to the appellate court in the event of an appeal, but these opinions should be no longer than necessary to accomplish their purpose.

Dignity

No list would be complete if it did not include dignity. This does not mean that judges should go around with their noses in the air. That is an affectation, not dignity. A judge should be aware, however, of the great prestige of the judicial office as symbolized by the occupant. If the symbol is tarnished, it reflects upon the office. A judge has the obligation to engage in dignified conduct in and out of court.

One should not, however, confuse dignity with stuffiness: a judge need not be a humorless stick-in-the-mud, nor is he or she barred from enjoying life. Nevertheless, a line must be drawn, and any judge who has the proper consciousness of the office and its responsibilities will know where that line is.

A proper degree of decorum in a courtroom, where civility must prevail, helps to maintain the proper atmosphere for the serious business at hand. The judge must set the example for others to follow. We have much to learn from our English colleagues in this regard. Some American courtrooms have become too informal and lack the dignity the place deserves. It is shocking when visiting a court to see the judge enter without a robe, lean back in his chair, and light up a big cigar. Some may scoff at wearing a robe, but it does something to a courtroom and to the judge. It is a constant reminder of the position and its obligations. The robe also provides a degree of anonymity, which in turn promotes a sense of impartiality and creates a desirable atmosphere of solemnity.

Honesty and Integrity

Finally, the qualities of honesty and integrity are of the utmost importance. The public and the lawyers expect, above all, that a judge be honest and upright, and possess the degree of integrity that is in keeping with the high office of a judge. As the old saying goes, "If you can't trust a judge, who can you trust?" So follow the advice of Polonius in *Hamlet* (Act I, Scene III): "This above all: to thine own self be true, And it must follow, as the night the day, Thou canst not then be false to any man."

4

THE FAMILY EFFECT

Candid sessions with judges' children and with groups of judges' spouses suggest that when a family member becomes a judge, the whole family makes a transition. Judges' children are particularly sensitive to parental reaction to the new job. One child said, "When dad was an attorney, we entertained informally. Now that he is a judge, he is a stuffed shirt, and entertainment is stiff and formal." Another said, "My grades have improved at school since mom became a judge, but not because I am a better student." Not all children express themselves as clearly, but many of them echo these remarks about how a parent's change in occupation affects them—"the family effect" of a lawyer becoming a judge.

Another change noted by children of judges is the reaction of other children toward them. Older children are sometimes set apart by at least some former friends because their parent, the judge, is regarded as part of "law enforcement." This is particularly true if the judge has duties as a juvenile court judge.

What about judicial spouses?

Some felt their lives enhanced: "The judge works fewer hours." "There is a new status in the community." "We see new people."

Others feel deprived: "He works longer hours." "He can't talk any more about what he does than he did when he was an attorney." "We can't entertain fellow lawyers as we once did." "She tells me to avoid politics because of the Code of Judicial Conduct."

These reactions indicate that judges bring a variety of changes to the lives of their spouses.

Standards of Conduct

What about the standards of judicial conduct?[1] The Code of Judicial Conduct affects not only the courtroom conduct, but also the extraju-

1. *See* AMERICAN BAR ASSOCIATION CODE OF JUDICIAL CONDUCT, Appendix A.

dicial life of the judge and the judge's family. Among the areas affected are finances, political conduct, and social life.

In the area of finance, the business dealings of the judge or the judge's spouse may be cause for disqualification.

The same thing is true for other members of the immediate family. While the judge may be quite impartial, someone else viewing the interests of the judge or the judge's family might assume that the judge is not impartial. It is a matter of not only propriety, but also the appearance of propriety.[2] Frequent disqualification is a burden upon the colleagues of the judge and is to be avoided. Thus business interests or investments causing or likely to cause disqualification are to be avoided.

Gifts and loans are also matters of concern. The judge operates under certain restrictions. A judge cannot accept a loan on terms that are better than those that would be offered to one who was not a judge. Gifts of certain kinds are prohibited. Compensation must be reported under the provisions of canon 6.

Does the code prevent political activity by the judge's spouse? The intent of canon 7 of the Code of Judicial Conduct was to establish a standard that would reduce or eliminate political activity by the judge and the judge's spouse, including discouraging contributions to a political organization or candidate, except under special conditions.[3]

It has been officially recognized in New Jersey and New York that the spouse may be properly involved in politics, at least to some extent. California has diluted the stringent requirement of canon 7A, and canon 7B is in limbo. As a result, in these three states at least, it is probably safe for the spouse of a state trial judge to run for the school board or for mayor.

There is another trend that affects political activity of spouses. In some formerly "safe" states, where 95 percent of judges had no opposition at reelection time, in recent years there have been more contested elections.

There are at least two possible sanctions for violation of the Code of Judicial Conduct. One is discipline by the ethical and enforcement agency within the judge's jurisdiction. The other is a more subtle sanction. In the increased number of contested elections for judicial office, a publicized violation of the Code of Judicial Conduct can give an opponent potent campaign ammunition.

Living with Change

When one becomes a judge, it affects the lives of each member of the family. These effects vary from family to family. Judges have prestige,

2. *See id.*, canon 20.
3. *See id.*, canons 7A, 7B.

community recognition, even honor. But these very things set the judge and the judge's family apart. They create real problems for spouses and growing children. Learning to accept the attention, the respect and the attitude of the people toward judges and their families is an important part of the transition from bar to bench, a part of the price of being a judge. Even so, judges should do their best to minimize "the family effect."

5

INTEGRATION OF WOMEN AND MINORITY JUDGES INTO THE AMERICAN JUDICIARY

In the past 10 years, we have seen a substantial increase in the number of women and minority judges appointed or elected to the bench. Despite these strides toward achieving the goal of a judiciary that is truly representative of the great diversity of American society, much progress remains to be made. According to 1985 statistics from the Fund for Modern Courts, only 7.2 percent of our state court judges are female, and only 5.7 percent are minorities, including blacks, Hispanics, Asian-Americans, and Native Americans. At the federal level, 7.4 percent of the federal bench are female and 10.6 percent are minorities.[1]

This means that our judiciary still remains, overwhelmingly, white and male. That fact has serious implications for the integration of "the new kids on the block"—women and minorities—into the mainstream of the American judiciary.

As in any situation where newcomers are entering a field, they will encounter a certain degree of resistance from those who have become comfortable and familiar with, as well as successful under, the status quo. However, while it took political change from *outside* the judiciary to open up the bench to those who were excluded, it will take change from *inside* the judiciary to allow women and minorities to function effectively in an atmosphere free of gender and ethnic bias. Most significantly—as we come to recognize and acknowledge the difficult, and usually uncomfortable, issues of gender and ethnic bias in terms of relationships with colleagues—we will also come to understand how those issues affect our decision making and the quality of justice dispensed in our courtrooms.

1. FUND FOR MODERN COURTS, INC., THE SUCCESS OF WOMEN AND MINORITIES IN ACHIEVING JUDICIAL OFFICE: THE SELECTION PROCESS (1985).

The aim of this chapter is to help judges understand how they may be exhibiting bias toward their female and minority colleagues, and to make female and minority judges aware of how ethnic and gender stereotyping by judicial colleagues and others may hurt them as they undertake the difficult task of learning their unfamiliar profession. How that same stereotyping affects the quality of substantive decision making in areas as diverse as sentencing, child support, domestic violence, and tort case damages is discussed in the next chapter.

The Assimilation of Female Judges

Recently appointed or elected women judges enter upon their new careers with all the excitement, enthusiasm, energy—and apprehension—of any of their male counterparts. Like most Americans, they retain an idealized view of judges as being fairer than the rest of us and free of the biases and stereotypes that plague most mortals. Thus, most women judges join the bench anticipating a warm welcome, total acceptance as a colleague, and treatment based on their ability to dispose of a heavy caseload and handle a busy courtroom. In many cases, events will prove them wrong.

Because it is better for new judges—particularly new women judges—to understand and thus be able to handle the problems they will face, this section is written to alert them to situations they may never have considered. These words do not apply to every jurisdiction; they certainly do not apply to every male or female judge. In many instances, male judges will be welcoming and supportive; in many instances they will run interference with less accepting colleagues and ensure that their new female colleagues are treated appropriately. But the problems that women judges face—as women—are still pervasive and unsettling enough to a new judge that these problems need to be openly addressed. To be forewarned is to be forearmed.

Acceptance and Treatment by Judicial Colleagues

Newcomers to the bench look to colleagues for the guidance and support (as well as substantive training) that every new judge needs. In doing so, new judges must remember that colleagues, while reflective of the prevailing legal community, will probably be older, more conservative, more "establishment," more white, and more male than the rest of the local bar. Given the relatively recent entry of women into the legal profession in large numbers, and the relatively low number of women who have been large-firm senior partners or government prosecutors (areas of practice from which many judges are selected), many of the sitting judges on the bench—especially those with substantial seniority—will never have maintained an easygoing, collegial working relationship with a woman as their peer.

For some of them, that will prove virtually impossible to do. Thus, having achieved the pinnacle of professional success with a judicial seat, a woman judge will still find some men colleagues addressing her as "sweetie," "doll," "honey," or the ubiquitous "dear." Some colleagues will never fail, no matter how many times a week they see a female judge on the same court, to comment on her clothes or ask about her husband, instead of asking about her assignment, discussing the latest appellate court decision, or trading political gossip about what the mayor is or isn't doing properly.

At judicial seminars and training sessions, a curious phenomenon can be perceived which one state appellate judge called the "you don't exist" syndrome—namely that a woman's comments are often not heard, or her suggestions are ignored, while the same idea is readily adopted when a male colleague proposes it a few minutes later.

At social functions with judicial colleagues, other issues emerge. Life is infinitely easier if a woman judge has a husband or "significant other" to whom male colleagues can relate and with whom they can comfortably discuss sports.

If a woman judge is single or does not choose to bring a male "security blanket" to judicial functions, she must be particularly alert to potential dangers arising from the loosening of inhibitions in a social atmosphere where alcohol usually flows freely. Although women have dealt with these problems throughout their professional lives, and have usually discreetly handled them, it is more than a little disconcerting when a sixty-year-old man she has always respected as a judge pats her on the derriere or asks about her sex life. And when a woman's chief judge makes unwelcome sexual overtures, she has the right to worry about what her future assignments will be. Finally, her equanimity may be stretched to the breaking point by attending a colleague's birthday party and finding that his birthday cake—to his evident delight—is molded in the shape of a woman's breasts.

While these experiences do not happen everywhere to everyone, each of them has in fact happened somewhere to someone. If male judges are acting in this manner toward their equals on the court, how are they acting in the courtroom toward the women lawyers and litigants who appear before them expecting equal treatment?

Acceptance and Treatment by Members of the Bar

One of the most difficult elements of the transition from bar to bench is the change that must take place in the relationship of the new judge to the lawyers the judge has known and practiced with throughout his or her professional life. That change dramatically affects male and female judges. Indeed, because the law is still a male-dominated and male-controlled profession, and because men are more actively involved in the mainstream of the law, it can be argued that they suffer more than women do in this transition, precisely because they have enjoyed greater collegiality and friendship among their peers than most women do.

However, new women judges encounter problems that are unique to them as women. Some are as simple, albeit annoying, as lawyers continually referring to a woman judge as either "sir" or "ma'am." When a lawyer continues to address a woman judge as "sir," it tells that judge that the lawyer is incapable of seeing her in a role of authority. It is particularly exasperating to women who sit on appellate benches when experienced and articulate advocates, looking at a panel of one female and two male judges, begin their argument with "gentlemen." As to the use of the patronizing term "ma'am" instead of "your honor" or "judge," it connotes to many women exactly what the term "boy" connotes to a black man.

One of the most significant issues faced by a new judge—female or male—is the need to demonstrate the ability to run a courtroom well, to manage the calendar efficiently, and to insist upon the appropriate respect and decorum. In attempting to develop these critical skills, many women judges face what can only be called the "damned if you do, damned if you don't" syndrome.

Many times, when a woman judge attempts to run a tightly controlled, highly organized court where tardiness, lack of preparation, and general sloppiness are not tolerated, she runs the risk of being labeled "bitchy," "difficult," "abrasive," and worse.

If, on the other hand, her personal style is more relaxed, and she tries to cultivate a relatively informal atmosphere where less pressure is put on lawyers and calendars move at a more leisurely pace, that woman judge runs the risk of being labeled "weak," "not in control," and "not tough enough."

Women judges are often subject to the same kind of automatic stereotyping by the bar that the bar criticizes in judges. For example, it was apparent to one relatively new woman judge that a defense lawyer was trying to transfer a rape case to a male judge. When questioned about it, he reluctantly noted her reputation for stiff sentences in "that kind of case." In response, she pointed out to him that she had never handled a rape case either on the bench or in private practice.

Many judges attend bar association functions because they enjoy socializing with their colleagues and because they feel it is part of their judicial responsibilities. A new woman judge making the transition from bar to bench will often find that her former colleagues are far less comfortable with that change than when men travel that path. Whereas a new male judge is addressed off the bench as "judge" from the day of his swearing in, it is not surprising to find many lawyers in a community continuing to call a new female judge by her first name long after that swearing in, or stumbling uncomfortably over the word "judge," or asking how she would like to be addressed when no such question is asked of her male counterpart.

The issue, again, comes down to the discomfort men experience when dealing with women who have been given power. For most, it is a brand-new experience for which time and exposure are the only antidotes.

Decision Making

Upon taking the oath of office, every new judge swears to rule fairly and impartially and to render justice for all. A new woman judge is keenly aware that she is more visible than her new male colleagues, and that she will be scrutinized more closely. Because of this, many women understand that they are under greater pressure to prove themselves because they are women. With that pressure may come a concomitant pressure to not only rule fairly (which is of course their obligation) but also bend over backward to avoid any appearance of partiality to women.

Thus, some women may find when they first sit on the bench that they develop an unfortunate tendency to rule against women whenever an issue is in doubt. In the close cases, there may be a tendency to choose to disbelieve a victim of domestic violence, or to blame the mother of small children for not being able to get a better job and therefore deny her an award of higher child support, or to heavily sentence prostitutes.

A woman judge who has reached the bench by virtue of her own excellence may find herself feeling personally threatened or uncomfortable when a woman lawyer appears before her who is not fully prepared or is dressed unprofessionally, or when a bitter homemaker vindictively demands excessive alimony because her husband abandoned her for another woman.

In short, it is not surprising when female professionals who have finally made it to the pinnacle of power in their community react to and internalize many of the stereotypes that have traditionally blocked the path of other women to success. This attitude may stem, in part, from the selection process by which that judge reached the bench. Many female applicants for judgeships report extensive questioning about whether they can be fair and impartial in lawsuits traditionally involving women such as sexual harassment cases or custody cases. Would a male applicant be asked if he could be fair and impartial in a rape case or a child support case?

The Role of the Woman Judge within the Courthouse

In the early days on the bench, a new judge will be acclimating herself to the courthouse and its staff. If that judge was fortunate enough to have been an active litigator, she may know well many of the clerks, secretaries, and administrative assistants who really turn the wheels of justice. In that event, a new woman judge may face the problem of establishing with them her new position and the respect it should be accorded. Both sides will have to make accommodations. Just as she can no longer enjoy the breezy, informal relationship she may well have had with court staff, they cannot maintain the first-name, bantering attitude that they may well have had with her as a practicing attorney.

Male and female court staff both may have problems adjusting to a female attorney who becomes a judge. Men working in the court system may have the same difficulties as male lawyers and judges accepting her as a person with authority and power. What may be much more hurtful to a woman judge personally, because unexpected, may be the hostility of some women employees in the court system.

One woman appellate judge recounts the story of another judge's secretary who literally intimidated the entire female support staff into ignoring her and harassing her staff. While such excessive conduct is rare, it is not surprising to find individual women court reporters or secretaries who do not welcome a woman judge's success or presence with open arms.

However, the reverse is more likely to be true. A new female judge may well find herself not only greeted with warmth and pride by female support staff, but also placed in the difficult position of being asked to champion their cause on grievances they have with the existing male power structure governing the court. Or, if she is not openly asked for help, she may come to learn of administrative or personnel problems affecting women within the court system, and then have to decide what, if any, role she will choose to play in ameliorating those problems. The choice to speak out on behalf of women in the court system may well hurt her own later career prospects in terms of preferred assignments, designation as presiding or assignment judge, or promotion to a higher bench.

Additionally, many women judges are asked to play a mentor role for the many lawyers who seek a role model. This can be a demanding and difficult task, but it is obviously an investment in the future of those to follow.

Finally, if there are enough women on an individual court, they may well wish to organize—whether informally for a dinner meeting or formally as a women's caucus—to focus on judicial issues particularly affecting women that they think they can effectively address. For example, few courthouses have facilities to care for the children of witnesses, litigants, and jurors who must transact business in the courthouse. Women judges could, in the name of efficiency and courtroom tranquility, work toward the establishment of such nurseries or playrooms, thus relieving the stress of parents and reducing court disruptions.

Private Life/Private Time

Becoming a judge will radically change one's life. Probably the best known of the side effects of judicial life is the isolation. There is no question that both male and female judges keenly feel the isolation, dislike its impact and ramifications, and acknowledge its necessity and inevitability.

In some ways, however, it does have a disproportionate impact on women judges. Because there are still so few women judges in this country and because of the problems just outlined, women find themselves even more isolated than when they were lawyers. Often there is only one woman on a court. That woman is denied the support, camaraderie, and nurturing that she probably enjoyed with other women lawyers in the days of practicing law. She is thrust into a new position, where every action she takes is public and where she faces the most demanding professional challenge of her career. Moreover, there is an unwritten law in the judiciary that "thou shalt not tattle on thy colleagues," so that she cannot share her sense of alienation and exclusion with former friends and peers.

Judicial life also greatly affects family relationships. New judges—male or female—often work much harder than they did as lawyers because of the awesome nature of their new responsibilities and so are too drained to contribute much to family life when they are present. On a day-to-day basis, they face harrowing personal tragedies for which the legal system can provide no solution, and that ongoing frustration takes its emotional toll.

But again, the impact often differs for women. If a woman has a steady male figure in her life, it is simply harder—given the cultural context of life in the United States at this time—for a man to accept overwhelming demands stemming from a woman's career. Consequently, significant as the stresses are for the families (children as well as spouses) of new judges, they are significantly greater for families of women judges.

If a woman judge does not have a steady male figure in her life, the situation is immeasurably complicated. Many women judges do their socializing out of town. (This practice led one judge to end up marrying a lawyer who lived hundreds of miles away from her town!) Others identify a "safe" local male friend whom they can take to local functions without gossip and speculation. For many, sadly enough, social life ceases.

These comments are intended to help women judges anticipate some of the problems they will encounter when they take the bench, and take comfort in knowing they are not alone in facing those problems. The comments are, as they must be, of a general nature, although every example is based on the personal experience of some woman judge sitting in a courtroom in this country. Just as some will have no problems of adjustment to the bench, others will face substantial difficulties.

Because the judiciary to a great extent reflects society at large, many of the difficulties encountered by women judges will be mirror images of those they encountered as practicing attorneys. As male judges come to understand and acknowledge the existence of gender bias—often subtle, often totally unintentional—they will be taking the first vital steps toward its elimination.

The Assimilation of Minority Judges

As demonstrated by the statistics from the Fund for Modern Court's 1985 study set out at the beginning of this chapter, minority judges are still a distinct rarity in the United States. Looking at numbers rather than percentages makes this even more apparent. Out of the 12,093 full-time, law-trained judges of the state courts in 1985, 465 were black, 155 were of Hispanic origin, 77 were Asian-Americans, and only 3 were Native Americans or Native Alaskans. At the federal level in 1985, out of 753 judges there were 53 blacks, 24 Hispanics, 3 Asian-Americans, and no Native Americans or Native Alaskans.

These very small numbers account for a phenomenon upon which many black judges have remarked: a tremendous demand for one's time from the community, and direct questions about what it is like to be a black judge.*

The new black judge is immediately elevated to a position of prominence in the black community and society at large. Demands are made on the judge's time for speaking engagements, radio and television appearances, community and civic involvements, and consultation with groups and organizations on many causes and issues. Which of these invitations the judge accepts is an individual choice, dictated by considerations such as work load and time constraints and the Judicial Canons of Ethics. It is important, however, to guard against the tendency to become overextended, and to learn how to decline these invitations without antagonizing the community.

A new black judge may be asked, "What is it like being a black judge?" This question may have several connotations. The judge should assess the setting in which the question is asked, and the person who is asking the question, to determine what is the real question. Such connotations might imply:

- That black judges only hear cases involving black litigants or black attorneys

*Other minority judges may consider the following examples in the light of their own situations.

- Concern that a black judge is isolated from other judges and, if the question comes from a judicial colleague, how that situation might be remedied
- Interest in what it is like for a black person to be a judge, or
- A combination of all these possibilities

Asking the questioner to clarify the question may yield a better perspective as to the response or answer to give. The new judge should not be annoyed or surprised at such questions. Black and other minority judges are still such a rarity that it is an educational process for the bench, bar, and public to become accustomed to their presence on the bench.

Acceptance and Treatment by Judicial Colleagues

Most newcomers to the bench have appeared before most of the judges with whom they will serve on the bench and thus are aware of these judges' biases. Becoming a judicial colleague to those already on the bench should bring few surprises. The curt manner directed by some judges to minority lawyers will still be present. If a judge virtually ignored the presence of the black as a lawyer, this same behavior will be exhibited toward the black as a judge. If a judge's attitude toward the presence of the black lawyer in the courtroom was a tolerating and subtle acceptance, that attitude will be reflected in the relationship with the new judge. There is little chance that these negative attitudes will change simply because the black is elevated to the bench. It would be wise for the new judge to analyze judicial colleagues' known attitudes toward black attorneys so he or she will be prepared to counteract most effectively any bias encountered.

Judges' biased attitudes can be manifested in the location of the minority judge's courtroom. The courtroom or office of the judge whom the minority judge is replacing may be claimed by judges already there. It may be a more desirable location in the courthouse in terms of larger space, easy accessibility to other judges or court activities, design, equipment, and other factors, and the denial of the use of this courtroom may be based on race. Some judges may take the attitude that, as a newcomer is the "new kid on the block," the new kid gets the least desirable courtroom. Or they may feel that because anything is OK for a black person, it is acceptable for sitting judges to claim the most desirable space, leaving the least desirable area for the new black judge.

Race bias is often detectable when meetings of the judges on a multijudge bench are in progress and it becomes obvious that the topics on the agenda have been previously discussed and decided among the white judges before the meeting, to the exclusion of the black judge. Many times explanations such as "you were not available" or "we met in the hallway" or "I saw (name of fellow judge) at church" are offered. These are weak excuses when a telephone call to the black judge to simply mention the issue would have eliminated the need for an excuse. This technique of exclusion can affect decision making, depending on the topic or issue to be decided. Court assignments, court procedures, handling of calendars, types of cases to be handled, vacation schedules, vacation leave, and other concerns directly affecting the judge's performance may be at stake.

One obvious demonstration of race bias can be observed when the group of white judicial colleagues is in a circle talking but quickly disperses when the black judge approaches. One would believe that whatever topic or discussion drew these judges into a huddle would be important enough to include all judges on the bench. This is particularly true when all of the colleagues are there to the exclusion of the black judge.

Many judicial colleagues will share legal materials with the black judge, as this is one common topic they can discuss without embarrassment. It can become a painful exercise when social involvement and fringe benefits are discussed; in some courts, the black judge is routinely excluded from social functions to which colleagues invite all other judges on the bench. Business decisions are occasionally made at social functions from which the black judge is excluded.

In meetings, black judges may experience the same demeaning treatment experienced by women judges. For example, black judges may find themselves ignored when they make points in a discussion of issues, then find that these same points are adopted when they are advanced by a white judge. When this happens, the black judge can specifically call it to the attention of the group so that the entire group can become sensitive to the problem, recognize it as racial in origin, and consciously work toward eliminating it.

In court systems where cases are supposed to be randomly assigned based on date of filing, equalization of caseload, and, in some instances, complexity of issues in the case, it sometimes becomes apparent that cases involving upper income or affluent white citizens, white well-known or public citizens, or highly publicized trials involving white or black persons are routinely assigned to white judges to the exclusion of black judges. Many black judges find themselves presiding only over cases involving poor whites, blacks, and other minorities. Such exclusion prohibits the black judge from growing and developing into a well-experienced judge, capable of handling complex cases with the most experienced and able lawyers arguing before him or her, weakens the entire bench, and makes decision making suspect.

When supposedly random case assignments are so skewed, it raises the suspicion that the bench in that jurisdiction has racial biases. This suspicion causes the entire judicial system to be looked upon as racist.

The presiding judge should make certain that case assignments are in fact being made randomly. In the highly unlikely event that a random system is yielding such peculiar results, the presiding judge should take affirmative steps to eliminate this disparity so the system will not continue to look as if it is being manipulated.

Some white attorneys will seek out a white judge to override a decision made by a black judge, and some judicial colleagues may find themselves a party to racism when they take on such a case without consulting the black judge. Such practices will affect decision making of the black judge and totally undermine the black judge's ability to be effective and respected by the bar. Since all judges have equal status, judicial colleagues should refuse attorneys' requests for review of the minority judge's actions. If judicial colleagues discourage such practices, attorneys will cease requesting them.

Acceptance and Treatment by Members of the Bar

The judge must establish the atmosphere of the courtroom, whether relaxed or formal, but always courteous, considerate, and respectful. When the judge's style has been established and becomes known, lawyers generally adhere to that standard. When the attorney does not conform, however, the client does not conform. Such disrespect must be dealt with directly and firmly by reprimand (private reprimand should be tried first), a contempt citation, then a report to the attorney's bar association for disciplinary action if disrespectful behavior continues.

Disrespectfulness can be exhibited in manners, such as failure to address the judge by title or respectful designation, such as "your honor," or "may it please the court," or the judge's name, or simply beginning talking or presenting the case while virtually ignoring the judge's presence. It can further be exhibited by calling minority clients or witnesses by given names rather than Mr., Ms., Miss, or Mrs., while referring to white witnesses or clients by such titles.

In jurisdictions where judge shopping is practiced, white attorneys who have racial biases may seek ways to avoid appearing before the black judge, especially if the client is white. If this practice is permitted, the black judge in these situations will find that cases in his or her courtroom become predominately those of black litigants. Because the open demonstration of racial preference respecting the judge who will hear their cases disadvantages lawyers' practices and their clients, the expression of these biases becomes subtle and difficult to detect. The existence of a pattern of selection may be the only indication of such bias.

Some attorneys are abrasive and disrespectful to all judges. Before concluding that such behavior is directed to the judge because of race, the new minority judge needs to determine whether such performance occurs only in his or her courtroom or also before other judges. A discussion with judicial colleagues could help determine this fact. Although disrespect to the judge should never be tolerated, no matter what the motivating factor, the minority judge has added concerns.

If the minority judge feels sure that an attorney's disrespectful behavior is prompted by racism, the judge must evaluate carefully the pros and cons of confronting the lawyer, even in the privacy of chambers. Individual black and women judges who have faced these situations have come to different conclusions. Some believe it is appropriate to be direct. Others believe that it will lead to the judge's being denounced by the offending lawyer to the entire legal community as paranoid and worse.

Relationships between whites and blacks in our country in many instances are guarded. Because of this fact, and the judge's position, many white attorneys with whom the judge did not have a previous acquaintance may be inhibited from approaching the judge. The black judge may need to break the ice by speaking to these attorneys, introducing himself or herself to the attorneys, so they can be comfortable and not have the impression that the judge is unapproachable.

Decision Making

Although anyone ascending the bench should be sensitive to his or her possible biases, minority judges, like women judges, are highly conscious of the fact that they are often subjected to greater scrutiny than their white male colleagues and must prove themselves competent and impartial.

The judge from a minority group should be neither so conscious of his or her race that it clouds the ability to see fairly, nor so determined to appear "impartial" that he or she discards the personal understanding of important issues that come from being a member of a minority group.

The Role of the Black Judge Within the Courthouse

The presence of the black judge in the courthouse gives black employees a feeling of hope and a sign of fairness operating within the courthouse system. The black judge may have to champion the causes of black employees: clerks, deputy sheriffs, court reporters, maintenance workers, probation officers, and other minority court personnel. When this is done, fairness and justice should prevail and be evident.

When the black attorney who ascends to the bench was known by and had a good relationship with the courthouse staff, these good relationships usually continue. In some situations, however, white courthouse personnel will try to avoid and circumvent the black judge and ignore his or her instructions or directions. The new judge should establish very early with support personnel the line of authority within the courthouse. Although first name calling might be in use, it would be well to take care that such usage does not weaken the authority which the judge must exercise.

Soon after taking the bench, the new judge should meet with support personnel and their supervisors (unless prohibited by the presiding judge), in order to develop a good working relationship and rapport with the courthouse staff. Staff members can sabotage the implementation of the judge's work in so many ways that the judge will appear inept. Deliberately inaccurate messages, delay in filing documents, and incorrect citation of authorities are examples of the kind of sabotage that creates this appearance. Initially, spot checks can be made of all work to determine whether these kinds of things are happening. When the judge acquires the reputation for monitoring work, such practices will not develop or will cease.

In the selection of immediate staff, the new judge has an opportunity to choose personnel in whom the judge has confidence and to manifest affirmative action. This approach can prove to be a role model for the court if it has previously made no conscious effort toward outreach to minorities.

Private Life/Private Time

The minority judge faces many demands on his or her time for community involvement. Social involvements present other problems.

Often social invitations are less readily extended to the new black judge than they were before he or she ascended the bench. Some people feel inhibited about conducting themselves as usual in the presence of a judge. Rather than restricting or repressing their social conduct, these people may cease to invite the judge to some social affairs. The new judge, however, can find solace in knowing that all social activity will not be curtailed. Most friends and acquaintances who once enjoyed the judge's company will continue to find his or her presence stimulating and enjoyable.

Although, as noted, minority judges may be excluded from white colleagues' socializing as they sometimes are excluded from their meetings, social invitations extended by white colleagues and associates may increase if the new judge is inclined to accept those that are offered. The judge need not be fully isolated if he or she endeavors to participate.

This chapter does not pretend to exhaust all attitudes or acts of racial bias that minority judges may experience. Many of the examples of gender bias recited in the section on women judges can well be applied to minority judges, who should read that section of this chapter for further suggestions about dealing with problems of bias.

Not all minority judges will be subjected to the incidents and attitudes described in this chapter. Nonetheless, as stated in the segment of this chapter about women judges, forewarned is forearmed. It is important for minority judges to realize that, even as judges, they may encounter racism. Of equal importance is that nonminority judges learn from this chapter that they may in some ways—perhaps totally unintentionally—be failing to exercise toward their minority colleagues the fairness and impartiality that are the hallmark of a judge.

6

AVOIDING RACE AND GENDER BIAS IN THE COURTROOM

Judges have an obligation to avoid race and gender bias in their own decision making and court interactions and to intervene to eliminate biased behavior on the part of attorneys, court personnel, witnesses, jurors, and others under their supervision. Despite this obligation, there is a substantial body of evidence demonstrating that race and gender bias continue to interfere with the fair administration of justice in our courtrooms. Some of this bias is conscious and overtly expressed. Much of it is unconscious, the product of unexamined and often unrealized adherence to cultural stereotypes, myths, and misconceptions.

This chapter summarizes the principal race- and gender-based problems in our courts that have been identified by legal and social science researchers and court-sponsored state task forces across the country and recommends ways to eliminate them. Manifestations of race and gender bias in decision making are treated separately. Race- and gender-based problems in court interaction are discussed together. A short bibliography follows this chapter to enable the reader to become familiar with these issues in greater depth.

The discussion of race bias in this chapter focuses on blacks because this is the minority group about whom the most extensive data exist. Many of the aspects of bias that confront blacks in our court system are also problems for Hispanics, Asian Americans, and Native Americans. A particular problem for Hispanics and Asian Americans is the need for interpreters. The bibliography includes reference materials on the due process implications of access to qualified interpreters in the courts.

Issues Regarding Race

Black Americans approach the justice system with trepidation and a good deal of ambivalence. It is in the courts of this country that they have suffered ignominy and denial on so many occasions, but it is also in the courts that they have witnessed the triumph of law and the promise of justice. The hope engendered by such decisions as *Brown v. Board of Education*[1] is often replaced by fear that, in substantive areas, there are lingering attitudes such as those expressed by Chief Justice Taney in the *Dred Scott* case[2] that blacks have "no rights which the white man [is] bound to respect." It is this feeling which the National Advisory Commission on Civil Disorders identified as a major source of racial unrest in urban areas:

> Some of our courts, moreover, have lost the confidence of the poor . . . The belief is pervasive . . . that lower courts in our urban areas dispense 'assembly-line' justice; that from arrest to sentencing, the poor and uneducated are denied equal justice . . . [T]he apparatus of justice in some areas has itself become a focus for distrust and hostility.[3]

Recent studies have indicated that the concerns of minorities may well be justified by measurable differences in treatment attributable to their race.

Background

The legacy of the American justice system is that black Americans are less worthy and therefore should be treated differently. Long before *Dred Scott*, American law accepted, indeed mandated, such differences. Slavery was part of the legal fabric of the original colonies. The Constitution sanctioned its continuance and decreed that a black was three-fifths of a person. Before the Civil War, most of the southern states had enacted "slave codes," which regulated the criminal and civil behavior of black persons, whether slave or free. Free black persons were severely restricted in northern states as well. Free blacks were prevented from bringing suit in some instances and were not allowed to testify against white persons. Statutes provided for more severe punishment for blacks for the same crime or made illegal conduct by blacks that was not illegal for white persons.

The end of the Civil War did not bring an end to the disparate treatment of black Americans. Shortly after the war, states began to enact "black codes," which retained many of the traditional differences in civil and criminal matters. Despite the Civil Rights Act of 1866 and the fourteenth amendment, these statutes continued to gain favor and were instrumental in establishing the Jim Crow segregation in the southern states. Meanwhile, blacks in northern states were suffering many of the same deprivations without the official sanction of the law. Equal justice simply was not available in the nation's courts.

1. 347 U.S. 483 (1954).
2. 60 U.S. 393 (1856).
3. National Advisory Commission on Civil Disorders, Report 183 (1968).

The Supreme Court's decision in *Brown* and the subsequent civil rights movement signaled a new era of equal treatment before the law. Yet there is evidence that the attitudes which place a lesser value on the rights and lives of blacks and which supported segregation continue to place blacks at a disadvantage in our courts.

Jury Selection

Apart from the judge, the jury has the most significant impact on the decisions in our courtrooms. Participants are entitled to juries that are fairly composed. For many years, blacks had been overtly prevented from participating in jury venires. As early as *Strauder v. West Virginia*,[4] the Supreme Court held that such a policy denied equal protection to a black defendant. Following its cases involving total exclusion, the Court established the principle that substantial underrepresentation could also be a constitutional violation and approved the use of statistical analyses to show such disparities.

Racial criteria, however, continued to be used in the selection of individual petit juries. Curtailed, officials still managed to exclude blacks from jury rolls. Blacks who succeeded in getting on the rolls, moreover, were systematically eliminated from petit juries by prosecutorial use of peremptory challenges. In *Swain v. Alabama*,[5] the court held that to make out an equal protection violation, a defendant would have to show that there was a pattern of excluding blacks from juries.

Prosecutors in criminal cases thereafter continued to use their peremptory challenges to exclude blacks based on the type of case and the race of the defendant. Similarly, attorneys in civil cases have excluded blacks from juries in cases where there were black participants. This practice is based on the erroneous assumption that black persons as a class cannot be fair in certain types of civil and criminal cases. Rather than increasing the fairness of the jury, the exclusion of any class of persons subverts the intent of our jury system. In *Peters v. Kiff*,[6] the Supreme Court noted the importance of diverse views in a jury:

> When any large and identifiable segment of the community is excluded from jury service, the effect is to remove from the jury room qualities of human nature and varieties of human experience, the range of which is unknown and perhaps unknowable. It is not necessary to assume that the excluded group will consistently vote as a class in order to conclude, as we do, that its exclusion deprives the jury of a perspective on human events that may have unsuspected importance in any case that may be presented.

4. 100 U.S. 303 (1879).
5. 380 U.S. 202 (1965).
6. 407 U.S. 493, 503-04 (1972).

The Court's recent decision in *Batson v. Kentucky*,[7] however, holds that a defendant may make out a prima facie violation of the Equal Protection Clause in an individual case and now provides an opportunity for the judge to actively police jury selection practices. Whether in a criminal or civil context, the judge should be cognizant of the possible impermissible use of the peremptory challenge. "Selection procedures that purposefully exclude black persons from juries undermine public confidence in the fairness of our system of justice."[8] To minimize the problem, the court should counsel attorneys that such practices will not be tolerated. One approach is to make it clear that the court's policy is to discourage the racial use of peremptories. Since *Batson* allows defendants to challenge peremptories, attorneys would be forewarned that the use of peremptories in an apparently racial manner will result in the attorney being required to state on the record the reason for the use of the peremptory. While *Batson* was decided in the context of a criminal trial, the racial use of peremptories in a civil trial is similarly at odds with the concept of equal justice before the law. "[B]y denying a person participation in jury service on account of his race, the State unconstitutionally discriminate[s] against the excluded juror."[9] If attorneys are aware of the court's policy, misuse of peremptories will be less likely because attorneys will not want to risk embarrassment, sanction, or loss of credibility, and a record will be developed that may be useful in spotting problems and initiating reforms.

Sentencing

Research continues to add to the considerable body of data concerning racial disparities in the criminal justice system. The evidence indicates that, from the beginning of the process until the end, racial considerations affect decision making. As the National Minority Advisory Council on Criminal Justice (NMACCJ) found:

> [M]inorities are not only more likely to be suspected of crime than whites, but also more likely to be arrested and less likely to secure bail. Further, after being arrested, minorities are more likely to be indicted than whites and are less likely to have cases dismissed. If tried, minorities are more likely to be imprisoned and more likely to serve full terms without parole.[10]

One area within the system that has received an enormous amount of attention and research is sentencing practices. Studies have sought, for example, to explain why blacks, who make up just over 10 percent of

---

7. 476 U.S. 79 (1986).

8. *Id.*

9. *Id.*

10. National Minority Advisory Council on Criminal Justice, The Inequality of Justice: A Report on Crime and the Administration of Justice in the Minority Communities (1982) [hereinafter cited as NMACCJ Study].

the population, comprise about 50 percent of the prison inmates. These investigations have shown that sentences are indeed a function of race, not only the race of the defendant, but also the race of the victim, and also that the racial impact increases in situations requiring the exercise of discretion. The pattern appears to be consistent with a devaluation of blacks by the system: Punishment increases when the defendant is black, but decreases when the victim is black. In a schematic manner, this can generally be represented by the following order of severity in sentencing, from most severe to least severe:

Defendant	Victim
Black	White
White	White
Black	Black
White	Black

The desire to punish the black defendant or to protect the white victim may cause the middle two combinations to be switched.

While earlier studies examined gross sentencing data, more recent studies that subjected data to more stringent statistical analysis have reached similar conclusions. A 1983 study by the Rand Institute surveyed the sentencing practices in three states—Michigan, California, and Texas—and concluded, "Controlling for the other major factors that might influence sentencing and time served, we found that minorities [blacks and Hispanics] receive harsher sentences and serve longer in prison—other things being equal."[11] The race of the victim was also found to be statistically related to the sentence received.

A comparable study, completed in 1985 by the New York State Committee on Sentencing Guidelines, examined sentencing patterns of more than 28,000 felony convictions within that state by comparing "offenders with similar offence severity and prior criminal involvement." Using regression analyses, the study found that "black, male, and young offenders were more likely to be sent to prison, even after controlling for seriousness" and that "black, male, and older inmates were likely to serve more prison time than the state average."[12]

These detailed analyses, by accounting for legitimate factors in sentencing, support the conclusion of the NMACCJ that "glaring disparities in the sentencing of the poor and minority defendants . . . lacks any rational basis and leads the researchers to the inescapable conclusion of

11. J. Petersilia, Racial Disparities in the Criminal Justice System, R-2947-NIC (1983).

12. New York State Committee on Sentencing Guidelines, New York State Sentencing Patterns: An Analysis of Disparity (1985).

institutional racism."[13] The task of the judge is to bring principle to the process and to ensure that only relevant factors enter into the decision to incarcerate.

Two possible kinds of impermissible considerations may taint the sentencing decision. First, there are factors overtly based on race. The Rand Institute study, for example, cites two such examples: (1) hesitancy to send white persons to prisons where they will be confronted by black majorities and (2) an attitude that white persons are more valuable and more rehabilitable than black persons. These considerations would be easy to detect, but are unlikely to be sanctioned and therefore are not generally expressed.

More prevalent, and perhaps more serious, are factors which, though not expressed in overtly racial terms, are clearly correlated with race:

> For example, long-term unemployment is generally thought to help predict criminal recidivism, and, therefore, may influence judges' sentencing decisions. Since the unemployment rate tends to be much higher among blacks, when employment status is considered at sentencing it tends to produce disproportionate incarceration rates for black defendants.[14]

If these racially correlated factors actually predict recidivism, it may be necessary to continue using them despite their racial impact. However, the Rand Institute report suggests that such indicators often do not predict recidivism, but only demonstrate the prevalence of these factors in an ethnic group.

A limited follow-up study concluded that the inclusion of racially related factors did not significantly enhance the ability to predict recidivism. These factors, however, continue to find their way into presentencing reports by probation officers and influence the input from other decision makers in the process, including prosecutors and defense attorneys.

The most important decision in the process belongs to the judge. The vast majority of the time, the judge relies on the input from these other persons and mainly on the presentence report. The Rand Institute recommends that socioeconomic factors be carefully studied to ensure that they are relevant to the sentencing decision and specifically recommends that:

> Judges and probation officers must begin to distinguish between information concerning the defendant's personal culpability and information that reflects his social status.[15]

---

13. NMACCJ Study, *supra* note 10.
14. THE CRIMINAL JUSTICE SYSTEM AND BLACKS 327 (D. Georges-Abeyie ed., 1984).
15. Petersilia, *supra* note 11.

Capital Punishment

It is often said that "capital punishment is different," and indeed it is. It is also similar in the sense that its imposition is correlated with both the race of the defendant and the race of the victim. Capital punishment, however, presents a special case; it directly implicates the relative worth of black and white lives within the criminal justice system. From the time of slavery, the imposition of capital punishment has been race-related. A number of offenses carried the death penalty for slaves and lesser penalties for white persons. The crime of raping a white woman, for example, carried a mandatory death sentence for blacks, while whites faced a term of imprisonment. Long after this result ceased to be dictated by statute, white juries continued to impose the death penalty for rape in a manner consistent with this requirement.

This pattern has been revealed time and time again. One such study of rape cases in the city of Baltimore and the state of Maryland from 1923 to 1966 showed that a black was 10 times more likely to receive a death sentence if the victim was white. All 30 persons executed were convicted of rape or attempted rape of white women. The documentation of such arbitrary uses of the death penalty led the Supreme Court to invalidate all then-enacted capital statutes in *Furman v. Georgia.*[16]

Furman did not eliminate the racial factor in the imposition of the death penalty. In practice a black life is still not valued as highly as a white life. Studies have continued to show that, as measured by imposition of the death penalty, the taking of a white life is considered more serious than the taking of a black life. In Florida, a detailed study of homicides between 1973 and 1977 showed that no white was sentenced to death for the killing of a black person and that, although there were roughly equal numbers of white and black victims, more than 90 percent of the persons on death row were sentenced for killing whites. Moreover, the probability of receiving the death penalty conformed to the general defendant/victim model described in the section on sentencing.

A comprehensive study of Georgia's capital sentencing structure, based on more than 2,400 cases from 1973 to 1980 and controlling for more than 230 separate variables, determined through multiple regression and other statistical analyses that race was as significant a factor in death sentencing as the commission of a prior homicide. The gross data showed that, although 61 percent of the homicide victims were black, only 13 percent of the cases imposing a death sentence involved black victims. White-victim cases were 11 times more likely to result in a death sentence. When the individual case factors were included, the odds of receiving a death sentence were still more than four times greater in white-

16. 408 U.S. 238 (1972).

victim cases. The study also showed that the racial disparities increased in a midrange of cases where there was more room for discretion.

In some jurisdictions, the judge has the authority to overrule a jury recommendation of life imprisonment and impose the death penalty. In these situations, the court should carefully consider the role of the jury in weighing the many diverse factors that go into such a decision and avoid substituting personal views. In those jurisdictions where the jury decides on punishment, the court must be alert to possible issues that could affect the composition of the jury. One such issue is whether a prospective juror who expresses concern about the death penalty should be excused because the "juror's views would prevent or substantially impair the performance of his duties as juror in accordance with his instructions and his oath."[17] The court must be sensitive to the difficulties in deciding whether to remove such a person from consideration and should not exclude persons for the mere expression of reservations.

Jury Decisions

Research has shown that the outcome of jury trials is correlated to the race of the participants, both in criminal and in civil matters. On the civil side, a 1985 study by the Rand Institute examined, among other things, the effect of race on the outcome of 9,000 civil trials in Cook County, Illinois, and found:

> Litigants' race seemed to have a pervasive influence on the outcomes of civil jury trials in Cook County. Even after we adjusted for differences in case type, injuries, and characteristics of other parties, we found that both liability decisions and awards differed significantly between black and white plaintiffs and between black and white defendants.[18]

The study found that "(b)lack plaintiffs won somewhat less often than white," and "(b)lack defendants also lost somewhat more often than whites."

In a manner similar to the defendant/victim pattern of punishment, the interplay of plaintiff and defendant showed a distinctive hierarchy of valuation:

Plaintiff	Defendant	Probability of Plaintiff Winning
White	Black	.61
Black	Black	.55
White	White	.51
Black	White	.45

When the amount of award was compared by race, the analysis showed

17. Wainright v. Witt, 469 U.S. 412, 424 (1985)

18. A. Chin & M. Peterson, Deep Pockets, Empty Pockets: Who Wins in Cook County Jury Trials (1985).

that, on average, black plaintiffs "received only three-fourths as much compensation as whites who had the same injury, lost income, and type of legal claim." The differences were greater for plaintiffs with major injuries. While these results are consistent with a difference in value placed on white persons and black persons, the study did not address actual juror attitudes.

More direct evidence of juror attitudes was uncovered during a study of rape cases in Marion County, Indiana. Based on interviews with more than 300 jurors, the researchers found that the race of the victim played a role in the likelihood of a guilty verdict:

> [I]n the consent-no sex cases [defenses that victim consented or no sex act took place] jurors were less likely to judge a man guilty when the complainant was a black woman. Perhaps jurors were influenced by stereotypes of black women as more likely to consent to sex or as more sexually experienced and, hence, less harmed by an assault. Or they may have simply accorded less priority to black victims' claims for justice.[19]

The authors noted one case involving the rape of a young black girl in which "one juror argued for acquittal on the grounds that a girl of her age from 'that kind of neighborhood' probably wasn't a virgin anyway."[20]

Jurors are not, and should not be, automatons. Whether black or white, they bring to the court their biases, their admitted and subconscious prejudices and stereotypes about people and groups. The judge should actively seek out persons for whom these biases will make it impossible to make a fair determination in the particular case before the court. As the Supreme Court held in *Ham v. South Carolina*,[21] the trial judge is required "to interrogate the jurors upon the subject of racial prejudice."

As a practical matter, some potential jurors who are biased will not acknowledge that fact. For some, this may be simply an unwillingness to admit prejudice in front of other members of the panel. This problem might be easily overcome by providing an opportunity for such persons to present the matter to the court privately. For the more intractable individuals, the judge must be aware of subtle or nonverbal indicators of bias that suggest the need for further inquiry.

Issues Regarding Gender

> The Task Force has concluded that gender bias against women litigants, attorneys, and court personnel is a pervasive problem with grave conse-

19. LaFree, Reskin, & Visher, *Jurors' Responses to Victims' Behavior and Legal Issues in Sexual Assault Trials*, 32 Social Problems 389, 401-02 (1985).
20. New York Task Force on Women in the Courts, Report 5 (1986).
21. 409 U.S. 524 (1973).

> quences. Women are often denied equal justice, equal treatment and equal opportunity. Cultural stereotypes of women's role in marriage and in society daily distort courts' application of substantive law. Women uniquely, disproportionately and with unacceptable frequency must endure a climate of condescension, indifference, and hostility. Whether as attorneys or court employees, women are too often denied equal opportunities to realize their potential.[22]

Like black Americans, women often feel considerable ambivalence about using the courts, wondering whether they will be treated with fairness or further victimized. Will they be blamed for the violence perpetrated against them, reduced to poverty after divorce while their husbands live in comfort, ignored in their efforts to enforce child support?

Although gender bias in the courts sometimes disadvantages men, overwhelmingly its victims are women. Stereotyped thinking about the nature and roles of the sexes, devaluation of women and what is perceived as women's work, and myths and misconceptions about the social and economic realities of women's and men's lives are as prevalent in the justice system as in the other institutions of society. In the courts these three aspects of gender bias distort decision making and create a courtroom environment that undermines women's credibility.

Background

Women's legal history parallels that of blacks, recording a difficult and ongoing struggle to secure the same rights granted white men in the Constitution and to see the remedial intent behind statutory reforms realized in the courts.

Women were not mentioned in the Constitution and remained subject to all the disabilities that circumscribed their rights at common law. Repeated legislation and litigation were necessary to secure the right to own property, contract, practice law, and serve on juries, to cite only a few of the areas in which women were denied full citizenship. Well into the twentieth century, numerous state laws classified women with children and idiots. It was not until 1971 that the U.S. Supreme Court used the Equal Protection Clause to strike down a statute that discriminated on the basis of sex;[23] not until 1986 did the Florida Supreme Court ban the Lord Hale jury instruction requiring strict scrutiny of the female complainant's testimony in rape cases.[24]

The last two decades have brought major reforms in laws affecting women's rights, but laws are only as effective as the judges who interpret and enforce them. Extensive studies by legal and social science research-

---

22. *Id.*, note 20.

23. Reed v. Reed, 404 U.S. 71 (1971) (mandated preference for males in estate administration).

24. Marr v. Florida, 494 So. 2d 1139 (Fla. Sup. Ct., 1986).

ers nationwide reveal that, because of gender bias, the remedial intent behind these laws is not being fully realized. As the New Jersey Supreme Court Task Force on Women in the Courts wrote of its 1983 study:

> Although the law as written is for the most part gender-neutral, stereotyped myths, beliefs and biases were found to sometimes affect judicial decision making . . . In addition, there is strong evidence that women and men are sometimes treated differently in courtrooms, in chambers, and at professional gatherings.[25]

Domestic Violence

The Attorney General's Task Force on Family Violence reported in 1984 that although "(b)attery is a major cause of injury to women in America . . . (t)he criminal justice system has responded inconsistently to acts of violence. Violence committed by a stranger is classified as an assault. Yet when one family member assaults another, it is commonly viewed as a family squabble, something less than a real crime."[26]

This inconsistent response is the legacy of a long cultural and legal heritage that condoned wife beating as a man's appropriate "correction" of his wife, whose role was to be subservient to him in all things. Current law condemns wife beating, but old attitudes persist. The New Jersey and New York task forces reported that battered women seeking court protection often encounter not only the attitude that the matter is a family squabble not worth the court's time, but also the assumptions that they provoked and deserved what they got, and that they are not credible absent serious visible injuries. Battered women are sometimes subjected to comments that trivialize the violence against them and may be shunted between family and criminal court until they abandon seeking relief.

Battered women often go to court seeking an order of protection and emerge with a *mutual* order of protection, although there has been no cross-petition from the respondent, and often no allegation that the petitioner was violent. This is a denial of due process and gives confusing directions to the police, who may refuse to take any action when called or else arrest both parents and put children in foster care. Unwarranted issuance of mutual orders is a particular problem in divorce cases. Although divorce is often a period of increased violence because the batterer is enraged by his wife's assertion of independence, some judges assume the wife is seeking only to bolster her case, and issue a mutual order. In addition to confusing the police, such an order creates a record

25. New Jersey Supreme Court Task Force on Women in the Courts, Report of the First Year 6 (1984).
26. Attorney General's Task Force on Family Violence, Final Report 11 (1984).

that may prejudice the woman in a custody dispute or in a subsequent award of property.

Many victims of domestic violence withdraw their complaints, frustrating the court and making it appear that they are stereotypically indecisive or manipulating. Judges need to be aware of the numerous causes of battered women's decisions to withdraw: pressure from family and church to reconcile; economic dependency and the well-founded fear of being forced onto welfare; the low self-esteem that afflicts victims of prolonged violence; threats of increased violence from the batterer; demeaning comments from court personnel, prosecutors, and judges that deter the victim from continuing. The need for judges to be aware of court personnel's actions in domestic violence cases is apparent in *Bruno v. Codd*,[27] which discusses how New York City Family Court clerks and probation officers deterred battered women from pursuing their legal remedies. Judges should also be aware that studies have shown that even if the complaint is withdrawn, when the judge states clearly to the abuser that his behavior is unacceptable and to the victim that she does not have to accept violence as a way of life, there has been a reduction in recidivism.

The stereotype of women as provoking and thus responsible for the violence against them is a factor in cases where the batterer who kills his victim receives a *de minimis* sentence[28] and the victim who kills her batterer in self-defense is victimized again at trial. Because women who respond to violence with violence violate the female behavioral norm of passivity, they may be seen as irrational and incapable of the "reasonableness" that is the core of the self-defense justification, in addition to being blamed for provoking the abuse and failing to flee their homes when faced with ongoing violence. *State v. Kelly*,[29] approving the admission of expert testimony about the battered woman's syndrome in self-defense cases, provides an excellent explanation of how stereotyped thinking about women and misconceptions about domestic violence can undermine fairness.

Rape

Among the stereotypes burdening women is that of the seductive, deceitful temptress. Until quite recently, rape laws were premised on the assumption that women invite and consent to sex, then cry "rape" afterward. A historical look at rape statutes reveals a profound mistrust

27. 419 N.Y.S.2d 901 (1979).

28. *See, e.g.*, People v. District Court of City & County of Denver, 673 P.2d 991 (Colo. 1983) (sentence overturned and judge investigated for accusing deceased wife of provoking acts).

29. 97 N.J. 178 (1984).

of women as witnesses, a presumed causal connection between a woman's (but not a man's) sexual behavior and her credibility, and a tendency to discourage prosecution by making it extremely difficult and unpleasant for the victim. New York's former rape law, for example, requiring corroboration of every material element of the crime, made prosecution so difficult that in a typical year only 18 rape convictions were obtained, despite thousands of complaints.[30]

Women's rights activists have achieved major reforms in rape laws over the last two decades, particularly enactment of rape shield laws limiting examination of the complainant's prior sexual history. Nonetheless, stereotyped thinking about rape victims, the myth of rape as a crime of sex rather than violence, and misconceptions about the consequences of rape for its victims persist throughout the justice system.

In a series of recent Wisconsin cases, one judge described rape as a normal response to a permissive society, another called a five-year-old victim "an unusually promiscuous young lady," and a third told a complainant he would dismiss her case if she did not stop crying on the stand. The New Jersey Supreme Court Task Force on Women in the Courts received reports of judges making and permitting lawyers to make comments on rape victims' appearance and physical attributes. Prosecutors from sex crimes units told the New York Task Force on Women in the Courts that in many instances women victims are still being put on trial and that some judges permit improper questioning about the complainant's life-style that subtly impeaches the witness's credibility by playing to juror prejudice.

Juror prejudice was explored in detail in the recent Indiana University study, noted earlier in this chapter, in which 360 jurors in sexual assault cases participated in lengthy posttrial interviews. The researchers concluded:

> Frequently, jurors voluntarily mentioned the victim's reputation in explaining how they reached their verdict . . . [J]urors, were more likely to believe the defendant's innocence when the victim violated rules of appropriate behavior for women, especially when the jurors themselves held sex-role conservative attitudes.[31]

Violations of appropriate behavior included holding a blue-collar job, being sexually active outside marriage, drinking, taking drugs, and being away from home at the time of the assault. The researchers also found that knowing the rapist diminished the victim's credibility. Jurors were reluctant to believe that a man could be guilty if the victim knew him,

30. Governor's Approval Memorandum No. 16, Ch. 373, New York, Laws of 1972 (approving partial repeal of corroboration requirement).

31. LaFree & Reskin, "Structural Analysis of Jurors' Verdict in Rape Trials: Final Report to the National Institute of Mental Health," Grant #R01 MH 29727 (1985), p. 8.

a particularly disturbing finding in light of recent studies showing that the majority of rapes are committed by someone known to the victim.

As these examples demonstrate, it is vital that judges be alert to the possibility of gender bias on the part of all the actors in a rape trial. Among the recommendations made by the New York Task Force on Women in the Courts in this regard are that judges become familiar with the substantial current data about the nature of the crime of rape, the psychology of offenders, the prevalence and seriousness of acquaintance rape, and the long-term psychic injury to rape victims; the difference between vigorous cross-examination that protects the defendant's rights and questioning that includes improper sex stereotyping and harassment of the victim; and the appropriate use of victim impact statements in the determination of sentencing.

This last point is important because there is a tendency to underestimate the injury done to rape victims, especially victims of acquaintance or marital rape. Cases are often reported in which, because the victim did not sustain the kind of physical injuries associated with a nonsexual assault, the judge asks questions such as "Was she injured?" failing to see that rape *is* an injury with profound, perhaps lifetime, psychological consequences. With respect to acquaintance rape, there is a widespread misconception that because the rapist was not a stranger, the victim was less traumatized. Research on the long-term consequences of rape demonstrates that, where a relationship of trust was violated, particularly in cases of marital rape, the long-term psychic injury is more severe.

Equitable Distribution, Spousal and Child Support and Enforcement

Gender bias in the distribution of marital property and the award and enforcement of spousal and child support is a nationally documented phenomenon. Devaluation of women's contributions as homemakers, myths about remarriage for women, misconceptions about the ability of women to support themselves and their children, unrealistic assumptions about the costs of child raising, and protectiveness of men's assets and incomes have reduced countless formerly middle class women and their children to the poverty line and below after divorce.

A University of Michigan study that followed a sample of 2,000 families, weighted to be representative of the country, for seven years after divorce (1968-1974) found that, at the end of that period, divorced men had incomes 17 percent over need level (need defined according to Department of Agriculture budgets), remarried men had incomes 31 percent over need level because they remarried younger women in the paid work force (there were too few remarried women to be statistically significant), but divorced women's incomes had fallen to seven percent *below* need level. The researchers pointed out that the women had to share their incomes with their children, that the alimony and child support awarded them was usually unrealistic and often unenforced, and that the women were unable to earn high wages because the only employment they could obtain was minimum-wage clerical and service jobs of the kind traditionally open to women.

A 10-year University of California study of 1500 California divorce cases from the late seventies found similar results. Often long-term homemakers were awarded no alimony at all, and child support bore little relationship to the cost of child raising. Using a representative sample of these cases for follow-up, the study found that, one year after divorce, men's standard of living had risen by 42 percent, while that of women and children had fallen by 73 percent. Similar findings have emerged from studies in Alaska, Cleveland, New Haven, Utah, and Vermont, and by the New Jersey and New York gender bias task forces.

Most state equitable distribution statutes direct the judge to take into account each partner's monetary and nonmonetary contributions to the acquisition of marital property. The evaluation of nonmonetary contributions is particularly important to women, who have traditionally borne most, if not all, responsibility for maintaining the home and parenting, often at the cost of their own ability to join the paid work force, become financially independent, and build a retirement fund. Equitable distribution decisions from all parts of the country reveal that judges often devalue the homemaker's nonmonetary contribution, resulting in highly inequitable divisions of marital property.

With respect to spousal support, there has long been a national myth that divorced women lead indolent lives on their alimony while their ex-husbands struggle to meet the payments. According to the U.S. Census Bureau's most recent data, in 1983 only 14 percent of the country's 17 million ever divorced or currently separated women had an agreement or award to receive alimony, and of the 791,000 women due to receive payments in that year, less than half received the full amount, and one-quarter received nothing. The average amount received was $3,980.

The national trend toward awarding short-term or no alimony at all, even if the marriage has been of long duration and the wife was a homemaker, has created stark postdivorce inequities between former husbands and wives. In most families the principal asset is the husband's earning ability, which the wife enhanced through her nonmonetary contributions. Women with young children and older homemakers have great difficulty establishing themselves in the paid work force. The demands of being primary caretaker to young children make it difficult to pursue a career absent support services such as high-quality child care, which few women can afford. Because long-term homemakers are usually without the education, skills, and recent employment experience that are valued in the paid work force, they are often limited to minimum-wage jobs in typically female occupations such as health care and clerical work.

Research from the University of Ohio has shown that younger women awarded rehabilitative alimony to enable them to obtain education and retraining after divorce are in a much better financial situation with better prospects for the future than are women forced to take the first job available. However, judges should be aware that for some women permanent alimony or a combination of rehabilitative and permanent alimony is essential to avoid reducing women to poverty while their former husbands enjoy financial comfort.

Courts' failure to make and enforce realistic child support awards has been recognized as a national disgrace, resulting in the federal Child Support Enforcement Amendments of 1984, requiring each state to study the problems in its own system and adopt stringent enforcement mechanisms and guidelines. The New York Child Support Commission reported that the greatest number of complaints it received related to judges' unwillingness to use the enforcement mechanisms that already existed. With respect to the adequacy of awards, the New York Task Force on Women in the Courts found that child support awards are often insufficient to furnish even half the actual cost of raising a child and that courts have a protective attitude toward fathers' incomes and lifestyles:

> [Some judges] are perceived to give disproportionate weight to what the father can comfortably afford. Testimony by the father as to his limited ability to pay tends to be accepted without substantiation while the mother must prove the expenses of the children. Moreover, there is a strong perception that the father is deemed entitled to retain for himself as much of his own income as possible . . . Consequently, the income of women and children is dramatically reduced from its level prior to divorce.[32]

To avoid gender bias in decisions respecting equitable distribution, spousal and child support and enforcement, judges need to reconsider their attitudes toward unpaid work in the home and to familiarize themselves with the paid work force potential for individual women, given their age, education, and employment background, as well as the real costs of child raising. Although all states were required to have child support guidelines by October 1987, each family should still be considered individually. Teenagers are more expensive than grade-schoolers; some children have special educational and medical needs. Children's needs cannot be reduced to a formula, and custodial mothers should not be required to bear a disproportionate share of child-raising costs.

---

32. New York Task Force on Women in the Courts, *supra* note 22, at 141-42.

Custody and Visitation

Custody and visitation are areas in which stereotyped thinking about the nature and roles of both sexes sometimes influences decision making. Despite the elimination of the maternal preference doctrine, some judges have great difficulty in awarding fathers custody, believing that it is the nature and role of women alone to be nurturers and to care for children. This belief can also affect visitation decisions. Some judges will not give fathers overnight visitation with infants, believing men cannot care for babies.

Because the maternal preference issue has received so much attention of late, some judges, determined *not* to appear biased against men, award fathers custody on little more than a showing of interest in postdivorce parenting. This results in bias against the mother who has been the child's primary caretaker. Many commentators have suggested and states have begun to adopt the primary caretaker standard as an objective measure against which to judge which parent has been most involved in daily child care and should probably be awarded custody.[33] Joint custody is the focus of much current research. It appears that where both parents agree, this is usually the best alternative for the children. However, as discussed in *Taylor v. Taylor*,[34] imposed joint custody often results in repeated litigation and strife, and judges must be alert to demands for joint custody made solely to gain bargaining leverage concerning the economic aspects of divorce.

Custody decisions evincing bias against mothers arise from the stereotype of the mother as pure, self-sacrificing and at home full-time. Personal relationships that are acceptable for fathers may not be acceptable for mothers. In a recent pair of Illinois cases, for example, a woman with a live-in boyfriend lost custody of her children, while a man with a live-in girlfriend retained custody of his.

Some judges have refused to award custody to women working outside the home, particularly those they perceive as "careerists," or readily transfer custody away from such mothers when the father remarries and tells the court that his new wife will be at home full-time. In 1986 the California Supreme Court ruled that neither a mother's work force participation nor a father's greater financial security could be the basis for denying a woman custody.[35] Given that, according to the U.S. Department of Labor, as of August 1986, 70 percent of mothers of children six to 17 and 54 percent of mothers with children under six were in the paid labor force, the majority of them full-time, judging a woman's parenting

33. Garska v. McCoy, 278 S.E.2d 357 (W.Va. 1981).
34. 306 Md. 290 (1986).
35. Burchard v. Garay, 724 P.2d 486 (Ca. Sup. Ct. 1986).

by whether she is at home full-time is out of touch with reality. The New York gender bias task force observed that because men earn so much more than women (1985 median earnings for year-round, full-time workers were $16,252 for women compared to $24,999 for men), basing custody decisions on parental income amounts to a paternal preference.

Custody and visitation decisions that ignore violence against the mother demonstrate gender bias in their indifference to women's safety and the model established for the children. Some judges mistakenly assume the abuse will stop at divorce and refuse supervised visitation, resulting in further violence against the woman. Judges have said in open court that a man's hitting his wife does not make him a bad father. As the Wisconsin Court of Appeals noted in overruling a trial court's refusal to admit evidence of the husband's violence in a custody dispute, children are secondary victims of the violence against their mothers and suffer both mentally and physically.[36] Research shows that boys from violent families grow up believing that violence against women is acceptable, girls that they must accept violence in their lives. Research also shows that children from violent families are more likely as adults to physically abuse their own children.

Courtroom Interaction

How an individual is treated in the courtroom significantly affects how that individual's credibility is assessed and whether the individual and others present believe that justice was done. When minority and women litigants, witnesses, and lawyers are treated with less dignity and respect than their white male counterparts, their credibility is undermined, and they feel that their cases were not fairly heard.

Judges need to be sensitive to the possibility of discriminatory verbal and nonverbal behavior on their own part and on the part of those under their supervision. Judges should also appreciate how difficult it is for the individual subjected to discriminatory behavior to object, and that when there is discriminatory behavior on the part of lawyers (cited in many studies as the principal offenders), court personnel, or others, it is the judge's obligation to intervene to eliminate it.

Consistency in forms of address and treatment are important to avoid the impression that one person is being favored over another, and to prevent denigration of one person's status as compared to another's. Calling a white male lawyer by his first name and inviting him into chambers while calling a black male lawyer "Mr." and leaving him behind in the courtroom demonstrates a relationship between the judge

36. Bertram v. Kilian, 394 N.W.2d 773 (Wis. Ct. App. 1986).

and the lawyer and implies favoritism. Calling a male lawyer "Mr." or "Counselor" while calling his female adversary "young lady" or by her first name detracts from the female lawyer's credibility and professionalism. Similarly, all witnesses should be addressed by their professional titles or surnames. It is a subtle but meaningful denigration of a witness's professional status to call a white male physician "Doctor" and a minority or female physician "Mr." or "Mrs."

Other behavioral indicia of bias include asking minority and women lawyers or lawyers representing minority or women parties to state their reasons for objections without requiring the same of opposing counsel; granting continuances or recesses for white male lawyers but not for minority and women lawyers in similar circumstances; and questioning black and women witnesses extensively after opposing lawyers have finished but not questioning white men, the implication being that their testimony is credible as given.

Avoid comments on women's personal appearance and physical attributes. Appropriate compliments on women's and men's appearance have their place in private, but in the courtroom a judge's remarks on a woman attorney's looks, even if well meant, draw attention away from her as a professional, causing those in the courtroom to evaluate her on the basis of her looks rather than her ability.

Hostile remarks, slurs, and "jokes" that reflect race and gender bias are absolutely impermissible. This should be obvious, but a number of judges have recently been disciplined for remarks such as "I will tell you what, little girl, you lose" and referring to women attorneys as "lawyerettes." In three recent incidents, judges were cited for using the phrase "nigger in the woodpile." Judges must also be alert to comments of this nature from counsel. In 1984 a New Jersey federal judge held an attorney in contempt for referring to a black civil rights plaintiff as "boy."

Attitudes toward Minority and Women Attorneys

Most judges on the bench today had few if any minority or women colleagues in law school or in practice. As a result, some judges are uncomfortable in treating these newcomers to the profession as professionals. For example, in appointing lawyers to challenging and lucrative civil and criminal cases, they may not think to appoint a minority or a woman because they don't think of them as able to handle the "big business" of a receivership. The Rhode Island Supreme Court Committee on the Treatment of Women in the Courts found that, because of the stereotype of women as intended for the domestic sphere, women are almost exclusively appointed to family law cases.

Another way in which women attorneys are stereotyped has to do with acceptable styles of behavior. Aggressive behavior is rewarded or tolerated from men but viewed as out of place or even unacceptable for women, who are supposed to be passive, quiet, and deferential. Women attorneys have been criticized and admonished for aggressive cross-examination tactics or any sarcastic tones toward male witnesses, while male attorneys are permitted to use exactly these tactics against all witnesses.

Gender-Neutral Language

Communications researchers have shown that masculine pronouns are not generic but evoke predominately male images. When a mixed-sex group is addressed as "gentlemen," the women become invisible. A jurors manual that employs only masculine pronouns for judges and attorneys sets up certain expectations about who the people in authority are.

Failure to use gender-neutral or gender-appropriate language in jury instructions can affect jury deliberations. In 1977 the Washington Supreme Court reversed a murder conviction in part on the grounds that it was impossible for the jury to assess the woman defendant's self-defense justification because the use of masculine pronouns in the instruction created the impression the defendant's conduct must be "measured against that of a reasonable male finding himself in the same circumstances" rather than in the context of a 5-foot, 4-inch tall woman in a cast facing a 6-foot, 2-inch tall intoxicated man.[37]

Nonverbal Communication

According to communications experts, nonverbal communication carries four times the weight of speech content. A judge may be unconsciously conveying powerful negative messages to everyone in the courtroom solely through posture, tone of voice, and quality of attention to the speaker. Some of the ways in which these messages are conveyed include listening attentively to and making eye contact with white men but shuffling papers and turning away from minorities and women; speaking to white men in a neutral, straightforward tone of voice but using a hostile or condescending tone to women and minorities, having nothing to do with what they are saying; consistently responding to white men's questions or statements within a few seconds but consistently delaying more than five seconds to respond to other kinds of speakers. A recent study of criminal trials in Santa Clara, California, concluded that judicial beliefs about guilt or innocence seemed to "leak" to the juries most in purely nonverbal forms of communication.

37. State v. Wanrow, 559 P.2d 548 (Wash. 1977).

Conclusion

Because fairness is the judicial norm, and because some aspects of race and gender bias are so accepted a part of our culture that they are not perceived for what they are, it is often difficult for a judge to acknowledge that he or she may have biases. Calling on his colleagues to recognize that judges, too, are subject to this human failing, Second Circuit Judge Jerome Frank wrote:

> Frankly, to recognize the existence of such prejudices is the part of wisdom. The conscientious judge will, as far as possible, make himself aware of his biases . . . and, by that very self-knowledge, nullify their effect.[38]

The judge has a unique role and responsibility in our justice system. The judge is the symbol of equal justice and must act to ensure impartiality and fairness. The judge must be alert for bias on the part of all the actors in the judicial drama, including unconscious biases which may affect his or her own decisions and courtroom behavior. It is only by avoiding such bias that a judge can maintain the integrity of the court for all participants.

Selected Bibliography

Issues Regarding Race

Bell. *Race, Racism and American Law*, 2d ed., 1980.

Chin and Peterson. *Deep Pockets, Empty Pockets: Who Wins in Cook County Jury Trials*, 1985.

Christianson. "Our Black Prisons." 27 *Crime & Delinquency* 364-75 (July 1981).

Georges-Abeyie (ed.). *The Criminal Justice System and Blacks*, 1984.

Gombossy. "Excluding Black Jurors Brings Sanctions," *National Law Journal*, November 10, 1986, p. 3, col. 1.

Higginbotham. *In The Matter of Color: Race and the American Legal Process: The Colonial Period*, 1980.

LaFree, Reskin, and Visher. "Jurors' Responses to Victims' Behavior and Legal Issues in Sexual Assault Trials." 32 *Social Problems* 389 (April 1985).

National Advisory Commission on Civil Disorders. *Report*. Washington, DC: U.S. Government Printing Office, 1968.

---

38. J. Frank, Courts on Trial: Myth and Reality in American Justice 414 (1949).

National Minority Advisory Council on Criminal Justice. "The Inequality of Justice: A Report on Crime and the Administration of Justice in the Minority Communities." Washington, DC: NMACCJ, 1982.

New York State Committee on Sentencing Guidelines. "New York State Sentencing Patterns: An Analysis of Disparity." May 14, 1985.

Ochi. "Racial Discrimination in Criminal Sentencing." 24 *Judges' Journal* 7 (Winter 1985).

Petersilia. *Guideline-Based Justice: The Implications for Racial Minorities*, R-3306-INC. Santa Monica, Cal.: Rand Corporation, 1985.

_____. *Racial Disparities in the Criminal Justice System*, R-2947-NIC. Santa Monica, Cal.: Rand Corporation, 1983.

Spohn, Gruhl, and Welch. "The Effect of Race on Sentencing: A Reexamination of an Unsettled Question." 16 *Law and Society Review* 71-88 (1981-1982).

Ware. *From the Black Bar: Voices for Equal Justice*, 1976.

Linguistic Minorities

Grossier. "A Right to Translation Assistance in Administrative Proceedings." 16 *Columbia Journal of Law and Social Problems* 469 (1981).

Pousada. "Interpreting for Language Minorities in the Courts," In *Life with Two Languages: An Introduction to Bilingualism*, Grosjean, ed., 1982.

Issues Regarding Gender

Berger. "Man's Trial, Woman's Tribulation: Rape Cases in the Courtroom." 77 *Columbia Law Review* 1 (1977).

Crites. "A Judicial Guide to Understanding Wife Abuse." 24 *Judges' Journal* 5 (Summer 1985).

Crites and Hepperle, eds. *Women, the Courts and Equality*. Sage Yearbooks in Women's Policy Studies, Vol. II, 1987.

Estrich. "Rape." 95 *Yale Law Journal* 1087 (1986).

Johnston and Knapp. "Sex Discrimination by Law: A Study in Judicial Perspective." 46 *New York University Law Review* 675 (1971).

Keenan. "Domestic Violence and Custody Litigation: The Need for Statutory Reform." 13 *Hofstra Law Review* 407 (1985).

New Jersey Supreme Court Task Force on Women in the Courts. *Report of the First Year*. Trenton, N.J.: Administrative Office of the Courts, 1984.

New York Task Force on Women in the Courts. *Report*. New York: Office of Court Administration, 1986.

Polikoff. "Why Are Mothers Losing: A Brief Analysis of Criteria Used in Custody Determinations." 7 *Women's Rights Law Reporter* 235 (1982).

Schafran. "Eve, Mary, Superwoman: How Stereotypes about Women Influence Judges." 24 *Judges' Journal* 12 (Winter 1985).

———. "Documenting Gender Bias in the Courts: The Task Force Approach." 70 *Judicature*, no. 5 (Feb-Mar 1987).

"Special Issue: Child Support Enforcement." 36 *Juvenile and Family Court Journal* (Fall 1985).

Weitzman. *The Divorce Revolution: The Unexpected Social and Economic Consequences for Women and Children in America*, 1985.

Wikler. "The Economics of Divorce." 25 *Judges' Journal* 8 (Summer 1986).

———. "On the Judicial Agenda for the 80s: Equal Treatment for Men and Women in the Courts." 64 *Judicature* 202 (1980).

Courtroom Interaction

Blanck, Rosenthal, and Cordell. "The Appearance of Justice: Judges' Verbal and Nonverbal Behavior in Criminal Jury Trials." 38 *Stanford Law Review* 89 (1985).

"Discipline Caselaw Reflects Gender Bias in the Justice System." 7 *Judicial Conduct Reporter* 1 (1985).

Schafran. "Women as Litigators: Abilities vs. Assumptions." 19 *Trial* 36 (1983).

7

STRESS MANAGEMENT AND HEALTH

More and more twentieth-century illnesses have been shown to be related to the smoking, drinking, eating, and hurrying behaviors of patients. It is estimated that as many as 75 percent of all medical complaints are stress-related.[1]

The change from lawyer to judge includes a new role, new responsibilities, new opportunities, and new sources of stress. To prepare themselves, judges should be made fully aware of the stresses inherent in the judiciary. Stress is not always negative and may provide the impetus for great achievements. Stress can, however, be a disabler and even a killer if not dealt with openly and reasonably.

Stress has many meanings, but most people think of stress as the demands of life. Technically, these demands are called "stressors," and the actual wear and tear on our bodies is the stress. The demands or challenges of life can come from people and events around us, as well as from our inner thoughts and struggles. When these demands increase, people often feel that they are under excessive stress.[2] Stress can also be described as an external stimulus requiring the body and mind to make a "nonspecific response" to the outside demand.[3]

When people suffer a stress overload, they experience certain effects, and "burnout" is a real potential. Those effects can be recognized as *behavioral*, e.g., heightened muscle tension, elevated blood pressure, rapid heart beat; *emotional*, e.g., heightened anxiety, depression, anger; and

---

1. E. Charlesworth & R. Nathan, Stress Management xix (1984) [hereinafter Charlesworth].

2. *Id.*

3. Zimmerman, *Stress: What It Does to Judges, And How It Can Be Lessened,* 20 Judges' Journal 4 (1981).

cognitive, e.g., increased distractibility, decreased concentration. Long-term effects can be even more serious, e.g., alcoholism, heart disease, personality changes, mental illness. The overall cost can be decreased productivity, enjoyment, or intimacy, and eventually burnout—the inability to cope with stress.[4]

Learning from Other Professions

Members of the judiciary do share similar personality characteristics that are typical of "supercharged," achieving individuals in other professions. Therefore, studies dealing with stress in other professions can provide insights. It is also clear that some types of stress inherent in the judiciary are unique, and more specialized care is needed to assist judges develop the ability to cope successfully with judiciary-related stressors and pressures.

Every person is different, but within specific classes or types of people, there are common themes. Professionals in general share two major characteristics: (1) they are highly motivated to achieve, and (2) they have undergone an extended period of formal education and apprenticeship. These two characteristics give judges the potential to develop spin-off personality traits that can lead to serious mental health problems.

Three such traits that have been identified by therapists are the overdeveloped capacity to defer gratification, a resume mentality, and emphasis on controlling the events and environment in which one lives.[5]

Deferring Gratification

The long period of education and apprenticeship of professionals provides few rewards during the process. Certainly money is the fewest of the few, and it is almost necessary to deny one's current needs or desires in favor of higher financial and other rewards expected in the future. There are certain benefits to "toughing it" during school and apprenticeship—developing the ability to work long and hard, a sense of accomplishment, and a positive self-image as an achiever. There is also a concomitant risk: "the risk that extensive years of education, preparation and apprenticeship will develop a psychological defense that renders one incapable of taking pleasure in the here and now naturally, openly and fully."[6]

The long term of personal deprivation under the guise of deferring gratification may actually render the licensed professional unable to care

4. CHARLESWORTH, *supra* note 1.
5. Sunan, *Psychological Disability of Judges and Other Professionals: Some Causes and Cures,* JUDICATURE Nov. (1982).
6. *Id.*

for his or her personal needs. For the professional, work is often not a job, it is a state of mind. If there is no room in one's life for family, play, leisure, social relationships, and other nonwork-related activities, the person is in grave danger of becoming a workaholic, forsaking a balanced life for a compulsive dedication to work. With the same compulsive nature, the addicted worker may attempt to "cure" his or her addiction by turning to alcohol, drugs, random sex, and wild spending sprees, searching for the immediate gratification and pleasure so long denied. The complications are obvious.

Resume Mentality

Another major trait can be labeled the "resume mentality," a focus on goals outside oneself as a person—in short, allowing external achievements or resume building to stunt one's personal development as an integrated human being. The compulsive professional is always seeking to gain professional experience and improve professional skills, and is achievement-oriented. Such a person may overlook the need to develop as a human being with a variety of needs. This person lacks a sense of personal renewal and is confused about the continuing need for personal growth and development. His or her world is external, not internal.

Psychologist Carl Jung was the first major analytic thinker to view middle life as the time of maximum potential for personal growth, and others have followed his lead.[7] The professional obsessed with achievement to the detriment of personal growth has ignored an important part of the personality. A person who places every bit of development energy into external affairs is probably encouraging a midlife crisis. Unity of one's personality, fully developed and integrated, is an antidote for preventing such a life event.

Gail Sheehy gives this advice to the vulnerable:

> Life does end. Time is short. Each of us travels alone. No one else can always keep us safe. And there are some parts of our personalities that we cannot change or ignore, even when the price is separation and loss, if eventually we are to find unity within ourselves.[8]

Need to Control

Often, professionals also have an exaggerated need to control their environment and the events of life. Independence is a strength, but the abnormal fear of being dependent upon significant others is a block to good mental health and a hindrance to healthy relationships.

The long dependence on professors, mentors, and others involved in training professionals is seen by some students as demeaning, and they

7. G. Sheehy, Passages (1974); Levinson, Darrow, Klein, Levinson & McKee, The Seasons of a Man's Life (1979).
8. G. Sheehy, *supra* note 7.

develop a burning desire to be rid of condescending superiors. The new professional is driven by the desire to control his or her own destiny and most often reach an accepted degree of independence after the third decade. As professionals grow older, however, they become less able to control the events of their own lives. Loved ones die, children leave home, marriages are dissolved. The professional become more vulnerable. Long-disguised dependency needs begin to emerge, but by this time these people are bewildered and unable to deal with the realities of the crisis. The underlying insistence on control has taken its toll.[9]

This discussion is not intended to be exclusive or complete. It describes professionals from various fields and with varied life and professional experiences. It is set forth to alert the new judge to the broad-based causes of stress and related complications that transcend professions. Each profession undoubtedly has stressors unique to the profession. Certainly that is true of the judiciary.

Stress in the Judiciary

Stress is inherent in the judicial career. Isaiah M. Zimmerman and other clinical psychologists have identified the narrow phenomena of judicial stress. Research indicates that the inherent stress can be recognized in a number of categories. The following discussion includes significant findings by Dr. Zimmerman and other experts, along with personal input from state trial judges.

The Transition and Social Isolation

Notwithstanding the increase in state and national orientation programs for judges, most judges enter their career with little assistance. The transition from lawyer to judge can be an overwhelming experience, and to assume the responsibility of a judge without orientation, education, and assistance from experienced judges is unfair to the judge and the community and unnecessarily stressful.

The requirements of the judicial office are barriers to many social relationships. Lawyer friends will refer to the judge as "your honor," and there is a clear deference to the new judge that signals, sometimes painfully, changes in long-term relationships. Such social deprivation contributes to the stress upon a judge.

Lack of Appropriate Feedback

Judges lack objective feedback to assist them in evaluating their judicial performance. Many bar polls are ill-conceived, inadequately planned, and inappropriately executed—some nothing more than pop-

9. Sunan, *supra* note 5.

ularity contests. Judges are often stressed by the results, especially if the results are announced to the public. Such an announcement most often creates an unnecessary ranking of judges, causing resentment and morale problems within the court. Under these circumstances, the bar does a disservice to the judge, the court, and the community.

A judge who does poorly on a valid, objective evaluation should feel stress, and that stress should provide the incentive to improve. That good judges are stressed by invalid polls is a reality, and new judges must be aware of this potential stress event. The judge's will to excellence is aided by a valid evaluation, but discouraged by an invalid poll.

Judges should consult the American Bar Association Guidelines for Evaluation of Judicial Performance. An evaluation under the guidelines could provide the appropriate feedback necessary to allow a judge to evaluate his or her performance for purposes of self-improvement. Under the ABA Guidelines, the judiciary is responsible for the entire evaluation process, including the criteria, sources, and distribution. The primary goal is self-improvement, and confidentiality is a major concern.[10]

Information Overload

The volume, variety, and complexity of litigation inundate judges with information that stretches the ability to understand, organize, weigh, and use the data as a basis for a sound decision. Time constraints, case loads, and administrative duties add to the problem. The broad spectrum of topics—one after the other, often without notice or adequate time to prepare—can be mind-boggling. Adding to the stress in the complicated case is the judge's fear that the lawyers are patronizing him or her because of their superior knowledge of the case. The lawyers have lived with the case for months or years, and in most complicated cases, they have become experts on the substantive factual issues as well as the law. The judge is most often a stranger to the facts, the law, and—perhaps less obviously—a stranger to the informal community that often develops between opposing lawyers and litigants over the months of trial preparation.

The pressure of such responsibility is awesome enough, but the pure mechanics of handling the information and mastering the factual topics, let alone the legal issues, is something not taught in law school or learned in the practice of law.

10. American Bar Association, Guidelines for the Evaluation of Judicial Performance (1985).

Midlife Years

Every adult is vulnerable to a "midlife crisis," a time when physical and psychological changes signal limits in activities and bring on a real sense of mortality. It is common knowledge that most women suffer unpleasant physical symptoms associated with midlife menopause—"the change of life." It is also understood that men often experience many of the same uncomfortable symptoms in a similar midlife transition. The male symptoms are generally related to the retrogression of the sexual function and other psychological factors. Such experiences in the lives of judges can be a disruptive force.[11] Aging can be a difficult process for anyone, but to those used to achieving, time the ally may be perceived as time the antagonist.

What is left to achieve? For some a higher court provides a possibility; for many the business of just being the best judge possible is not satisfaction enough. Add to these unresolved issues a marital problem, a delinquent child, or other vicissitudes of life, and the judge is a prime candidate for a midlife crisis. The passage can be a rough one.

Lack of Control

Judges do not select the cases that come to court, and they are subjected to the whims and emotions of the litigants. Cases that are unpleasant, emotionally taxing, or even boring routinely appear before the judge. Judges must face whatever and whoever is placed before them. A stream of unsatisfying cases or difficult people can taint the judge and chip away at the sensitive, caring nature desirable in judicial officers. The "luck of the draw" can be a serious psychological stressor.[12]

Criminal Justice Cases

Judges have been perceived in many communities as "soft on crime" and, indeed, even accused of being a major reason for the increase in crime. The difficult responsibility of protecting the rights of all citizens often puts a judge in the position of appearing to favor a criminal. Making an appropriate legal decision that may be unpopular in the community is the responsibility of a dedicated, independent judiciary, but the stress on the judge accompanying that responsibility is real and significant. This is especially true in a jurisdiction where judges are elected.

Judges who make such difficult decisions are entitled to the encouragement of colleagues and the active support of the bar association concerning any unjust criticism that may appear in the news media. A courageous and thoughtful, albeit unpopular, decision can be its own

11. M. Fishbein, The Modern Family Health Guide (1959).
12. Zimmerman, *supra* note 3.

reward, but that reward is unlikely to diminish the level of stress to any significant degree.

Unjust Criticism

The matter of unjust criticism is especially frustrating to judges. Of course, any public criticism may upset a judge, but unjust criticism is not only unfair and damaging to the judge, but also undermining of the public confidence in the system of justice.

It is frustrating to judges because correcting inaccurate or unjust criticism is often difficult if not futile. The Code of Judicial Conduct restricts a judge's ability to make certain responses or get into a public debate about a specific case or ruling. When the judge cannot properly respond, the appropriate bar association should speak in behalf of the judge and, in effect, the court system. This seldom happens.

Two major elements (stressors) of unjust criticism affect judges most. First, it is often impossible to correct an impression in the minds of news media viewers or readers. In fact, a response risks causing the unjust criticism to be republished, reinforcing a negative impression rather than correcting inaccuracies or balancing the comment. Responses are often interpreted as part of a debate on the function of the court or judge.

The second element involves the local or state bar association. Most lawyers recognize a responsibility to defend judges from unjust criticism. The American Bar Association Model Rules of Professional Conduct state the following in the commentary of Section 8.2:

> To maintain the fair and independent administration of justice, lawyers are encouraged to continue traditional efforts to defend judges and courts unjustly criticized.

The problem is that although most lawyers believe in the fundamental concept, few bar associations are organized or equipped to appropriately defend judges.

Concerned about a lack of organizational planning and preparation by bar associations, the National Conference of State Trial Judges followed the suggestions of the American Bar Association manual, *Meeting Criticism of Bench and Courts,* and developed a "Program to Meet Unjust Criticism of Judges and Courts." The program outlines the steps for a bar association to take in creating the ability to respond promptly and responsibly to unjust criticism. The program also sets forth guidelines to help bar associations determine whether or not a response is appropriate.

Several bar associations have used the National Conference of State Trial Judges outline to set up competent programs within their jurisdictions. The Washington State Bar Association was one of the first, joining with the Washington State Superior Court Judges' Association to develop a plan of action. The ABA manual for *Meeting Criticism of Bench and*

Courts and the "Program to Meet Unjust Criticism Of Judges and Courts" can be obtained from the office of the National Conference of State Trial Judges at the American Bar Association in Chicago.

Decision Making

Some people have difficulty making the everyday decisions of life; a major responsibility of a judge is to make significant decisions affecting the freedom, lives, reputations, and fortunes of others. Some judicial decisions are relatively stress-free, e.g., evidentiary rulings, ex parte matters. Others are pregnant with high levels of stress, e.g., sentencing, awarding child custody, any final decision after a trial. Some judges are paralyzed by the awesome responsibility of decision making; most judges feel stress in making difficult decisions but are able to compensate by developing a personal philosophy of a trial judge's role.

The trial judge's role is to make a decision as promptly and efficiently as possible. Lawyers and litigants must have a decision, right or wrong. The trial judge does not have the final responsibility in a lawsuit. If the judge has done the best job possible under the circumstances, he or she need not fear an appellate review. At least the stress of having to be right the first time can be alleviated.

It can be safely stated that if decision making is a source of stress, then stress is written into the job description of a judge.

Emotional Demand

An important source of stress, especially in the helping professions, is the emotional demand of working with people who have problems. While judging is not, strictly speaking, a helping profession, judges regularly face the emotional, psychological and poignant circumstances of others. Cases involving child abuse, child custody, dependency or termination of parental rights, bitter divorces, involuntary commitments, or serious crimes are examples of matters that draw emotional energy from the judge and add to the level of stress.[13]

Lack of Monetary Reward

The office of judge offers many potential rewards. The honor and prestige accorded the office is a significant reward for most, as is the power inherent in the position. There are other rewards less obvious, e.g., no overhead, no bill collecting, special committee work, opportunities to teach, some control over scheduling, and the satisfaction of providing a just result.

The lack of reward, however, is also a reality and often centers around salaries and pensions. As perceived by many judges, most jurisdictions

13. J. Ito, Judicial Burnout: Stress and Coping among Judges (1982)

do not pay judges close to what the judges could earn in private practice. Given most judicial salary levels, the pressures of raising a family in a reasonably comfortable environment are a nagging problem for judges. Many arguments support the proposition that most judges are underpaid. Special concern arises, however, when the compensation is so low as to cause some judges to resign and most of the remaining judges to have low morale. The stress increases as judges reasonably perceive that they are being treated unfairly.

Judges should take a systematic approach to keeping compensation at a reasonable level. Some judicial organizations have special committees to work on the problem year-round. These committees often have access to professional consultants and legislative representatives financed by personal assessment of the judges affected. The knowledge that the judge's own collegial group is taking every reasonable action to provide fair compensation tends to lessen the stress on individual judges. In the meantime, the judge should concentrate on the rewards available and leave the compensation issues to those responsible.

Role Ambiguity

Lawyers are not trained to be judges. Most often the new judge knows less about judging than he or she thought. The responsibilities and expectations within the system of justice are quite different for lawyers and judges. Good orientation programs for new judges are essential to a smooth transition and a reduction of role ambiguity. Role ambiguity has been defined as the lack of information necessary to meet the role requirements of an organizational position.[14]

Certainly a new judge lacks a good deal of specific information needed to perform efficiently and comfortably. Given the diverse matters presented to a court, it is often difficult for even the experienced judge to keep fully informed. Laws, rules, and procedures change with alarming frequency, and judges have to be continually alert to new roles and responsibilities.

Rotating assignments also contribute to stress. Moving from a domestic relations department to a motions calendar to juvenile court during the span of six months or a year challenges a judge to leave one role and immediately meet the expectations of a new one. Sometimes the change is stimulating and welcome, but often negative stress is present even under the best of circumstances.,

14. R. Kahn, et al., Organizational Stress: Studies in Role Conflict and Ambiguity (1964).

Judicial Immunity

Judicial immunity has been significantly eroded during the last few years and judges' personal resources have been threatened. More and more judges have been sued for a variety of claims, but most claims allege violations of the plaintiff's civil rights. The status of judicial immunity is confusing largely because of two U.S. Supreme Court cases. In *Stump v. Sparkman*,[15] the court upheld judicial immunity where a judge ordered a 15-year-old girl sterilized without her knowledge.

In 1983, however, the court decided *Pulliam v. Allen*,[16] a case in which two individuals brought an action in Federal District Court under 42 U.S.C.S. § 1988 seeking an injunction to stop a magistrate from incarcerating persons charged with a nonjailable offense when they could not put up bail money. The district court granted the injunction and awarded attorney fees to the plaintiffs and against the judge personally. The Supreme Court affirmed.

There is confusion about the future of judicial immunity, and in the meantime judges may be vulnerable. Some states defend the judge as a state officer; other courts rely on the county to provide protection. Some judges have obtained specialized insurance at their personal expense. At least one state, Nebraska, has an indemnification statute to repay the judge for any loss. In the midst of the confusion, judges are subject to a good deal of uncertainty and stress.

Judicial Discipline

All 50 states now have judicial discipline commissions to handle complaints against judges. Some commissions are perceived as out to get judges, while others are more passive. In any event, judges are constantly aware that anyone may complain about anything concerning a judge—and although most complaints are groundless, a judge lives under the cloud that some day he or she may be required to respond to a complaint. Representation by counsel will cost money, and the strain on the judge may be incalculable.

To meet this relatively new national phenomenon, many judges are obtaining special insurance to cover the cost of such proceedings. Feelings of vulnerability and helplessness add stress to the life of a judge.

Cameras in the Courtroom

During the past few years, news media cameras and equipment have moved into the courtroom. Many states have court rules allowing cameras in the courtroom under the control of the trial judge with certain conditions.

15. 435 U.S. 349 (1978).
16. 466 U.S. 522 (1983).

The reality is that judges are hard-pressed to deny access to the courtroom, and in fact most judges have come to agree that news media cameras and equipment have a role in the courtroom.[17]

Most often the news media are interested in a few highly publicized criminal cases and, in fact, have generally conducted themselves appropriately within the orders of the court. The judge, however, is faced with one more complication in a criminal trial fraught with inherent problems of constitutional rights. The presence of a third party, with the requirement of serious judicial attention to the circumstances, is bound to stress the judge. Prejudicial action by the news media could cause a mistrial or create reversible error.

Change as Stress

Change itself is stressful. What could be described as a positive or pleasant change can still be a significant source of stress. Obviously the change secondary to the death of a spouse, loss of a job, or divorce will take its toll, but such changes as promotions, vacations, or a new house can also provide serious degrees of stress. It is the total amount of stress on an individual at any one time combined with that individual's ability to adjust or cope that makes a difference in health patterns.[18]

The studies of Holmes and Rahe, and other scientists, have provided a way of looking at life changes. Holmes and Rahe have developed a social readjustment rating scale which calculates a change in numerical values. In general, a score of 150 to 300 is considered moderate, while a score above 300 is considered high. High scores have been correlated in large group studies with susceptibility to illness and accidents. A score in excess of 300 does not mean the individual will actually become ill or have an accident. It merely points to the correlation between the amount of stress and susceptibility of the individual.[19] The Holmes-Rahe scale is reprinted in the accompanying chart.[20]

17. *See* AMERICAN BAR ASSOCIATION, STANDARDS FOR CRIMINAL JUSTICE, Ch. 8 (1980).

18. CHARLESWORTH, *supra* note 1.

19. *Id.*

20. Reprinted with permission from JOURNAL OF PSYCHOSOMATIC RESEARCH, Vol. 11, pp. 213–217, Thomas H. Holmes and Richard H. Rahe, *The Social Readjustment Rating Scale,* 1967, Pergamon Press plc.; *and from* Atheneum Publishers, an imprint of Macmillan Publishing Company, from STRESS MANAGEMENT; A COMPREHENSIVE GUIDE TO WELLNESS by Dr. Edward A. Charlesworth and Dr. Ronald G. Nathan. Copyright © 1982, 1984.

THE SOCIAL READJUSTMENT RATING SCALE

Directions: Read each life event and indicate in the space provided the number of times you have experienced the event in the last year. Multiply the number of times you experienced the event by the points next to it, and total up the products.

Life Event	*Stress Values*	*Number of Times You Experienced the Event Last Year*		*Your Total Life Change Scores*
1. Death of spouse	100 times	______	=	______
2. Divorce	73 times	______	=	______
3. Marital separation from mate	65 times	______	=	______
4. Detention in jail or other institution	63 times	______	=	______
5. Death of a close family member	63 times	______	=	______
6. Major personal injury or illness	53 times	______	=	______
7. Marriage	50 times	______	=	______
8. Being fired from work	47 times	______	=	______
9. Marital reconciliation with mate	45 times	______	=	______
10. Retirement from work	45 times	______	=	______
11. Major change in the health or behavior of a family member	44 times	______	=	______
12. Pregnancy	40 times	______	=	______
13. Sexual difficulties	39 times	______	=	______
14. Gaining new family member (e.g., birth, adoption, oldster moving in, etc.)	39 times	______	=	______
15. Major business readjustment (e.g., merger, reorganization, bankruptcy, etc.)	39 times	______	=	______
16. Major change in financial state (e.g., a lot worse off or a lot better off than usual)	38 times	______	=	______
17. Death of a close friend	37 times	______	=	______
18. Changing to a different line of work	36 times	______	=	______
19. Major change in the number of arguments with spouse (e.g., either a lot more or a lot less than usual regarding childbearing, personal habits, etc.)	35 times	______	=	______

20. Taking on a mortgage greater than $10,000 (e.g., purchasing a home, business, etc.)	31 times______	=	______
21. Foreclosure on a mortgage or loan..........................	30 times______	=	______
22. Major change in responsibilities at work (e.g., promotion, demotion, lateral transfer)	29 times______	=	______
23. Son or daughter leaving home (e.g., marriage, attending college, etc.)...........................	29 times______	=	______
24. In-law troubles	29 times______	=	______
25. Outstanding personal achievement	28 times______	=	______
26. Wife beginning or ceasing work outside the home	26 times______	=	______
27. Beginning or ceasing formal school.........................	26 times______	=	______
28. Major change in living conditions (e.g., building a new home, remodeling, deterioration of home or neighborhood)	25 times______	=	______
29. Revision of personal habits (e.g., dress, manners, associations, etc.)..........................	24 times______	=	______
30. Troubles with the boss	23 times______	=	______
31. Major change in working hours or conditions	20 times______	=	______
32. Change in residence.............	20 times______	=	______
33. Changing to a new school	20 times______	=	______
34. Major change in usual type and/or amount of recreation...........	19 times______	=	______
35. Major change in church activities (e.g., a lot more or less than usual)........................	19 times______	=	______
36. Major change in social activities (e.g., clubs, dancing, movies, visiting, etc.)..................	18 times______	=	______
37. Taking on a mortgage or loan less than $10,000 (e.g., purchasing a car, TV, freezer, etc.)	17 times______	=	______
38. Major change in sleeping habits (e.g., a lot more or a lot less sleep, or change in part of the day when asleep)	16 times______	=	______

39. Major change in number of family get-togethers (e.g., a lot more or a lot less than usual)	15 times______	=	______
40. Major change in eating habits (e.g., a lot more or a lot less food intake, or very different meal hours or surroundings).........	15 times______	=	______
41. Vacation	13 times______	=	______
42. Christmas	12 times______	=	______
43. Minor violations of the law (e.g., traffic tickets, jaywalking, disturbing the peace, etc.).........	11 times______	=	______
GRAND TOTAL			______

Reprinted with permission from *Journal of Psychosomatic Research*, Vol. 11, pp. 213–217, Thomas H. Holmes and Richard H. Rahe, "The Social Readjustment Rating Scale," 1967, Pergamon Press plc.; *and from* Atheneum Publishers, an imprint of Macmillan Publishing Company, from *Stress Management; A Comprehensive Guide to Wellness* by Dr. Edward A. Charlesworth and Dr. Ronald G. Nathan. Copyright © 1982, 1984.

Spousal Emancipation

During the career of some judges, a spouse, most often a wife, may reach a new level of growth that calls for significant changes in the marital relationship. Most of the time this involves a wife's need to find new avenues of expression and a claim of independence and personhood. The comfortable acceptance of traditional husband and wife roles may be upset and altered significantly by the wife's new direction. Each situation is unique, and no generalization will suffice to explain the life-changing transition. The issue is raised here as part of the catalog of stresses affecting many professionals, including judicial officers.

Coping and Prevention

One expert defines the coping process as "an array of covert and overt behavior patterns by which the organism can actively prevent, alleviate or respond to stress-inducing circumstances."[21] He distinguishes between "anticipatory" coping mechanisms and "preventive" coping. The former mechanisms are planned to alleviate stress, while the latter involve elimination of stressors. Coping mechanisms minimize the negative effects of stress on job performance and the quality of life.

Other experts have divided coping strategies into two groups: organizational (actions an organization can take to alleviate or eliminate

21. J. McGrath, Social and Psychological Factors in Stress (1970).

stressful working conditions) and intrapersonal (techniques individuals use to deal with stress in their lives).[22]

A judicial organizational strategy could include the following actions:

- Make efforts to clear up the confusion about judicial immunity, giving judges sound information on each judge's status.
- Inform judges of the role of the judicial discipline commission and give advice on how to lessen the possibility of a complaint.
- Explore the possibilities of a judicially operated judicial performance evaluation system, as recommended by the ABA guidelines, to provide valid feedback for self-improvement.
- Provide an ongoing, well-financed effort to ensure that salaries and pensions are fair and equitable.
- Help bar associations establish programs to meet unjust criticism of judges and courts.
- Provide updated information and full descriptions of all assignments so that judges are clear on what is expected on special calendars and departmental assignments.
- Provide a comprehensive judicial education program designed to meet the judge's needs on planning a personal strategy to cope with stress.
- Provide sound liaison with appropriate bar associations on subjects affecting stress on judges, e.g., unjust criticism of judges and courts, professionalism of lawyers, compensation.
- Maintain appropriate communication liaison with the news media through bench-bar-press committees, and provide judges with information and support concerning issues of fair trial and free press.[23]
- Provide ongoing public information programs to educate the community on the role of a judge and the attendant pressures.

On the intrapersonal side, each judge should recognize the stress factors abundant in the judiciary. A personal strategy should recognize that personality development is an ongoing element of living, creating the necessity to give continuing attention to matters of personal growth in addition to professional improvement and achievement. In developing a personal strategy, a judge should seek out appropriate programs to eliminate or alleviate personal stress. Here are some suggestions:

- Get a regular physical examination.
- Engage in a regular exercise program.
- Study written materials on the general subject of stress management.

22. A. Pines & E. Aronson, Burnout: From Tedium to Personal Growth (1981).
23. *See* ABA, *supra* note 17.

- Read books, articles, studies, and other self-help literature concerning personal growth and development.
- Seek faith and spiritual renewal.
- Develop a hobby or enjoyable avocation.
- Plan high-quality family time, e.g., vacations, special events, reunions.
- Establish improved communication ties with spouse.
- Reexamine personal goals regularly.
- Become active in an appropriate nonlaw-related group activity, e.g., church, service club, fraternal group, alumni association.
- Make full use of opportunities for collegiality.
- Take time for play and leisure. Have fun! (Arthur, in the movie of the same name, exclaimed with glee, "Isn't this fun? Isn't fun the best thing to have?")

These lists are not in any order of importance and certainly not exhaustive. They are included here to encourage judges to do something about stress management before the consequences of stress diminish the quality of life and interfere with judicial responsibilities.

At the end of this chapter is Dr. Isaiah M. Zimmerman's "Personal Burnout Prevention Plan." It first appeared in the *Judges' Journal* (Summer 1981), a publication founded by the National Conference of State Trial Judges.

Judges can win the battle with stress, but only if they are continually alert and willing to take the necessary steps to cope.

Neglect a danger and it will take you by surprise.
—Proverb

Personal Burnout Prevention Plan

Isaiah M. Zimmerman

Select only one action from each track; then undertake all four actions together over a two-week period

I. Professional Track (choose only one)
   1. Discuss your thoughts and feelings about your work with your closest friend and your spouse.
   2. Resign from one committee or board.
   3. Read one book in a totally unfamiliar field or topic.
   4. Ask a respected law professor or colleague to critique a sample of your recent writing.
   5. Tell several close colleagues that you are going through a period of important personal reassessment. Do not be apologetic, defensive, or humorous about it.

II. Personal Track (choose only one)
   1. Meditate, pray, or simply relax, with eyes shut, for a brief period each day.
   2. At home, finish one house repair or gardening project.
   3. By telephone, "visit" and chat with three friends you have not seen for a long time.
   4. Ask your spouse to be the initiating and active partner in sex and affection for two weeks.
   5. Go through your family photo albums. Think about the course of your life and discuss it with your family.

III. Physical Track (choose only one)
   1. Do an alternating tensing and relaxing exercise for three minutes, twice each day.
   2. After medical consultation, start light jogging, rapid walking, or swimming daily.
   3. Arrange not to be disturbed, and take a short nap daily in the office, or as soon as you come home.
   4. Cut out all sugar and salt in your diet, and limit coffee, tea, and liquor to one drink a day.

IV. Administrative Track (choose only one)
   1. Exchange your briefcase for a larger in-basket and take no work home.
   2. Take an hour off each week to visit around your courthouse and get acquainted with the people who work there. Show an active interest in their jobs and problems.
   3. At the end of each day, take 15 minutes to talk the day over with your whole staff and go over plans for the next day.
   4. Find funds and time for a course or workshop not directly related to your work: a "mini-sabbatical."
   5. Invite your administrative staff to two "brainstorming" sessions (one week apart) where no ideas will be criticized during the session.

It is suggested that the above program, or a similar concept, be carried out once every six months as a form of personal renewal and as an "early warning system." The value inherent in such an approach is that no matter how heavy the work at the court gets, the quality and liveliness of one's personal life must not yield to the pressures involved.

II

The Work of a Judge

8

ALTERNATIVE DISPUTE RESOLUTION

In some places and on some occasions, the judge's work load becomes so great and the delay so long that people look wistfully toward methods that might prevent so much work from reaching the courts. The problem of finite court resources and expanding litigation creates widespread interest in alternatives to adjudication. Couples would like to see some alternative to hotly contested divorce cases. People without means to afford expensive attorneys need to find an inexpensive and prompt method for resolving their disputes.

The result of this interest is a variety of remedies that are now often referred to as *alternative dispute resolution* (ADR). Some of these mechanisms for dispute resolution have been available for many years. Others have been devised more recently. Court sponsorship of some of them is a relatively new phenomenon.

What are some of these methods? Among them are arbitration, mediation, early neutral evaluation, summary jury trial, minitrial, and private courts or rent-a-judge programs.

Arbitration-Mediation

Let us first look at some of the older ADR methods, mediation and arbitration. Many business professionals, even lawyers and judges, are unaware of the differences between arbitration and mediation. This confusion is fostered by dictionaries, statutes, and library reference cards, each of which often defines one term by referring to the other. Actually, there is a considerable difference.

The most basic difference between the two is that arbitration involves the decision by an intervening third party, or "neutral"; mediation does not.[1]

---

1. Bedikian. *Overview of Alternative Dispute Resolution Techniques,"* MICHIGAN BAR JOURNAL 876-77 (1986).

Mediation also differs from arbitration in that the mediator lacks authority to decide the dispute, or even to recommend a decision to the parties; rather, this person acts to assist the parties in reaching agreement.

This difference in authority calls upon different skills:

> Another way to distinguish the two is by describing the processes in terms of the neutral's mental functions. In arbitration, the neutral employs mostly 'left brain' or 'rational' mental processes—analytical, mathematical, logical, technical, administrative; in mediation, the neutral employs mostly 'right brain' or 'creative' mental processes—conceptual, intuitive, artistic, holistic, symbolic, emotional.[2]

The arbitrator is passive, determining the outcome. The mediator is active, attempting to bring the parties to reconciliation and agreement, regardless of who or what is right or wrong. The nature of the role therefore complicates the mediator's job:

> Because the role of the mediator involves instinctive reactions, intuition, keen interpersonal skills, the ability to perceive subtle, psychological and behavioral indicators, in addition to logic and rational thinking, it is much more difficult than the arbitrator's role to perform effectively. It is fair to say that while most mediators can effectively perform the arbitrator's function, the converse is not necessarily true . . . Mediation is used where there is a reasonable likelihood that the parties will be able to reach an agreement with the assistance of a neutral. Usually, mediation is used when parties will have an ongoing relationship after resolution of the conflict. Arbitration, on the other hand, is generally appropriate for use when two conditions exist: there is no reasonable likelihood of an negotiated settlement; and there will not be a continuing relationship after resolution.[3]

Obviously, these processes are different.

The role of the judge in a settlement conference has been likened to mediation. However, to the extent that a settlement conference judge assigns a value to the case or in some other way makes a decision that is not final, the settlement conference may be more of a hybrid.

Each of these two processes has been used to resolve disputes for many years. Contracts frequently provide for arbitration, whether to resolve a building contract dispute or a dispute between an athlete and the management of the team.

These techniques also are increasingly popular within the judicial system. Some states now provide for arbitration in certain kinds of cases. Mediation is frequently used to resolve questions of child custody and visitation and other domestic relations issues.

2. Cooley, *Arbitration vs. Mediation—Explaining the Differences,* 69 JUDICATURE 263 (1986).

3. *Id.* at 264.

Early Neutral Evaluation

Early neutral evaluation is an experimental process designed in the Federal District Court for the Northern District of California.[4] This procedure can take place early in litigation and encourages each party to confront and analyze its own situation in the lawsuit. The evaluation provides an inexpensive opportunity to hear the other side present its case, and ultimately it affords a confidential, frank, thoughtful assessment of the relative strengths of the parties' positions and the overall value of the case.

The central feature of the procedure is the confidential two-hour evaluation session that takes place early in the life of the litigation. The session is hosted by a neutral, experienced, highly respected private lawyer who is appointed by the court under its inherent power to appoint special masters. The parties, accompanied by counsel, attend the session at which four major things happen:[5]

1. Each party takes 15 to 30 minutes to present its position.
2. The evaluator works with counsel to reduce the scope of the dispute. Together, they identify areas of agreement, and the evaluator urges the lawyers to set aside tenuous theories until they have thoroughly explored the settlement possibilities.
3. The evaluator candidly assesses the strengths and weaknesses of arguments and evidence. By estimating the likelihood of liability and dollar range of damages, the evaluator evaluates the case.
4. The evaluator helps the litigants devise a plan for sharing information and/or conducting discovery in a way that will bring the case to serious settlement negotiations as expeditiously as possible.

Summary Jury Trial

The *summary jury trial* was created to provide a summary presentation of a civil case to an advisory jury for the purpose of showing the parties (as well as the lawyers and the judge) how a jury reacts to the dispute.[6] It is the creation of the Hon. Thomas D. Lambros, U.S. District Judge for the Northern District of Ohio.[7] It has been endorsed by the Judicial Conference of the United States as a means of promoting fair and equal

---

4. Brazil, Kahn, Newman & Gold, *Early Neutral Evaluation: An Experimental Effort to Expedite Dispute Resolution,* 69 JUDICATURE 279 (1986).

5. *Id.*

6. For an excellent article on summary jury trial *see* Brenneman & Wesoloski, *Blueprint for a Summary Jury Trial,* 65 MICHIGAN BAR JOURNAL 888-91 (1986).

7. Lambros, *The Summary Jury Trial—An Alternative Method of Resolving Disputes,* 69 JUDICATURE 286 (1986).

settlement of potentially lengthy civil cases. The entire trial takes place in one day.

The first step in the summary jury trial process is a pretrial conference conducted by a magistrate who will preside at the trial. In federal court the conference is scheduled in a referral order issued by the district judge assigned to the case.

The pretrial conference reduces evidentiary disputes. At the conference, attorneys are required to exchange exhibits before the hearing. Issues are narrowed. Since they do not present live evidence, the attorneys summarize the evidence, present slides, charts, and notebooks, and furnish to each juror a copy of documents presented.

The parties themselves must be present at the summary jury trial. Thus they see and hear a presentation of their opponents' arguments as well as their own and personally gauge the impact of the case on the jury. While the jurors are deliberating, the court speaks to the parties and cautions them that six disinterested strangers are about to decide their case, but should the case go to a full-scale trial, a regular jury of strangers would do the same thing with the result likely to be the same.

While the jurors are selected in the usual way, they are told that they are participating in an experimental procedure. They are *not* told that their decision is not binding. As a matter of fact, most often it is binding because the parties are able to reach agreement. After the verdict has been returned, the procedure is explained to the jurors.

The Minitrial

A similar procedure is called the minitrial.[8] It is a voluntary, expedited, nonjudicial process whereby the top management officials of each party meet to resolve a dispute. The actual hearing is informal and usually lasts only one or two days. Each side is represented by an attorney, but the presentation is made not to a jury, but rather to the principals on the respective sides. No transcript of the hearing is produced, and the rules of evidence and procedure are not enforced.

In some cases, a neutral adviser assists the parties in assessing the merits of the claim, but the use of such an adviser is optional. The role of the adviser must be well defined.

Cases appropriate for this procedure are those which have complex factual situations, involve large sums of money, and do not involve questionable areas of law.

8. *See* Edelman & Carr, *The Mini-Trial: An Alternative Dispute Resolution Procedure,* 42 Arbitration Journal 7-14 (1987).

Private Courts or Rent-a-Judge Proceedings

Private courts or the so-called "rent-a-judge" proceedings[9] were authorized by California law in 1872.[10] The procedure was little used until the mid-1970s, when it was first used to avoid the backlog of cases in court. Now it is fairly common in California, in those large urban areas which have a backlog of civil trials, to have cases resolved by private judges who are paid by the parties to those cases. Five other states have similar statutes,[11] but the use in those other states appears to be far less extensive than it is in California. This proceeding can be used in any case in which the parties are willing to pay for the services of a private judge.

The proceeding commences with the filing of a petition or stipulation with the trial court. The court then appoints a referee to hear the case, usually after a stipulation by the parties, who have selected the person they desire to act as the "judge" in their case. The person selected is most often a retired judge.

After the appointment of the referee or judge, the court system is not involved and no public notice is filed until the conclusion of the proceedings. The parties determine the time and place for the proceedings, provide a place for the trial, pay the judge $100 to $250 per hour, and provide any other facilities they agree upon. Within 20 days after deciding the matter, the referee files a report with the court. The report contains the referee's findings of fact and conclusions of law. At this time, the matter does become a part of the public record.

Multidoor Courthouse

One of the most comprehensive efforts to make available many of these methods in one place is the so-called multidoor courthouse.[12] This is a result of a 1976 paper by Professor Frank Sander of the Harvard Law School identifying the need for a multifaceted "dispute resolution center."

With American Bar Association support, Houston, Texas; Tulsa, Oklahoma; and the District of Columbia were selected as "multidoor" project

9. *See* Myers, *Rent-a-Judge in California,* 131 NEW LAW JOURNAL 1042 (1981); Coulson, *Private Settlement for the Public Good* 66 JUDICATURE 7 (June-July 1982); Glantz, *Analysis of a First Amendment Challenge to Rent-a-Judge Proceedings,* 14 PEPPERDINE LAW REVIEW 989-1005 (1987).

10. CAL. CIVIL PROCEDURE CODE § 638 West 1976 and Supp. 1987.

11. New York, Oregon, Rhode Island, South Carolina, and Washington. *See* Myers, *supra* note 9, at page 1044.

12. Address delivered at the National Conference on the Causes of Popular Dissatisfaction with the Administration of Justice, St. Paul, Minnesota, April 7-9, 1976, as found in *Varieties of Dispute Processing,* 70 F.R.D. 79, 111-134 (1976).

sites. The concept is that a court would increase the range of options offered citizens in the resolution of their varied disputes and would acquaint them with the various alternatives available, helping them select those most suitable to their particular dispute.

In the District of Columbia, the superior court offers a sophisticated screening and referral operation that is both visible and accessible to the public. Over 40 dispute resolution programs are operating in the District of Columbia community. Intake centers are located at the courthouse and at the District of Columbia Bar's Lawyer Referral and Information Service. A referral manual describes more than 300 programs. During one period, more than three-fourths of the people who sought assistance were directed to programs *outside* the court system.

Obviously, such a system requires funding and commitment. With funding and commitment, however, the potential litigants can often find alternative methods of resolving their dispute at far less cost than going to court.

Summary

Early neutral evaluation and summary jury trial are court-centered. Arbitration and mediation usually are accomplished outside the court system. However, courts at the federal, state, and local levels are actively working to bring mechanisms for alternative dispute resolution within the control of the judges. Court-sponsored mediation programs have proliferated during the 1980s. Mandatory court-annexed arbitration has vastly increased. Minitrials and rent-a-judge are accomplished outside the court system, though rent-a-judge is in a sense court-validated by the appointment of the referee and the filing of the findings of the judge. Where the size of the court warrants its use, the "multidoor courthouse" affords a buffet table of dispute resolution techniques that should be helpful to litigants and courts.

Not all of these efforts prevent cases from getting to the courthouse, but they all attempt to resolve disputes more readily and more quickly.

9

COURT MANAGEMENT AND DELAY REDUCTION

One of the most startling discoveries of new judges is that their decisions on legal issues, whether good or bad, right or wrong, do not in any way affect a major source of public dissatisfaction with the courts. The public's greatest irritation with the court system is not the quality of judicial decisions but calendar congestion and trial delay.[1] In other words, judges are expected to do more than decide legal issues sagely; determine guilt or innocence, fault, duty, and damages; conduct trials fairly; and see that justice is done. Like it or not, it is the court's obligation to manage its docket. Case and docket management is not only the court's prerogative, it is also its obligation.

This administrative responsibility is not always acknowledged or well received by trial judges. One well-respected judge stated that if he wanted to be an assignment clerk or court administrator, he would have applied for the job. As Colorado Justice Anthony F. Vollock points out, judges have retained their responsibility for decision making on legal and substantive issues, and have largely abdicated their managerial responsibility.[2]

The trial court is the public's principal contact with the judicial system. The performance of our courts is critical, and success or failure inspires or undermines confidence in the entire judicial system.[3] Serving the public at large includes managing the docket. There is no doubt that

1. YANKELOVICH, SKELLY AND WHITE, INC., THE PUBLIC IMAGE OF THE COURTS (1978); CITIZENS' COMMISSION TO IMPROVE MICHIGAN COURTS, FINAL REPORT AND RECOMMENDATIONS TO IMPROVE THE EFFICIENCY AND RESPONSIVENESS OF MICHIGAN COURTS (1986).

2. Vollack, *Keeping Abreast of the Flood: How Judges Can Control Caseflow,* 4 STATE COURT JOURNAL, no. 5 (1981).

3. AMERICAN BAR ASSOCIATION, ACTION COMMISSION TO REDUCE COURT COSTS AND DELAY, ATTACKING LITIGATION COSTS AND DELAY (1984).

unless the court actively controls the progress of cases, the caseload will control the court.[4]

Not only is the concept of administering a docket a surprise to new judges, it is also foreign to many experienced judges. Judges receive no training for this. In addition, most courts have an unfortunate lack of information to assist in this regard. Many judges and administrators lack reliable information to assess the pace of litigation in their court.[5] In some instances, a lack of personnel aggravates the situation.

There is no question that it would be easier to ignore the judicial administrative responsibilities. The temptation is always to avoid the difficult and take a laissez-faire attitude. Let the lawyers, who will profit from their control of cases, continue to perpetuate that system. The public be damned. Yet we know that justice is not served by an inefficient and protracted litigation process. The tired and overworn expression "justice delayed is justice denied" remains indisputable.

Caseflow Management

According to a study prepared for the ABA Commission on Standards of Judicial Administration, "Caseflow management connotes supervision or management of the time and events involved in the movement of a case through the court system from the point of initiation to disposition, regardless of the type of disposition."[6] Another observer of judicial administration writes that the goal of good judicial case management "is to help all participants in the process understand the dispute as clearly as possible, focus on what is central to it, develop expeditiously the information needed to resolve it, and either facilitate a negotiated disposition or deliver up the matter promptly and tidily to a trial court."[7]

The judge is the symbol of the legal system. Judges accept the praise and honor of the position as well as the obligation to dispense justice promptly at the least cost to all participants. While some judges are able to avoid the day-to-day administrative responsibilities of budgeting, purchasing, hiring, firing, and negotiating salaries, no judge can avoid the obligation of managing the court's docket. "While the case is in the hands of the lawyers, before it is filed in the court, it is their business—but after it reaches the court, it is the public's business; and it is the duty of

4. Vollack, *supra* note 2.

5. Mahoney & Sipes, *Zeroing in on Court Delay: The Powerful Tools of Time Standards and Management Information,* 4 Court Management Journal (1985).

6. M. Solomon & D. Somerlot, Caseflow Management in the Trial Court 3 (1987).

7. Brazil, *Case Management: The Panacea has its Side Effects,* 24 Judges' Journal, 4 (1985).

all to see to it that it is moved along to final disposition."[8]

Some may argue that the judge's responsibility in the management of the docket depends on the calendaring system involved. Not so! All judges, whether on an individual or master calendaring system, are accountable for the court's performance on case processing. The type of system used for case assignment does not determine the success or failure of caseflow management.[9]

The most important component in the successful management of the docket is the judge's commitment to controlling caseflow, improving the pace of litigation, and recognizing his or her responsibility for eliminating delay.[10] Strong adherence to the following principle is the most effective assurance of a successful docket: "From the commencement of litigation to its resolution, whether by trial or settlement, any elapsed time other than reasonably required for pleadings, discovery and court events is unacceptable and should be eliminated. To enable just and efficient resolution of cases, the court, not the lawyers or litigants, should control the pace of litigation. A strong judicial commitment is essential to reducing delay and, once achieved, maintaining a current docket."[11] The judge is the key element in this process. Research has established that the leading cause of delay is the judge's failure to maintain control over the pace of litigation.[12]

Management of Information

To be a successful manager, the judge must first take the time and make the effort to understand his or her own court. Simply stated, the judge should take off his or her robe, step back, and take a good hard look at the system in which he or she is working. Familiarity with such statistics as the number of cases filed and disposed in a given period of time, the number and age of the pending cases, and the age of cases at disposition is essential to assessing the pace of litigation and the extent

8. Alfred P. Murrah, Chair of Pretrial Committee of the Judicial Conference and Chief Judge of the Tenth Circuit Court of Appeals.

9. Solomon & Somerlot, *supra* note 6.

10. Neubauer et al., *Managing the Pace of Justice: An Evaluation of LEAA's Court Delay Reduction Programs,* National Institute of Justice (1981).

11. American Bar Association, National Conference of State Trial Judges, Standards Relating to Court Delay Reduction, § 2.50 (1984).

12. Friesen, *Cures for Court Congestion,* 23 Judges' Journal 4 (1984); Flanders et al., Case Management and Court Management in United States District Courts (1977); Friesen et al., *Justice in Felon Courts: A Prescription to Control Delay,* 2 Whittier Law Review 7 (1979); Sipes et al., Managing to Reduce Delay (1980); Trotter & Cooper, *State Trial Court Delay: Efforts at Reform,* 31 American University Law Review 213 (1982); Sipes, *The Journey toward Delay Reduction in Trial Courts: A Traveler's Report,* 6 State Court Journal 5 (1982). *See also* Church, *Who Sets the Pace of Litigation in Urban Trial Courts?* 65 Judicature 76 (1981).

of delay. The judge must have a working knowledge and understanding of the number and age of the cases on his or her docket. In addition, the judge should monitor these data regularly.

Whether retrieved manually or through the use of a sophisticated computer system, information is necessary to identify delay problems, develop a strategy for reducing delays, and control the progress of cases on an ongoing basis.[13] Initially this may require a manual listing of cases, the date of filing, and the date of disposition. Modifications can include an age breakdown of pending cases, the percentage of trial dates that are continued or adjourned, the percentage of scheduled trials that are settled or dismissed before trial, and the median age of cases disposed of by court and jury trial. If special expertise is available to assist in developing information systems, the judge should take advantage of it. This expertise can come from a local university or the business community. Without information about the size and age of the cases, a judge cannot effectively control his or her caseload.

Judges should be able to assess the success of their procedures against standards developed or adopted by the court. Needless to say, a most effective device is feedback and information comparing judges within the same court system. Detroit Recorder's Court provides the judges with a weekly status report that ranks the individual dockets according to age and size. The report includes the number of pending cases in the pretrial stage and the number in the trial stage. It is a form of accountability. Few judges would acknowledge that they are in a competitive position with their colleagues. Yet no judge wants to have the largest or oldest docket. Human nature dictates that everyone wants to avoid being last on the list.

Time Standards

"Effective case management begins by defining general time standards for the disposition of cases."[14] The National Conference of State Trial Judges (NCSTJ) and the Conference of State Court Administrators adopted national time standards in 1983 for processing civil and criminal cases. The NCSTJ standards suggest that 90 percent of all civil cases should be disposed of within one year, 98 percent within 18 months and 100 percent within two years.

These time measurements must commence with the filing of the complaint. The litigant is not interested in the problems of serving the summons or the delay of counsel in filing an answer. The injured person

13. Mahoney & Sipes, *supra* note 5.

14. Lieber, *Maximum Case Management with Minimum Judge Time,* 25 JUDGES' JOURNAL 4 (1986).

only measures time from the injury until the ultimate resolution of the matter.[15]

Similarly, in criminal cases, the public is most likely to measure time from the moment the crime was committed and the victim sustained injury.

The decision to establish standards for processing time should not be governed by the size of the caseload or the size of the court. Research conducted by the National Center for State Courts has established that case-processing time bears little relationship to the size of the court's individual caseload or the percentage of trials. Some of the fastest courts in the country have the heaviest caseload per judge.[16] In other words, when adopting time goals, the focus should not be on the complexity of the existing docket but rather on the goal sought to be achieved.

These time standards should not be seen as a basis for discipline. Rather, they should be viewed as an objective against which the judge can measure his or her achievements. The tendency is to fear promulgated time standards because judges tend to focus on the highly complex multiparty case that requires more time and attention. These cases are few, with the vast majority being routine and relatively simple. Time standards should not be developed for the most protracted litigation. The standards must cover the realities of the entire docket, while recognizing that the exceptionally complex case will require special handling and accommodation by the court.

Once the judge has committeed to managing his or her docket by controlling the flow of cases and has a grasp of the size and age of the cases under his or her control, the judge must develop a management plan. Management systems vary widely. Special expertise is helpful in developing a plan, but it is not essential. Many articles offer advice, techniques, and suggested plans for caseflow management. Systematic research by the National Center for State Courts, the Federal Judicial Center, and others provides approaches to reducing court delay.[17] Absorption and adaptation of these proposals with a significant overlay of old-fashioned common sense will more than likely lead to a suitable program of caseflow management.

15. Connolly & Smith, *The Litigant's Perspective on Delay: Waiting for the Dough,* 8 Justice System Journal 271 (1983).

16. B. Mahoney, L.L. Sipes & J. Ito, Implementing Delay Reduction and Delay Prevention Programs in Urban Trial Courts (1985).

17. Church, *Civil Case Delay in State Trial Courts,* 4 The Justice System Journal (1978); Friesen, *supra* note 12; Flanders et al., *supra* note 12; Lawyers Conference Task Force on Reduction of Litigation Cost and Delay, Defeating Delay (1986).

Court Supervision

The most significant factor in any successful caseflow management program is the continuous control of case progress by the judge. Equally important is a recognition and adherence to the maxim that it is the courts, not the lawyers, that control the pace of the litigation. The concept is relatively simple, but the implementation requires perseverance and commitment.[18] It is not easy to wrest control of the pretrial phase of litigation from the attorneys.

Establishment of, and adherence to, firm dates for the completion of discovery and/or the termination of filing of motions will often generate some resistance from the lawyers. Every judge would find it easier to yield to the plaint of a lawyer who asks for more time to prepare or an additional opportunity to amend a witness list, which will then necessarily lead to more discovery, time, and cost to the litigant. Lack of preparation is no excuse. However, an unforeseen event is.

Resistance to the attorney's plea for adjournments or continuances can be made easier by keeping in mind that if counsel knows the dates are firm, settlement will occur earlier. Since over 90 percent of all civil cases filed are settled without a trial, the emphasis should be on generating the early incentive to settle by expediting the prospect of going to trial. Thus, judges have to risk attorney displeasure in establishing a firm policy of denying requests for continuances or adjournments. There is no question that a judge's reputation in this regard will be reflected in the age, size, and status of the judge's docket. The stricter the no-continuance or adjournment policy, the shorter the median time to disposition.

A firm approach and resistance to attorney pressure is made easier when the judge keeps in mind that the majority of cases require little preparation for trial in the form of pleadings, motions, and discovery.[19] In addition, the judge should never forget the perspective of the litigant. Delay only increases the parties' anxiety level and sense of frustration.[20] Rightly or wrongly, the judge will invariably be blamed for the delay. Further, the feeling of justice achieved is directly related to the early and prepared resolution of the dispute.

18. Gage, *How to Reduce the Docket: What One Judge Can Do,* 23 JUDGES' JOURNAL, 1 (1984).

19. CONNOLLY ET AL., JUDICIAL CONTROLS AND THE CIVIL LITIGATIVE PROCESS: DISCOVERY, at 31 (1978) (the typical federal case going to trial totalled only five discovery requests; only 10 percent of federal cases totalled ten or more discovery requests.) The results of this study comport with the findings of other such studies, e.g., TRUBEK ET AL., CIVIL LITIGATION RESEARCH PROJECT FINAL REPORT, part A at 11-58-59 (1983).

20. Connolly & Smith, *supra* note 15.

Court Delay Reduction: One Judge's Approach

The author establishes early control by setting a calendar conference within 90 days of the date of filing of the complaint. This conference is not permitted to be held on the telephone, since a face-to-face meeting often results in an opening of files with an exchange of documents and sharing of photographs. The attorneys attend; their clients do not. The purpose of this conference is to establish dates for discovery cutoff, mediation, exchange of witness lists, and the trial. The attorneys are thus compelled to examine their files and establish commitments early in the process.

The calendar conference order is on a prepared form with only the dates to be inserted.[21] Therefore, when the attorneys leave the judge's office, they carry with them an order signed by the judge. Also, the form has a place for any additional orders, so that if there are outstanding interrogatories or amendments to the pleadings to be made, the judge can order them during the conference and thus avoid the necessity of the attorneys appearing for an additional motion.

This early conference provides the attorneys with advance notice of dates and additional orders of the court. Further, the attorneys have had an opportunity not only to participate in the selection of the dates, but they have had, in an informal setting, an opportunity to discuss various anticipated problems in their respective cases. Approximately 20 percent of the cases settle during these pretrial conferences.

This conference is usually the only one that must be held. A settlement or subsequent pretrial conference is rarely held unless requested by the parties for a specific purpose. Early control is accomplished with a commitment to dates and an understanding that any requests for adjournment will be resisted by the court. This policy is respected by the bar.

The calendar conference order points out that certain events will occur during the process while the case is moving toward the trial date. As each event occurs, whether it be rapidly approaching the discovery closing date, the mediation date, or the filing of the witness list, it forces the attorneys to look at their files. Statistics have proven time and again that whenever an attorney is compelled to do something on a file, a certain percentage of cases will be settled. The job of the judge is to ensure that these settlements occur early in the process so as to minimize the parties' emotional investment and the cost to the public.

If one accepts the proposition that cases will settle once the expectation of actually going to trial becomes a reality, then the importance of setting the trial calendar is evident. Setting too few cases for trial will often leave the judge with nothing to do—a/k/a "downtime." It is generally

21. See Calendar Conference Order form on page 115.

unacceptable practice to set only one trial on a given day, blocking out a specified number of days to be used for the trial. The overwhelming majority of cases settle on the eve of trial. The judge is then left scampering to find a trial to fill the void. On the other hand, the court should not set too many cases for trial, resulting in too many court-generated continuances. Experimentation and an analysis of the dynamics of the judge's own trial lengths will assist the judge in developing the appropriate number of case settings. An occasional dark courtroom cannot be avoided. Similarly, two cases will sometimes be proceeding to trial at the same date. One will have to wait, resulting in a manageable trailing docket. Setting three to four civil cases per day is manageable for this author and generally achieves the best results. With 1,800 new cases per year, the author's docket is in compliance with the time standards of NCSTJ.

Conclusion

The citizens involved in litigation hold the court responsible for the progress of the case.[22] Judges serve the public, not the lawyers. The public expects prompt justice at the least cost.

No one can honestly deny that the public's greatest complaint with the courts is that litigation takes too long, and the public is not wrong. Delay results in an overuse of the courts, increased costs, and needless extra activity without a corresponding benefit to the client. In the end, the litigants are ill-served and they know it. Regardless of the result, as time passes waiting for the case to settle, the litigants' mental investment generally increases to the point that results are unsatisfactory no matter what the outcome. It was not worth all of the waiting and worrying. Judges must be sensitive to the destructive effects of delay so as to ensure "that the contending parties do not find themselves more effectively ruined by delay than they could have been by the injustice of any decision."[23]

22. Connolly & Smith, *supra* note 15.

23. Edmund Burke (1759) as cited in Falsgraf, *The Quest for Justice: Cost and Delay Threaten Equal Access to the Court System,* 9 STATE COURT JOURNAL (1985).

STATE OF MICHIGAN
IN THE CIRCUIT COURT FOR THE COUNTY OF OAKLAND

Civil Action
No. ____________________

____________________________________ /

CALENDAR CONFERENCE ORDER

At a session of said Court, held in the Courthouse
Tower, City of Pontiac, County of Oakland, State of Michigan,

on the ____________ day of ____________, 19______.

PRESENT: Honorable HILDA R. GAGE
Circuit Court Judge

This matter having come before the Court for a calendar conference and the parties, through their respective counsel having been present and heard, and the Court being fully advised on the premises;

IT IS HEREBY ORDERED that the within cause shall be set for mediation on

______________________________.

IT IS FURTHER ORDERED that the list of witnesses for each party shall be submitted to opposing counsel and the Court not later than ______________________________.

IT IS FURTHER ORDERED that discovery shall be completed by ____________________.

IT IS FURTHER ORDERED that the within cause of action shall be set for trial the week of ______________________________.

IT IS FURTHER ORDERED that all depositions to be used at trial shall be purged not later than two weeks prior to trial or the objections shall be waived.

IT IS FURTHER ORDERED that the appearance of counsel upon a pleading shall be deemed to be the appearance of every other member of his/her law firm. Such appearance shall require the presence of either the attorney who files the pleading or a member of his/her law firm at the mediation or trial. No adjournments of the mediation or trial shall be allowed.

IT IS FURTHER ORDERED

____
HILDA R. GAGE
Circuit Court Judge

Acknowledged and Approved:

____

____

10

PRETRIAL AND SETTLEMENT PROCEEDINGS

Pretrial proceedings—all of the things that happen before a trial—cover a wide spectrum of activities: motions, discovery, trial-setting conferences, "settlement conferences," and "pretrial conferences." Under rules adopted by the federal courts and by the courts of a number of states, the formal pretrial conference is one of four major procedural devices used in the pretrial stage, the others being pleadings, motions, and discovery.

The judge conducts a pretrial conference, either mandatory or voluntary, in order to formulate a pretrial order that identifies the nature of the action, the parties' positions as to facts affecting liability, damage claims, admissions, and expert witnesses; specifies legal issues; makes any allowance of further discovery; estimates the length of the trial; and fixes the date on which the case will be called to trial. Either during or after the conference, the judge signs the pretrial order.

Under most rules, the issues are defined by pretrial conference order, which supersedes the pleadings if there is a difference between the two. The pretrial conference was first considered as something so valuable that it should be required and later as something that could be held on a voluntary basis if the court felt it to be advantageous or if the parties desired it.

Effectiveness of the Pretrial Conference

Professor Maurice Rosenberg of Columbia University was asked by the State of New Jersey to evaluate the effectiveness of the pretrial conference. He conducted a controlled test in civil litigation in New Jersey.[1]

---

1. M. Rosenberg, The Pretrial Conference and Effective Justice: A Controlled Test in Personal Inquiry Litigation (1964).

He found that one of the primary problems with mandatory pretrial conferences was that they were conducted by judges who felt that they were useless ritual. When judges conducting such conferences felt that they were wasting their time, they tended to be perfunctory, to not explore, to accept whatever the attorney said or did not say, and to make orders that were speedy and meaningless. On the other hand, judges who were conscientious used the pretrial conference as a tool to dispose of the case without trial, to get it settled.

In fact, the federal rule and the majority premise as stated by Professor Rosenberg were that the pretrial conference was designed mainly to develop and clarify the issues so that they could be resolved in a way that reflected the merits of the case. New Jersey rules declared that the "matter of settlement . . . shall not be mentioned in the order."[2] However, this failure to mention settlement in the order does not mean a relegation to minor importance. While settlement was not the primary end sought, it was nevertheless a valuable by-product.

Over the years, the courts have tended to abandon mandatory pretrial conferences but to use pretrial conferences in selected cases where they may be of considerable value. If the goal of the pretrial conference is to define the issues to be resolved and to eliminate those matters not in dispute either factually or legally, where the issues are complex and where there are many parties, such a conference may be beneficial.

If settlement is a by-product of the pretrial conference and not its primary goal, it still is an important event. Ninety percent of civil cases settle before trial. *When* that settlement occurs is of very considerable importance to the court. The earlier it occurs, the better not only for the litigants but also for the court. The court should do anything it can to cause settlement to occur as early as possible. Any meeting of the attorneys for the opposing sides in the presence of the judge has a potential for settlement discussion. Of course, the purpose of the conference is clearer when it is called a settlement conference.

Most attorneys would rather settle a case than try it, provided the interests of their clients are properly protected. Settlement conferences, whether formal or informal, are widely held. The rules of most jurisdictions contain some provision for settlement conferences.

The Trial-Setting Conference

Another useful pretrial proceeding is the trial-setting conference, whether held in person or by telephone conference call. The parties set the date of the trial, determine whether the matter is to be tried to a

2. Rules Governing the Courts of the State of New Jersey, 4:25-1(b)(16) (West Publishing 1988).

jury and, if so, who demands the jury and posts the fees, how many challenges are allowed to each side, the time at which discovery and motions are to be terminated and experts named, and, in many places, the date for the settlement conference.

A settlement conference is probably a waste of time in short cases. In almost any kind of case where the conference can be held in far less time than the trial, such a conference is likely to be valuable.

The settlement conference should be held near trial time. The closer to trial, the greater the pressure to settle. While the adrenaline may flow even more rapidly just a few days before trial, a conference held somewhat earlier will allow witnesses, including experts, to be called off, saving an appreciable amount of money. Therefore, many courts hold such conferences two or three weeks before the date of trial.

Techniques for the Settlement Conference[3]

The most successful technique in any given jurisdiction is the one that works in that jurisdiction. Judge Homer Thompson of the California Superior Court of Santa Clara County uses the "soft-sell" approach. He operates substantially as a mediator, attempting to determine the case's settlement value by negotiation. He tries not to give an opinion on value, but rather to bring the parties to some middle ground acceptable to both sides. Judge Thompson describes his procedure for the soft-sell method as follows:

1. All attorneys are brought into chambers and each side explains the liability and damages issues to the judge.
2. All data regarding special damages are given to the judge.
3. The judge asks any questions necessary to gather information not covered by the attorneys.
4. The judge then asks what settlement figures, if any, have been given by either side before the conference.
5. The judge then explains the soft-sell method to the attorneys as follows and asks them to agree to its use.
   a. The judge will meet with each attorney in private.
   b. Any figure given to the judge by either side is confidential and may not be disclosed to the other side, without specific authorization, until the case is settled.

3. For an excellent book on settlement conferences, see K. Conn, Settlement Conference, A Handbook for Judges and Lawyers (San Joaquin Eagle Publishing, Visalia, Calif., 1988).

c. Neither side may disclose to the other side what is being said in private until the case is settled or negotiation fails. If no settlement is reached, either side is free to tell the other anything that was said in private.

d. Should the figures given by each side cross, *i.e.*, plaintiff's figure be lower than defendant's figure, it is the judge's duty to advise both sides of this immediately.

6. The judge then meets in private, first with plaintiff's attorney and then with defendant's attorney.
7. During each private meeting, the judge attempts to ascertain the very lowest demand and very highest offer of each side.
8. The judge then continues meeting with each side, alternately, until he or she brings them together on a common figure. The judge then brings in both attorneys and announces the case settled and states the figure at which it is settled.

During the opening session, the judge sits at a desk. During the private talks he or she moves to an easy chair so that both judge and attorney may relax. At the first private meeting with plaintiff's attorney, it is helpful to set the tone at the outset by saying something confidential in nature, such as 'This case sure has its problems'; 'This is really a dog'; 'You have good liability, but no damages'; or 'You have all the damages in the world, but lousy liability.' Counsel will accept the court's realistic assessment in private, but would resent this approach in front of the other attorney. To defense counsel the court might open with 'This is a case that ought to be settled' or 'You have some real exposure here.'

As soon as the ice is broken, the judge should start probing for the actual top and bottom figures. Counsel will want to spend a lot of time talking about liability and/or damages, and the judge must keep bringing the conversation back to dollars. Some tangential information given in private is very helpful, such as counsel's assessments of plaintiff and defendant as witnesses, the secret bit of evidence or strategy about which the other side knows nothing, or client or witness problems that are unknown by the other side. As soon as these helpful confidential bits are gathered, however, the judge should bring counsel back to the subject of money.

Often while the judge is probing, counsel is also probing, trying to find out where the other side is on figures. Counsel will say, 'Well, Judge, what do you think the case is worth?' or 'I figure he is at so and so.' The judge should parry these thrusts.

The reason the judge should try not to reveal his or her personal evaluation is that too many cases settle for more or less than any judge's opinion of their value. Sometimes the judge can meet this thrust by stating a range of figures, especially after talking to both

> sides. He or she may say the case is worth between $2500 and $3500 when it appears both sides can be squeezed into that range and the judge feels that range represents a fair settlement value. The court is really working toward what brings the attorneys together, not what he or she may think the case is worth based on a very limited knowledge of all its facts. The judge may avoid giving a direct figure by saying, 'It [surely is] worth more than that,' or 'less than that,' referring to the figure given by counsel.
>
> Another approach is to ask counsel what they believe the other side's top or bottom dollar is. It is surprising how often counsel will name the figure that is the other side's limit. This approach may be followed up by saying, 'Well, if $5000 is as high as he will go, how are we going to settle the case at $7500?'
>
> The secret to success is to keep probing. If counsel says his or her bottom dollar is $5000, ask if the client would take $4500. If the attorney says "yes," ask about $4000. A judge can soon get a feel for how strong or weak counsel's figure is.[4]

Another technique puts the judge more nearly in the role of arbitrator who assists counsel by providing an opinion of value. Under this procedure, the judge usually reads the file and is informed about the pleadings and any orders previously made by the court. The judge asks questions necessary to gather information that has not previously been covered by the pleadings or by the attorneys in the preliminary discussion. After the attorneys assure the judge that the facts are on the table, the judge meets with the attorneys for each side in private. The figures given to the judge are confidential, and the judge will not disclose them to the other side without specific authority.

Before meeting with the attorneys in private, the judge has written down an opinion of the value of the case. After talking with the attorneys on each side and obtaining from each their opinion of the value of the case, the judge states his or her opinion. If the judge's opinion is outside the range given by counsel, the judge may want to think carefully about whether that figure should be changed. On the other hand, it is often of value for the court to state its opinion even though counsel on each side disagree and the court is not within the range of the opinion of counsel. The court may state a specific figure, perhaps more frequently a range within which the case may be settled. The parties may then accept or reject the judge's figure as the area in which settlement will take place.

4. Thompson, "Settlement Conference Techniques," *Court Administration and Judicial Ethics,* 4 CALIFORNIA JUDICIAL COLLEGE NOTEBOOKS, 3d rev. ed. (Emeryville, Cal.: Center for Judicial Education and Research, 1982), 102-86 to 102-88. Reprinted with permission.

Often the judge's figure is a starting point for counsel, who then reach their agreement, sometimes at a figure higher than that expressed by the judge or, less frequently, lower than that set by the judge.

Any tool that can be devised, any method that can be used which will be accepted by counsel or which counsel can be educated to accept, is of value in the ultimate goal of disposing of litigation and matters before the court.

11

TRIAL BY JURY

The culmination of the duties of the trial judge is to preside over a jury trial. The task requires patience, knowledge of the law, knowledge of the rules of evidence and other procedural rules, leadership, and luck. The very quality of letting 12 citizens, unknown and unknowledgeable, decide the rights of the litigants in an open arena produces tension and excitement.

Juries are perceived as truthsayers, the process of a jury trial as a public uncovering of the truth. Hence there are greater interests at stake than the mere positions of the litigants. A jury trial is a melding of the government and the people, the public and the private, a process to be carried out with all of the solemnity due such an important event.

A judge should keep in mind that the jurors, though proud to serve as jurors, may be somewhat awed by the task of deciding. A jury is not a "decision machine," but rather 12 mere citizens, taken from their ordinary chores, each separate and different, each similar and alike, each complex and yet simple. A judge should at all times be sensitive to their situation.

A jury trial is also often a major event for the attorneys. Though they have prepared earnestly for the effort, they may not have anticipated all contingencies. A judge should be considerate of the role of the attorneys and the litigants.

Lastly, a jury trial is tradition. It is the stuff of headlines and history, an almost instantly recognized symbol of a system of resolving disputes. It is a key part of the legal process, though by no means all of it, and it ultimately must be considered a key part of American life.

A Fair Pool of Prospective Jurors

All citizens should be afforded equal access to juror pools. The recent ABA Standards for Juror Use and Management set as their first standard:

The opportunity for jury service should not be denied or limited on the basis of race, national origin, gender, age, religious belief, income, occupation, or any other factor.

Judges are responsible for examining policies for compiling jury lists, granting excuses, and supplementing jury lists to ensure full participation of the total community.

Lawyers' use of peremptory challenges has also recently come under increased court scrutiny. In *Batson v. Kentucky*,[1] the U.S. Supreme Court increased the trial judge's responsibilities to monitor the fair and nondiscriminatory use of peremptory challenges.

Fair Selection of the Particular Jury: Voir Dire

Counsel have the right to gain enough information about prospective jurors to properly use peremptory challenges and hence select a fair and impartial jury. The means of gaining this information is the voir dire examination of prospective jurors.

Court rule or practice may determine whether a judge conducts all of the voir dire examination, with counsel tendering desired questions to the judge, or whether the attorneys are granted the opportunity to question the prospective jurors. Some jurisdictions have found that attorneys having the unlimited right to examine has been unduly time-consuming and might lead to undue invasions into areas of juror privacy.

Voir Dire Examination of Jurors

The basic purpose of voir dire examination is to impanel 12 fair and impartial jurors, and to safeguard the rights of the litigants to have their case tried according to law. The procedure of voir dire allows counsel to ascertain whether the prospective jurors are willing and able to be impartial. In conducting the voir dire examination, the trial court is accorded broad discretion in determining what procedures are to be followed and what questions are to be asked of the prospective jurors. The test of a proper voir dire examination is whether it can be said with reasonable assurance that any prejudice or bias would be discovered.

Trial courts have many and varied procedures for voir dire examination. A key difference is whether only the judge should question the jurors, with the lawyers merely gathering the information and making decisions about each juror, or whether the lawyers should question the prospective jurors, with the trial judge sitting by as a sort of referee. Or there could be a combination of the two systems.

One argument for permitting the lawyers to ask some questions of the prospective jurors is that they know the details of their cases, and are sensitive to the types of relationships that could produce fairness or

1. 476 U.S. 79, 90 (1986).

unfairness. A second argument is that questioning by the trial judge seems to lend his or her authority to a particular fact setting or theory of the case. The downside to allowing lawyers to question jurors is that they often tend to seek to condition jurors to their point of view, rather than merely uncover information. Also, the process often takes too long.

One method of proceeding would be for the judge to ask certain basic questions of the jurors: their name, generally where they live in the county, their occupation, their marital status and family composition, and whether they have ever experienced the type of incident involved in the case ("Have you ever been injured at work?"or "Have you ever been the victim of a crime or criminal?"). The judge can also ask the basic "catchall" type of question: "Do you believe that you can give both sides a fair trial in this case?"

Having accomplished this, the judge could turn over the proceedings to the lawyers for limited questioning. By asking questions such as "Do you have any prejudice against police officers?" or "Would you be able to follow the law as to self-defense? Could you be open-minded about a law that allows a person, under certain circumstances, to use force to protect himself?" the lawyers could probe areas that are key to each case. If the judge wishes to ask all questions of the prospective jurors, he or she should permit the lawyers the opportunity to submit questions to him or her in writing, and the judge can ask whatever questions seem fair and appropriate.

Challenges of Prospective Jurors

Impaneling a jury is the process of rejecting jurors rather than selecting them.[2] As stated by Justice Story, "The right of peremptory challenge is not of itself a right to select, but a right to reject jurors. It excludes from the panel those whom the prisoner objects to, until he has exhausted the challenges, and leaves the residue to be drawn for his trial according to the established order or usage of the Court."[3]

In addition to the peremptory challenge, parties are also permitted challenges for cause or challenges based upon the prospective juror's specific inability to meet statutory or other bases for fairness.

Peremptory Challenges

The lawyers are generally permitted challenges to excuse jurors that they feel should not be on the jury. The number of peremptory challenges available varies as to the type of case (civil, criminal felony, criminal misdemeanor) and often as to the number of parties involved. Therefore,

2. United States v. Marchant & Colson, 25 U.S. 480 (1827).
3. *Id.*

the judge should consult the statutes or court rules. Before the start of jury selection, the judge should ascertain on the record whether the parties agree as to the number of peremptory challenges available.

The purpose of peremptory challenges was stated in *Pointer v. United States*:[4] "(T)he accused was at liberty to exclude from the jury all, to the number of 20, who, for any reason, or without reason, were objectionable to him . . . He was only entitled of right to strike the names of 20 from the list of impartial jurymen furnished him by the court."

Traditionally, the right to peremptory challenge was unlimited. As stated in *Lewis v. United States*, citing Blackstone, "[It is] an arbitrary and capricious right, and it must be exercised with full freedom."[5] Though the right of peremptory challenges grew from the distrust of the English Crown in criminal cases, the right is now established in both criminal and civil cases.

Limitation on the State's Use of Peremptory Challenges

In criminal cases, the state is barred from using peremptory challenges to exclude black citizens from jury service because of their race.[6] The standard of proving a violation of the equal protection clause, on which *Swain* was based, was expanded in *Batson v. Kentucky*[7] in order to relieve black defendants from the "crippling burden of proof" imposed by the *Swain* decision.

Now, under the *Batson* decision, "a defendant may establish a *Prima Facie* case of purposeful discrimination in selection of a petit jury solely on evidence concerning the prosecutor's exercise of peremptory challenges at the defendant's trial."[8] The Court continued:

> To establish such case, the defendant must first show that he is a member of a cognizable racial group, [citation], and that the prosecutor has exercised peremptory challenges to remove from the venire members of the defendant's race.[9]

The trial court should consider, the Court said, "all relevant circumstances," including a "pattern" of strikes against black jurors, and any statements made or questions asked by prosecutors during the voir dire. Once the defendant has made a prima facie showing, the burden shifts to the state to come forward with a neutral explanation for challenging black jurors.

The Court related the *Batson* test to the traditional peremptory challenge, saying, "Though this requirement imposes a limitation in some

4. 151 U.S. 396, 408 (1894).
5. Lewis v. United States, 146 U.S. 370, 378 (1892).
6. Swain v. Alabama, 380 U.S. 202, 223 (1965).
7. 476 U.S. 79 (1986).
8. *Id.*
9. *Id.*

cases on the full peremptory character of the historic challenge, we emphasize that the prosecutor's explanation need not rise to the level justifying exercise of a challenge for cause."[10] This statement would seem to permit a peremptory for a valid nonracial reason, if such reason rested on a good faith rationale. The court closed one door for some prosecutors by stating that a prosecutor could not rebut a prima facie case of exclusion by stating that the prospective black juror "would be partial to the defendant because of their shared race."[11]

The court in *Batson* concluded with a reminder: "The core guarantee of equal protection, ensuring citizens that their State will not discriminate on account of race, would be meaningless were we to approve the exclusion of jurors on the basis of [an assumption that the prospective juror would side with the defendant of his same race]."[12]

The trial judge will have to scrutinize the pattern of explanations set forth by prosecutors, where the defendant has established a prima facie case, to determine whether peremptory challenges were really used in good faith for the proffered reason.

It would seem, because of *Batson*'s underpinnings on the Equal Protection Clause, that *Batson* would not be extended to a civil case where one of the litigants is a member of a cognizable racial group. However, only time will tell on that issue. The fair and just administration of justice may, in the long run, be as important to our goals of a just and safe society as the outcome of any given case.

Challenges for Cause

If a prospective juror shows unwillingness or inability to be a fair and impartial juror, he or she should be excused for cause. A juror may be stricken for cause upon the motion of either attorney or by action of the judge.

A juror may be excused for cause because of relationship with or a strong affinity for one of the parties; a significant prior contact with the case, through publicity or otherwise; a prejudice toward one of the parties or one of the issues in the case; or some other feeling that would keep that prospective juror from being open-minded as to all of the issues of the case. A juror may be excused for cause for an inability to hear or some other physical ailment that might make jury service painful or unpleasant.

A judge can, and in most cases will, rely on a prospective juror's stated answers in determining qualifications, but there may be times when a judge might have to deduce a prospective juror's state of mind from his

10. *Id.*
11. *Id.*
12. *Id.*

or her situation in life, as well as from the juror's answers. For example, if a victim in a criminal case had a certain occupation and worked in a certain area, and the prospective juror had the same occupation and worked in the same area, a judge will have to scrutinize the juror carefully even though the juror's answers were that he or she could be fair. A judge is not bound by a juror's stated answers but may look deeper to determine impartiality or bias.

On the other hand, a prospective juror's hesitation or uncertainty at one point in the questioning need not amount to grounds for a challenge for cause if the totality of the juror's answers indicate a person who could be fair to both sides. A judge should evaluate the juror's life situation as well as all of the answers to voir dire questions.

The mere possibility of bias should not lead to dismissal of a juror for cause. For example, in some cities, one large business employs many prospective jurors. In the District of Columbia, many prospective jurors work for the federal government. If the large employer is a party to a lawsuit, is it necessary to excuse all the employees of the company for cause just because of their connection with one of the parties? The cases have held that the employer-employee relationship presents no more than the mere possibility of bias, and that the judge should not excuse for cause on that fact alone. A judge should consider the size of the employing company, the particular juror's actual job, the juror's attitude, and any possible stake in the case.

As trends seem to indicate a reduction in the number of peremptory challenges available to the parties, the focus of jury selection will turn to challenges for cause, increasing the significance of this procedure.

Swearing the Jury

When the 12 jurors have been selected, they should be sworn in as a jury to "well and truly try the issues" of the case. This is an especially important point in a criminal case, because the swearing of the jury attaches jeopardy under the Fifth Amendment protections against double jeopardy. At this point, a defendant in a criminal case is "in jeopardy."[13]

Keeping the Jury Informed of the Work of the Court

Jurors are citizens undertaking an important duty. They are not a decision-making machine. When jurors are not in the courtroom hearing evidence, they should be informed of the reason for the delay. They

13. *See* Serfass v. United States, 420 U.S. 377 (1975).

should be informed, however, in a way that protects both sides' right to a fair trial.

It is important to the judge, not only as a public official but also as the chief administrator of the trial, to tell the jury that he or she is on the job and that the delay is caused by matters beyond the court's control. Jurors will feel better, and the judge will be relieved of the pressure to work with the jury rather than leaving them sitting idly in the jury room.

This applies to delays caused by other matters as well as delays in the case on trial. The judge might say to the jury:

> Ladies and gentlemen—we will work on the case on trial just as much as possible. Sometimes delays occur, however, through nobody's fault. Witnesses may be delayed in getting to court. At other times, other cases unrelated to the case on trial come before me for emergency action. I have to give these matters my attention, of course. There may be times when you are sitting in the jury room not hearing evidence, but that does not mean that we have forgotten you or that the court is not busy. I will try to keep you informed about these matters. Thank you.

In addition to this initial advisement, the jury should be informed in a vague way about other delays during the trial. It is sufficient to tell the jury, "We are waiting for a witness," rather than "Mr. Soandso, the defense attorney, is late again." What is important is not that the jury be told the exact truth, but that the situation be considered and understood.

In some jurisdictions, jurors evaluate the judges. That system makes it more important than ever for the judge to keep an eye on public relations.

Determinations of the Admissibility of Evidence

Whenever one side objects to the introduction of certain evidence in a jury trial, the judge must be ready to rule upon the objection. The judge alone must determine whether the jury shall see and hear the challenged evidence. In evaluating the admissibility of the evidence, the trial judge should consider its relevance, its competence, whether its probative value outweighs its prejudicial effect, and the total reliability of the proffered evidence in the light of all of the circumstances.

Key in the trial judge's decision making is that a litigant should be permitted to put before the jury his or her theory of the case. It is not within the judge's sphere of authority to evaluate the soundness of that theory, but only to permit the jury to exercise its common sense on the subject. In evaluating the admissibility of any particular item of evidence, the judge should again rely on the common sense of the jury.

When an item of evidence has some probative value but also some considerable prejudicial effect, the trial judge should minimize the prejudice if that can be done without making the evidence appear unrealistic.

For example, if a prosecutor wishes to counter a defendant's testimony that he was injured and could not walk on the day of the crime, he could call a police officer to testify that he saw the defendant running earlier in the day. That testimony need not include that the defendant was running from the scene of a bank robbery.

If the defendant in this example questions the veracity of the police officer by asking how a police officer could remember at trial some six months later a person merely running, the defense has opened the door to why the police officer could remember such a seemingly insignificant event. Then the prosecution could bring out the totality of the events, including the bank robbery.

Sometimes the admissibility of certain evidence rests upon the resolution of certain other factual issues. In that case, the judge should decide the preliminary issues of fact before the question of the admissibility of other evidence. For example, the coconspirator exception to the hearsay rule rests on the determination of whether a conspiracy existed and whether it was ongoing at the time of the conversation in question. The trial judge should make a preliminary decision of the question of the conspiracy. If there is not sufficient evidence to make that determination, the trial judge could take the matter under advisement for a short time until more evidence has been provided on the subject, or ask the proffering attorney for an offer of proof.

Instructions for the Jury

Since trials often take several days, weeks, or even months, the system of instructing the jury on the law only at the conclusion of the case is somewhat dubious. A better system is to instruct the jury at the time the evidence is admitted, when evidence is received for a limited purpose only. For example, if a witness has testified and the party about to cross-examine the witness proposes to show that the witness was convicted of robbery, that prior conviction is offered for the limited purpose of impeaching the witness's credibility and not to show that the person had a predisposition to commit crimes. The party offering the witness might make a motion in limine to keep out the evidence of the prior robbery conviction, because the prejudice outweighs the probative value. Here the judge has the option of admitting the evidence but giving the jury a contemporaneous limiting instruction about the proper use of the evidence.

Near the close of the average jury trial, the judge should call the attorneys together to make sure that they are prepared for an instruction conference. During that conference, the attorneys will advance various instructions that they wish to use to aid the jury to decide the case. If the case is long or complicated, some judges may set aside a morning or a whole day to permit an unhurried and thoughtful review of the instructions. No issue on appeal is as important to reviewing courts as proper instructions and proper verdicts.

Many states have pattern jury instruction for civil and criminal trials. Under that sort of system, or where attorneys craft their own instructions based upon their perceptions of the law, each side should tender to the court the instructions they wish the judge to give the jury. After a conference, the judge ascertains whether there is any objection from the opposing party to any of the tendered instructions. If there is, the judge should carefully consider the law and the facts before deciding whether to give any particular instruction.

Ordinarily, the record of objections and rulings for each instruction should be placed upon the record, just before the start of closing arguments.

Instructions to Follow the Law

Traditionally, it was common for the trial judge to instruct the jury that "the jury is the judge of the facts, and the trial judge is the judge of the law, and just as the judge respects the jury's finding of the facts, it is the jury's duty to follow the law that the judge gives them."

The question of whether jurors have a duty to follow a law that they might perceive as unjust involves the issue known as "jury nullification." It is clear that juries often exercise their discretion to do what they believe is right, and that power is unreviewable and irreversible. The question at issue is whether the jury should be told, either through argument of counsel or instruction of the court, that the jury has the right to nullify the law in a particular case. *United States v. Doughtery*[14] provides a good discussion of this issue.

Court opinions place great value upon the jury's views of "community standards." In *Duncan v. Louisiana*,[15] a case involving the right to a jury in a misdemeanor case, the Supreme Court exalted the right to a jury trial complete with its unlimited powers. Justice White stated, "Providing an accused with the right to be tried by a jury of his peers gave him an inestimable safeguard against the corrupt or overzealous prosecutor and against the compliant, biased, or eccentric judge. If a defendant preferred the common-sense judgment of a jury to the more tutored but perhaps less sympathetic reaction of the single judge, he was to have it."[16]

14. 473 F.2d 1113 (D.C. Cir. 1972).
15. 391 U.S. 145 (1968).
16. *Id.*

Though all the folklore is projury and antijudge, any observer of courtrooms, and anyone with any sense of the community, knows that juries can be misled by lawyers, blinded by prejudice or misjudgment, and capable of incredible misweighing of the evidence, as well as capable of doing a good job. All errors do not fall on one side of the fence. The role of a trial judge is to see that the jury is free to issue a proper verdict, but also to be cautious about the work of jurors.

Outside Influences upon the Jury

A jury is to decide the case based upon the evidence heard in the courtroom. Hence, the judge must be watchful of outside influences that might effect the integrity of the jury's fact-finding and decision-making process.

There should not be outside communication with the jurors about the case, and the judge should instruct the jurors at the close of the first day of trial that they "should not discuss the case among themselves, or allow anyone to discuss it with you, and if anyone attempts to do that to inform the court."

Media accounts of the trial should be scrutinized, and jurors should be instructed not to read newspapers, listen to the radio, or watch television news. If the media carry a story that includes prejudicial details about the case not heard by the jury, the jurors should be individually questioned about whether each read, saw, or listened to the feature or heard anyone discuss the news item. A mistrial might have to be declared if jurors are hesitant about whether the media story might influence their judgments in the case.

Care should be taken about items brought into the jury room, both during the trial and when the evidence closes and the jury goes to deliberate. One Supreme Court reversed a death penalty verdict because a written paper with racial content, purporting to be a joke, was found in the jury room.[17] Where items are in evidence and approved by the judge for consideration, care should be given to any contents of such articles, items within pockets of clothing, documents within containers, and police markings on tested materials or exhibits.[18]

Jurors are not permitted to make their own excursions to check the scene of the crime or to gather evidence on their own.

If any event occurs to the jurors during the case or during deliberations, the judge should carefully scrutinize the situation. For example, if a juror's property is stolen while the jury is deliberating, each juror should

17. People v. Jones, 105 Ill. 2d 342, 475 N.E.2d 832 (1985).
18. *See* People v. Hughes, 434 N.E.2d 828 (Ill. App. 1982).

be carefully examined about whether he or she could continue to be a fair juror in the case.

Altering or Setting Aside the Verdict of the Jury

The verdict of the jury is to be set aside only under the most unusual situations. In determining whether there is satisfactory evidence to support the jury's verdict, the judge must view the evidence in the light most favorable to the prevailing side. The judge must not reassess the credibility of any witness, for that was within the province of the jury. So long as the evidence was such that a rational mind might fairly agree with the verdict, the judge should uphold the verdict.

In *Jackson v. Virginia*,[19] the Court was deciding the appropriate standard of review in a federal habeas corpus case. The court stated that, in reviewing the sufficiency of the evidence to support a criminal conviction, the question was not simply whether the jury had been properly instructed, but instead to determine whether the evidence on the record could reasonably support a finding of guilt beyond a reasonable doubt. The court made it clear that the judge's role was secondary:

> (T)his inquiry does not require a court to 'ask itself whether it believes that the evidence at the trial established guilt beyond a reasonable doubt.' [citation] Instead, the relevant question is whether, after viewing the evidence in the light most favorable to the prosecution, any rational trier of fact could have found the essential elements of the crime beyond a reasonable doubt.[20]

The court concluded that the test for review of a jury's decision making should impinge upon the jury's discretion "only to the extent necessary to guarantee the fundamental protection of due process of law."

Remittitur and Additur

The U.S. Supreme Court case of *Dimick v. Schiedt*[21] summed up the law of remittitur and additur, as it traced the common-law origins of these doctrines: "Where the verdict is excessive, the practice of substituting a remission of the excess for a new trial is not without plausible support in the view that what remains is included in the verdict along with the unlawful excess—in that sense that it has been found by the jury—and that the remittitur has the effect of merely lopping off an excrescence."[22]

"But," the Court continued, analyzing additur, "where the verdict is too small, an increase by the court is a bald addition of something which in no sense can be said to be included in the verdict." To allow an

19. 443 U.S. 307 (1979).
20. *Id.*
21. 293 U.S. 474, 486 (1935).
22. *Id.*

additur, the Court stated, was to "compel the plaintiff to forgo his constitutional right to the verdict of a jury and accept an 'assessment partly made by a jury which has acted improperly, and partly by a tribunal which has no power to assess.' "[23]

A judge faced with questions of remittitur or additur should consult local legal authorities. The power to cut verdicts seems well established; the power to add money to a verdict is much less clear.[24]

Granting a Motion for a New Trial

A trial judge has significant powers in ordering a new trial, based upon his or her conclusion that the jury's verdict was against the weight of the evidence and would result in a "miscarriage of justice."[25] Motions for a new trial are directed to the discretion of the trial court, and in considering such a motion, the court has broad power to weigh the evidence and assess the credibility of the witnesses.[26]

This power also is to be used with caution. As the First Circuit Court of Appeals stated in *Rothrock*, "To protect the fragile power given to the jury, we must ensure that 'the remedy of a new trial is sparingly used, and then only where there would be a "miscarriage of justice." ' "[27] Where a trial judge feels that he or she must grant a motion for a new trial after a jury verdict, the judge should state that he or she understands that the power is to be used sparingly, and that the verdict of the jury is to be granted great weight, and that serious errors have occurred, and that the judge feels that the errors led to the result, an obvious miscarriage of justice.

A Prompting Instruction: The *Allen* Charge

When the jury has been deliberating for a substantial period of time and it appears through communication from the jury that the jurors believe themselves to be deadlocked, the judge may give the jury an additional instruction aimed at prompting the jury to reach a verdict.

This instruction, approved in the early case of *Allen v. United States*,[28] is not surprisingly called the *Allen* charge or the "dynamite charge" or

---

23. *Id.*

24. *But see* Chief Justice Traynor in Jehl v. Southern Pac. R.R. Co., 59 Cal. Rptr. 276, 427 P.2d 988 (1967).

25. *See* United States v. Rothrock, 806 F.2d 318 (1986) (holding that trial court lacked power to enter a judgment of acquittal after a guilty verdict, but did have the power to order a new trial).

26. United States v. Indelicato, 611 F.2d 376, 387 (1st Cir. 1979).

27. *Rothrock, supra* note 25.

28. 164 U.S. 492 (1896).

the "shotgun charge," or by names tied to particular cases in particular states.[29]

Such instructions have been criticized not only for coercive language, but also for presenting an opportunity for a judge to deliver the instruction in a coercive manner. If a judge elects to give a prompting instruction, he or she should read it temperately, with concern, and not with impatience or anger.

The prompting instruction should not be given prematurely. The jury should be given full opportunity to decide the case, considering the number of days of evidence it heard. The instruction is generally approved for use only after the jury tells the judge that the jurors believe they cannot reach a verdict. If a jury has been out deliberating for an inordinate period of time, the judge may call the jury into court with the parties present and ask the foreman whether he or she believes that the jury can reach a verdict. The judge should caution the jury not to tell the vote or who the jury is favoring, because the party who is losing will immediately begin urging that the court declare a mistrial.

Jury Questions During Deliberations

Frequently juries, while deliberating, seek information on the law or the facts of the case from the trial judge. The judge should at all times, unless a governing statute prohibits it, seek to aid the jury.

Whenever the jury makes a request, either through a deputy sheriff or bailiff or by a note from the jurors to the judge, the attorneys should be summoned, told of the communication, and heard as to their views on the just way of responding.

As to jury requests to review certain trial testimony, three tests have emerged.[30] Some reviewing courts have held that a judge must grant the jury's request, others have held that the request should be granted if reasonable, and yet others have held that the matter is discretionary. The ABA Standards for Trial by Jury, have adopted the "reasonableness" test.[31]

Often practical problems arise when the jury asks that certain testimony be read back to it. Frequently no transcript is available, so the

29. *See* State v. Ortega, 2 Cal. App. 3d 884, 889, 83 Cal. Rptr. 260 (1969); People v. Prim, 53 Ill. 2d 62, 463 N.E.2d 1044 (1972).

30. *See* United States v. Jackson, 257 F.2d 41 (1958).

31. American Bar Association Standards for Criminal Justice, 15-3.7(b)(2d. Ed. 1980), which reads: "The trial judge should require a record to be kept of all communications received from a juror or the jury after the jury has been sworn, and he or she should not communicate with a juror or jury on any aspect of the case itself (as distinguished from matters relating to physical comforts and the like), except after notice to all parties and reasonable opportunity for them to be present."

court reporter who took the testimony in question must be found and brought to court. If this is not possible, the jury should be told that fact and told the jurors must use their best and collective memories about the issue in question. It is a good practice to have two court reporters working during a readback, one reading the notes and a second rewording the readback and any other statements or events.

If a jury asks for certain portions of a witness's testimony, fairness might dictate that all of that witness's testimony be read back. For example, even if the jury asked merely for the cross-examination, it may be wise to read both the direct and the cross-examination.

Whenever a jury asks a specific question of law, the judge should attempt to answer the question. A judge could respond by saying or writing in a return note, "The law governing the case is stated in the instructions. Read them," but such a brusque answer is neither very helpful nor good public relations. The judge should attempt a few sentences, stated neutrally, on the subject raised by the jurors. Sometimes jurors ask for dictionaries. One recently asked for a magnifying glass. Usually, these requests are denied as leaving the jurors without guidance in their determinations.

When a deliberating jury asks a question of fact, such as "After the car turned, did it go north or south?" the judge should refer the jurors to their collective memories. Any aid on these issues will be fiercely opposed by one side or the other.

Thanking the Jurors

In thanking the jurors and excusing them from the case or from jury service, the judge should not tie his or her thanks to whether he or she agrees with the verdict reached by the jury. One way to handle the matter is to thank the jury before the verdict is read in court. This procedure would make it clear to the jury and to courtroom spectators that the thanks were for the jury service and not for the particular verdict rendered.

Justice is seldom, if ever, served by criticizing the verdict of the jury. The public perceives the jury as the arbiter of truth and the judge as the moderator of the trial proceedings. It is difficult for outsiders to understand why the "neutral" moderator of the trial has any interest in criticizing the verdict of the jury.

It is proper for a judge to talk with the jurors informally after the verdict. One famous judge did this with his robes on but unzipped—as if to remind them that he was still the judge but to signal that the case was now over, so that they could talk together just as citizens. A judge should always be circumspect about his or her remarks and remember that at the time immediately after the verdict, the jurors are likely to be engaging in second-guessing of themselves and to need some reassurance.

The jurors should be reminded that it is their right to talk to, or refuse to talk to, trial attorneys. Though attorney criticism of the jurors is unlikely, jurors are likely to be concerned about that possibility. Professional canons of ethics or bar association opinions often set standards of aloofness for attorneys in postverdict situations.

Attorneys or investigators who interview jurors after verdicts do so at some risk.[32] If jury misconduct has been shown by the jurors themselves, the matter will likely be viewed in a different light.[33]

The court's role in protecting jurors does not end with the verdict. Their convenience, comfort, and safety should be uppermost in the thinking of the court. If a verdict is returned in the late evening, the judge should see that transportation is available for the jurors. In situations of postverdict harassment, the court's powers of indirect contempt could be used to protect jurors.[34]

32. *See* Rakes v. United States, 169 F.2d 739 (1948).

33. *See* Parker v. Gladden, 385 U.S. 363 (1966); United States *ex rel* DeLucia v. McMann, 373 F.2d 759 (1967).

34. *See* United States v. Crosby, 294 F.2d 928, 950, *cert. denied*, 368 U.S. 984 (1962).

12

TRIAL BY COURT

When the judge hears a case without a jury, the judge is "the court." In many respects a bench trial is more demanding than a jury trial because the judge must resolve both the facts and the law. Some judges feel that deciding the facts is more onerous than having to instruct the jury and manage the courtroom and the jury. Others find that the courtroom is more relaxed without a jury, and that a bench trial is easier.

It is of the utmost importance that the judge, as finder of fact, keep an open mind until all of the evidence has been presented and the arguments made. This can be extremely difficult. If a judge prepares for the trial by reading the file, he or she may tend to feel that one side should prevail. That tendency must be guarded against. If the judge's initiation into the subject matter of the trial is through the opening statements, there also may be a tendency to gravitate toward one side or the other on the basis of the opening statement. That also must be resisted. At every stage of the proceedings, the judge must heed the same admonition as that given to the jury about keeping an open mind.

When the facts have been presented, what about the law? Some attorneys present briefs on the law at the conclusion of the trial. Others ask, at the conclusion of the trial, for additional time to present briefs.

A brief presented at the beginning of a trial can be very helpful. Although it may miss one or two points that arise during the course of the trial, it can be supplemented. It also gives the judge an opportunity to review the law before the trial ends. Some judges are willing to do their own research on the law that applies to the case. However, unless the judge has time to spare or has a law clerk, such research can be expensive in terms of time. Knowing the law before the end of the case is of particular help because it then lets the judge rule at the conclusion of the trial.

When the facts have been received and argued and the law has been "found," when should the judge decide the case? A strong argument can be made for the prompt oral decision:

The judge will never know more about the case than he does at that moment. If he makes the fatal error of delaying his decision, his knowledge of the pending case will begin to fade from his memory when he starts to try another case tomorrow . . . [New Jersey] judges have learned that to delay decisions means casting a heavy and useless burden on themselves.[1]

Robert Lukowsky cites advantages for making the decision an oral one:

Unimpaired familiarity with the case is not the only advantage. The oral decision gives the Judge a unique opportunity to communicate with the litigants and to explain to them in simple, plain language the reasons for his action. Perhaps he cannot make them happy with it but he can make them understand it and thus enhance the therapeutic effect of the trial.

. . . (T)he oral decision should [not] be used in every case, but . . . it should be used in every case other than the most complex and protracted.

The criteria of a good oral decision are:

1. It determines all contested issues.
2. It does not discuss collateral issues.
3. The language is plain, definite and concise.
4. The Judge may resort to the use of slang or the vernacular for the sake of simplicity.
5. It is not filled with quotations from legal authorities nor filled with rolling phrases.
6. Long words and sentences are avoided.
7. Unusual and obscure words are not used.
8. It is delivered in a conversational manner.
9. It rings of complete sincerity.[2]

David Harris, writing in the *Judges' Journal,* made an argument for the written decision, however, once there were steps the judge could take to improve that process:

It must be conceded that the trial judge knows more factual detail immediately on submission of the case than he ever will again. But this advantage need not be lost merely because there is to be a memorandum decision. There is nothing to prevent the judge from immediately dictating, in chambers, his findings of fact. Indeed, such a practice is almost mandatory. And with it there must be a pledge of loyalty to those initial findings. To be sure,

---

1. Vanderbilt, *Improving the Administration of Justice—Two Decades of Development,* 26 UNIVERSITY OF CINCINNATI LAW REVIEW 155, 176 (1957).

2. Lukowsky, *The Case for the Oral Decision,* 4 JUDGES' JOURNAL 3 (1965). Reprinted with permission.

there is often a temptation to conform memory of facts to later research of the law. As a matter of judicial integrity, it seems obvious that we should be pledged to the view of the facts as seen at the time of the submission. This view need not be lost if they are promptly dictated for use in the memorandum.

We instruct our juries, and we bind ourselves, to keep a perfectly open mind about a case until it is finally submitted. Litigants, particularly losing litigants, are generally scandalized by a decision made in a matter of minutes after submission of a case long and carefully prepared. Such a litigant tends to feel that he has been dealt with summarily and without full consideration being given him. Or, he feels that the judge had his mind made up before the case was over. In either event, he feels an injustice which detracts more than would be gained by the personal touch of hearing the decision from the judge's own lips.

A memorandum decision is bound to be more careful. Few judges speak as well as they write. And, though few write well enough to assuage the feelings of a losing litigant, the language of the memorandum will come closer to doing so, because it is bound to be more logical.

The time between submission of the case and filing of the decision is traditionally a time when attorneys make their peace with their client. It is an ideal time for the attorney to evaluate his own work. Both the attorney and the client are in the best possible position to settle their relationship and the fee after the work is done and before the decision is filed.

. . . (T)he interests of justice demand a memorandum decision in all but the most simple and clear type of case . . . The determination of just which case is really a 'complex' case often takes sober and careful research. Some of the simple and clear-cut cases change complexion after being run through a library.

Judges who argue for the oral decision as a matter of judicial practice tend . . . to be decisive and effective. They get their work done promptly and the wheels of justice turn. A judge who habitually files a tardy memorandum decision would be a poor substitute. But a judge need not lose his decisiveness or promptness merely because he chooses to commit his thoughts and research to writing. If he does so promptly, . . . the written memorandum answers the demands of justice far more effectively than does the oral decision.[3]

---

3. Harris, *The Case for the Written Decision—A Reply,* 5 JUDGES' JOURNAL 6 (1966). Reprinted with permission.

Whether you decide orally or in writing, do not delay. Judges have acquired ulcers, bad reputations, even disciplinary sanctions by being indecisive.

The absence of a jury gives the judge greater latitude in the conduct of the trial—less formality, fewer people, no explanations to a jury. The judge handles and decides the whole case,[4] but must take particular care with that decision.

4. *See* Chapter 15, "Decision Making."

III

The Techniques of Judging

13

LISTENING

"Will the reporter read the question?"

Most judges have asked that question. On rare occasions it may be because there is a need to make sure that the questioner meant the question as it was asked. Far more probable, however, is that the judge did not hear the question. Occasionally, that is because of some distraction in the courtroom. But it can also be because the judge was not listening.

Listening is one of the most important things a judge does. As a judge soon learns, it is not as easy as it seems.

It occupies more than half the time of most judges. We assume that we get so much practice at it that training in listening is unnecessary. But the experience of most judges is that it is difficult to listen attentively for a full court day.

Listening concentration is said to be difficult because when we listen, we have spare time. The average American speaks at the rate of 125 words per minute. But our 13 billion brain cells can comprehend speech at the rate of 300 words per minute, and we can read and comprehend 1,200 words per minute. (One University of Florida student read 10,000 words per minute with an 80 percent comprehension rate!)

The result is that we fall into bad listening habits. Among these habits are:

- Faking attention— Oliver Wendell Holmes said that one of the traits of a good judge is to be able to look at an attorney and act as if he were listening, but not to hear a word the attorney says.
- "I-get-the-facts" listening—by body language, the listener says, "I am not trying to listen to everything you say, I am just trying to listen for the important parts."
- Avoidance of difficult listening.

- Premature dismissal of the speaker's subject as uninteresting.
- Criticizing the delivery or physical appearance of the speaker rather than listening to what the speaker has to say.

While it may seem obvious, in order to be a good listener one must be able to hear. A judge who finds it easier to hear while watching people's lips, or who becomes irritated with someone who does not speak loudly enough, might find it worthwhile to consult an audiologist or an ear, nose, and throat doctor. The cause may be some loss of hearing. If so, there are usually ways to enhance hearing.

Poor listening is an ancient and still prevalent problem. Three centuries before the birth of Christ, Aristotle and Socrates reportedly complained about the poor listening skills of their students. Because listening is one of the skills essential to being a judge, judges especially need to improve their skills in this area.

Those who hear well may improve their listening skills by following these ten guides:

1. Find areas of interest in what the speaker is saying. What is usable? Worthwhile? Workable? What can you use in what the speaker is saying?
2. Judge content, not delivery. Concentrate on what the speaker is saying, not how the speaker is saying it.
3. Do not get overstimulated. Do not allow your personal opinion or bias to interfere with what is being said.
4. Listen for central ideas.
5. Be a flexible mental note taker. Not every speech is well organized, and sometimes the speaker makes listeners work for the idea that is being presented.
6. Work at listening. Eye contact, posture, and facial expressions say something to the speaker. This feedback aids in communication. Give the speaker full attention.
7. Resist distraction. Either eliminate or mentally shut out any noises or sights that divert your attention. And be careful that you do not yourself create diversions to keep from listening.
8. Exercise your mind. Develop a mental appetite for difficult listening (and there is some in the courtroom).
9. Keep your mind open. Decrease the hampering effect of words that are emotionally upsetting.
10. Use your thought speed. The differential between your "listening speed" and the speed with which people talk gives you an opportunity to think while paying attention: "Why is the attorney asking that question?" "To which element of the case is this question relevant?"

We can train ourselves to be better listeners. Judges surely have the opportunity to practice.

Selected Bibliography

Burley-Allen. *Listening: The Forgotten Skill,* 1982.

Nicholas. "Ten Guides to Effective Listening." 45 *Nation's Business* 56 (1957).

Nichols and Stevens. *Are You Listening?,* 1957.

Roach and Wyatt. *Successful Listening,* 1988.

Wolff, Marsnik, Tacey and Nicholas. *Perceptive Listening,* 1983.

Wolvin and Coakley. *Listening,* 3d. ed., 1988.

14

NOTE TAKING

Why?

The judge's clerk noted that the judge was taking notes furiously. It would not have been unusual, except that it was during the argument of counsel to the jury, and that seemed very unusual. After the attorneys had completed their arguments, and the jury had been instructed and had retired to begin its deliberations, the judge wadded the notes into a ball and threw them into the wastebasket. After the judge left the courtroom, the clerk was so curious that she retrieved the notes. She pressed them, framed them, and gave them to the judge for Christmas.

The notes said, "I must stay awake. I cannot fall asleep. I have to do something to stay awake." All of this was repeated many times.

In addition to keeping oneself alert, or even awake, there are other good reasons for taking notes. It refreshes the recollection, helps to organize thoughts, and allows the recording of some of the nuances of the trial. Also, it requires careful listening. When the trial is long, deciding the case may depend on refreshed recollection, organized material, and notes about the little things.

What?

Many kinds of listening can be satisfied by "getting the main idea." Judges take notes in many different ways. Some take notes that are very abbreviated; others occupy all of their time making notes.

If the decision must be delayed, the judge will find it useful to have noted some things that may help determine whether he or she believes or disbelieves the witness. Hesitation in answering, nervousness, and other body language may cause the judge to believe the witness is not telling the truth. Of course, there may be other explanations. Writing a note concerning them may be helpful.

How?

Those who try to take down everything that is said must develop some form of shorthand. Those who have had formal training in shorthand find it easy to take notes. Those who have not learned formal shorthand develop their own methods of abbreviation.

A book called *Shortrite*[1] offers a new self-taught shorthand that is said to be easy. There are signs for vowel sounds, and consonants are only slightly modified. This can be helpful for the judge who is looking for an easier way.

Some judges find that using different colored pens assists in organizing the material. For example, the plaintiff's questioning is in black. The defendant's questioning is in red. If there are more parties, more colors are added. Another way to do it is to use a different color for each issue.

Another method useful to those who don't try to take down everything that is said is a sort of organizational chart on which the issues are numbered across the top and the witnesses are lettered or numbered down the side of the page. If witness A talks about issue 2, the testimony is put into that column. In many ways, this is a great deal more work, but the finished product allows the judge to see at a glance what was said about each issue and by whom.

Where?

One of the problems a beginning judge faces is what paper to use. For some people, the only way is to take notes on loose-leaf paper (the size is a matter of choice). Others find that bound notebooks afford the best place to keep notes. The judge who keep notes in a bound notebook likes the security of of knowing where the notes are, can reflect on past cases, and has a more permanent record. One who uses loose-leaf paper finds the paper easy to obtain, can store the notes in a loose-leaf notebook, and may have the advantage of being able to remove notes on part of a case should the occasion require it.

Few judges are flexible about their note taking. The way they started is the way that is comfortable to them. However, judges should not be afraid to experiment; it may keep them alert.

1. R. Greenburg, Shortrite (1986).

15

DECISION MAKING

How does the judge decide a case? The basic formula, embellished and modified by numerous theories of jurisprudence, is that the judge listens to the evidence and from that evidence finds facts. To those facts the judge applies the proper law. Facts plus law equals decision. This simple formula has many variations, each of which adds words telling of new qualifications concerning facts or law.[1]

Even the simple formula of "facts plus law equals decision" points out that the system is not foolproof. Since the evidence presented concerning facts is usually the testimony of witnesses, we have only to recall the four blind men and the elephant to realize that there may be honest differences in the testimony of witnesses who saw the same thing.

Furthermore, the law is not always clear. While a judge may go for a long period of time without meeting a case that has not previously been decided, that kind of case is eventually presented. Even if it has been decided in jurisdictions A and B, it has not been decided in the jurisdiction in which the judge sits. There may be conflicts of law, factual differences, or other matters that cause differences of opinion as to what law applies to such a case.

The Judge as Decision Maker

The differences of opinion regarding facts and law point out the importance of the personality of the judge in the process of decision making.

What do judges do? As part of the decision process, they listen. They take notes. They read. They think. They communicate.

The techniques for doing these things may make the judge's job easier or faster, but techniques for communicating, listening, or note taking do

1. One variation says the formula should be: Facts (as Found) + Law (as Found) + Social Goal = Decision.

not necessarily affect the decision. What factors do come into play? One could hypothesize that the judge's personality type[2] is a controlling factor. However, a correlation of personality types with decisions made by judges indicates with some assurance that personality type has little effect on final decisions.[3]

If a judge's personality type is not a significant factor, on what variables does the decision-making process depend? What are the steps involved in making a decision? Most judges recognize that they find the facts, apply the law, and reach a decision without having thought about the process or the factors influencing that process.

One method of describing the process is to say that it has six steps:

1. Defining the problem
2. Getting the facts
3. Finding the correct law
4. Reaching the tentative decision
5. Justifying the decision
6. Announcing the final decision

Step One: Defining the Problem

An essential part of any kind of problem solving is to define the problem. In judicial decision making, defining the problem means defining the issues before the court. This may be accomplished at a pretrial conference. At that conference, a formal order may be made defining the issues that remain before the court. Or the issues may be defined without a formal order.

If the problem is not defined before the time of the trial, the judge may well want to commence the trial by asking the lawyers to define the issues to be decided. The net effect of any of these methods is that all parties involved in the case are talking about the problems they agree are before the court.

---

2. Observers have usually noted four varying characteristics of personality. The Meyers-Briggs Type Indicator uses four dimensions to describe a given person:

Extrovert (E) —Introvert (I)
Sensing (S) —Intuitive (N)
Thinking (T) —Feeling (F)
Judging (J) —Perceptive (P)

Thus a person may be ESTJ or INTP, etc., combining one characteristic from each of these dimensions.

3. Judge Donald R. Fretz of the National Judicial College Faculty and Dr. John Chappell of the University of Nevada, Reno Medical School compared the Meyers-Briggs Personality Types of more than 150 judges with the decisions of those judges in two realistically presented court trials. No significant correlation was found between personality type and decisions reached.

Step Two: Getting the Facts

The next step—getting the facts—sounds simple but it can be complicated. Trial judges estimate that they spend 75 percent of their time getting the facts.

What is a "fact"? If witness 1 testifies that an incident occurred one way, while witness 2 says that it happened in an entirely different way, what really happened? Each of those witnesses testified to what he or she thought was the fact. But unless their conflicting versions can be explained in some way, the court must decide which is correct.

There are rules that apply in cases like this, and judges usually instruct jurors as to what factors they may consider in determining which witness is telling the truth. Judges should follow those same rules. Among the factors affecting getting the facts are attitudes, personality, cognitive style, stress, perceptions, nonverbal communication, probability, and memory.

Like the witnesses who testify before them, judges *perceive* certain information. Perception is the complex process human beings use to collect information, organize it, and integrate it.[4] The brain receives information through the senses of sight, hearing, touch, smell, and taste.[5] Each of these senses sends signals to the brain in a manner more complicated than we realize. By such a process, we see a three-dimensional world in colors and shades. Hearing distinguishes loudness, pitch, and the direction from which the sound comes.

Some of our senses give us "perceptual dilutions." We are familiar with optical illusions which cause a line to appear longer or shorter than another:

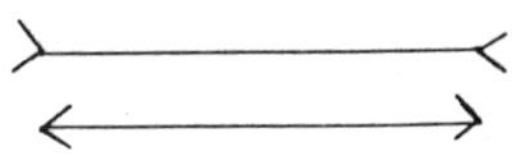

Now look at the next figure. What do you see?

4. L. Kaufman, Perception, The World Transformed (1979).

5. A modern view is that there are three additional senses: kinesthetic, vestibular, and organic.

You may see a side view of two faces facing each other, or you may see a vase. It depends upon which is the background and which is the foreground.

There are many such optical illusions. When we can see only one of the things portrayed, we are at a loss as to how anyone can see anything else. Then after we have given up and the explanation comes, we wonder how we could have failed to see the other thing. How many times does that happen in the courtroom to points of view and arguments? The judge hears both arguments but understands only one.

Another important part of human thinking, fact finding, and decision making is memory. Elizabeth Loftus, in her excellent book on memory,[6] uses the following diagram to illustrate the memory process:

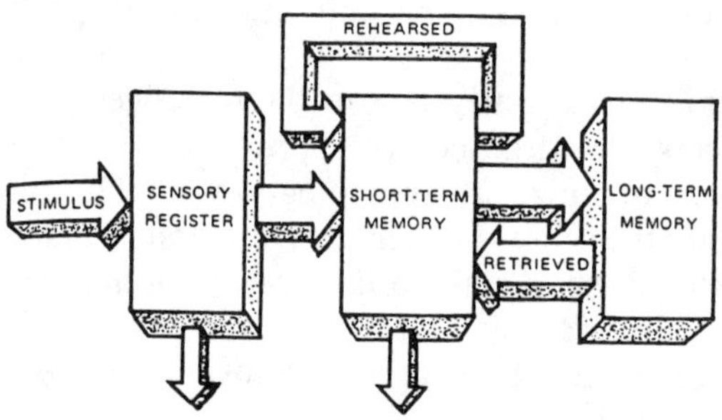

The memory process: Incoming information enters short-term memory, where it can be maintained by rehearsal and successfully transferred to long-term memory, or forgotten.

The senses register a stimulus. That stimulus may or may not be transferred to short-term memory. If it is not, it is forgotten. If it is transferred to short-term memory, it will ordinarily be retained for not longer than thirty seconds. If we rehearse it, however, we can remember it for a longer period of time. Telephone numbers are an example. We find the number we want. If we close the book, we may have to look it up again. If we repeat the number aloud, it will stay with us for a period of time. The more it is repeated the longer we will remember it.

A single rehearsal will cause the information to be retained for a period of time, but additional rehearsal is usually required before information

6. ELIZABTH LOFTUS, MEMORY: SURPRISING NEW INSIGHTS INTO HOW WE REMEMBER AND WHY WE FORGET © 1980, Addison-Wesley Publishing Co., Inc., Reading, Massachusetts, page 15. Memory model reprinted with permission.

is transferred to long-term memory. Long-term memory is information stored "for a lifetime." We are sometimes surprised that a name or a date that we thought we had forgotten comes to mind. It was buried in the card file of the mind, and somehow the mental index found it for us in our long-term memory.

From this brief discussion, it is clear that the minds of judges, like the minds of other people, are filled with rehearsed information. Some of the information in our subconscious minds has been heard or seen so repeatedly over the course of our lives that it has solidified into beliefs, unconscious images, and even prejudices.

Professor James Adams, in his book *Conceptual Blockbusting*,[7] speaks of perceptual, emotional, cultural, environmental and organizational, and intellectual and expressive blocks to fact finding and decision making. Professor Adams describes a block as a "mental wall" that prevents the proper perception of a problem or a solution. Here is a list of some of Adams' conceptual blocks.

1. Perceptual blocks
   a. Seeing what one expects to see; stereotyped seeing; premature labeling
   b. Inability to view problem from various viewpoints
   c. Saturation
   d. Difficulty in isolating the problem
   e. Tendency to delimit the problem area too closely
2. Emotional blocks
   a. Fear of making a mistake, of failing, of taking a risk
   b. Excessive zeal; overmotivation to succeed quickly; ability to see only one direction to go
   c. Inability to tolerate ambiguity: overriding desire for security, order; "no appetite for chaos"
   d. Inability to relax, incubate, "sleep on it"
3. Cultural blocks
   a. Taboos
   b. Belief that fantasy and reflection are wastes of time, lazy—even crazy
   c. Belief that playfulness is for children only
   d. Belief that reason, logic, number, utility, practicality are *good*, while feeling, intuition, qualitative judgments, pleasure are *bad*
4. Environmental and organizational blocks
   a. Distractions—phone, easy intrusions
   b. Lack of support to bring ideas into action

7. J. Adams, Conceptual Blockbusting, 2d ed. (1980).

c. Lack of cooperation and trust among colleagues—insecurity in job
d. Autocratic boss who values only his or her own ideas and does not reward others
e. Inhibiting organizational management styles

5. Intellectual and expressive blocks
a. Lack of information; incorrect information
b. Inflexible or inadequate use of intellectual problem-solving strategies
c. Formulating problem in incorrect language (e.g., verbal, math, visual)
d. Inadequate language skill to express ideas (verbally, visually, musically, etc.)

These blocks apply to judges. You will think of others, and of applications of these, but one application will serve as an example. The inability to tolerate ambiguity is described as an emotional block. In a courtroom, the judge inevitably deals with ambiguity.

Any lawyer can recall instances of simply being unable to find an essential piece of evidence or of presenting some evidence that was susceptible to several interpretations. Judges face such ambiguities daily and are required to reach decisions even without all the information that could be helpful for reaching the final and best decision. Under such circumstances, a perfectionist can suffer.

An appointed California judge resigned at the end of one year. He had not decided the very first case (or any of those heard thereafter) that had been tried before him as judge, and as a result he had not been paid for nine months. He was a perfectionist who was unable to deal with ambiguities in the cases presented to him.

It may be surprising to lay people, but it can be no surprise to an experienced lawyer that two different trial judges hearing the same evidence can reach different conclusions about the facts. Lawyers, where possible, "judge shop" based on what they think they know about different judges and how they will decide different kinds of cases.

Step Three: Finding the Correct Law

Once the judge has the facts, he or she must find and apply the correct law.[8] The attorneys usually present to the judge the law that they believe to be applicable to the case. After considering the presentations of the several sides, the judge can analyze, choose, and apply the correct law.

How does the judge do that?

8. For a good discussion and excerpts from many writers on the subject, *see* R. ALDISERT, THE JUDICIAL PROCESS 777 *et seq.* (1976).

The judge searches for authority. Pound said authoritative materials are of five types.[9]

1. Rules—precepts attaching a definite, detailed legal consequence to a definite, detailed state of facts, e.g., a criminal statute
2. Principles—authoritative starting points for legal reasoning, which are the work of writers and teachers rather than the work of lawmakers or the courts. They are best formulated in doctrinal writing, and often compete.
3. Conceptions—chiefly the work of law teachers and law writers, "categories to which types or classes of transactions, cases, or situations are referred, in consequence of which a series of rules, principles, and standards become applicable"
4. Doctrines—writings, as by code
5. Standards—general limits of permissible conduct

From the first day of law school, the admonition is to see whether there is an applicable statute. The admonition applies as well to judges. When the meaning of the statute is disputed, the judge resorts to rules or canons of statutory construction.[10] Then the judge turns to case law:

> The essence of the common law tradition is the rule of the case. The essence of the rule of the case, or case law, is . . . precedent or *stare decisis.*[11]

Cases often contain chaff along with wheat. The precedential part of a case is the *ratio decidendi*, that considered by the judge as necessary to the decision. The chaff, nonprecedential, is the *dictum*, a thing said that is not necessary to the decision.

Writers argue about the vitality of precedent and the average length of its life. Even trial judges hear challenges to precedent, but the far greater number of cases require no great effort to find and apply the law. Usually, the rule of law is clear and its application is simple.

Step Four: Reaching the Tentative Decision

There are said to be at least three methods or theories of decision making: cogitative, aleatory, and intuitive.[12] Most judges would like to think of themselves as using the cogitative or logical, thoughtful method of making decisions. Certainly the aleatory method, that is by the casting of dice or other forms of chance, is unacceptable for a jury and for a judge. The third method, the use of intuition, is one upon which most

9. Pound, *Hierarchy of Sources and Forms in Different Systems of Law*, 7 TULANE L. REV. 475, 482-87 (1933).
10. ALDISERT, *supra* note 8, at p. 170 *et seq.*
11. *Id.* at 777.
12. Hutcheson, *The Judgment Intuitive: The Function of the "Hunch" in Judicial Decision*, 14 CORNELL L. Q. 274 (1929).

judges initially frown. The idea of using a hunch as a basis for a decision seems improper.

The cogitative approach is one the judge can comfortably profess. But while the use of intuition seems improper, some respected legal scholars make it an acceptable part of decision making:

[Max Radin] tells us, first, that the judge is a human being; that therefore he does not decide causes by the abstract application of rules of justice or of right, but having heard the cause and determined that the decision ought to go this way or that way, he then takes up his search for some category of the law into which the case will fit.

He tells us that the judge really feels or thinks that a certain result seems desirable, and he then tries to make his decision accomplish that result. 'What makes certain results seem desirable to a judge?' he asks, and answers his question that that seems desirable to the judge which, according to his training, his experience, and his general point of view, strikes him as the jural consequence that ought to flow from the facts, and he advises us that what gives the judge the struggle in the case is the effort so to state the reasons for his judgment that they will pass muster.

Now what is he saying except that the judge really decides by feeling, and not by judgment; by "hunching" and not by ratiocination, and that the ratiocination appears only in the opinion?

Now what is he saying but that the vital, motivating impulse for the decision is an intuitive sense of what is right or wrong for that cause, and that the astute judge, having so decided, enlists his every faculty and belabors his laggard mind, not only to justify that intuition to himself, but to make it pass muster with his critics?[13]

Roscoe Pound, writing on intuition, said:

> Nor need we be ashamed to confess that much that goes on in the administration of justice is intuitive. Bergson tells us that intelligence, which frames and applies rules, is more adapted to the inorganic, while intuition is more adapted to life. In the same way rules of law and legal conceptions which are applied mechanically are more adapted to property and to business transactions; standards where application proceeds upon intuition are more adapted to human conduct and to to the conduct of enterprises.[14]

It is difficult to articulate the process by which a decision has been made. Dean Pound says, "The trained intuition of the judge continually leads him to right results for which he is puzzled to give unimpeachable

---

13. *Id.* at 285.

14. Pound, *The Theory of Judicial Decision*, 36 HARVARD L. REV. 940, 951 (1923).

legal reasons."[15] The tentative decision which the judge has reached often seems the result of an unconscious process. Because judges would like the assurance that the decision they have reached is the correct one, an incubation period or an opportunity to contemplate and justify the decision can be an important part of the decision-making process.

When is the decision made? A hoped-for result of the necessity for finding the facts and applying the correct law is that the decision is only made after the completion of the evidence and the arguments of counsel. Unfortunately, the judge is tempted, at least in some cases, to reach a decision far earlier than that.

The problem in doing so is that psychologists tell us that, once we tend to favor a particular side, we discount evidence that is contrary to that and thus give undue weight to evidence that favors the side for which we have at least tentatively decided. After the "initial leaning," it becomes difficult for counsel on the other side to say anything or produce any evidence that is persuasive. We discount the evidence that challenges our increasingly firm belief. Judges instruct jurors to keep an open mind until the case has been submitted to them. There is good cause for such a requirement, and judges should also be bound by it.

Step Five: Justifying the Decision

In the process of reaching the final decision, it is possible to reach, test, and abandon several tentative decisions. When there is time to do so, it may be helpful to examine the question in the fresh light of a new day. But it is also possible to reach an initial decision; believe that it is correct; think about it overnight; reach a new conclusion; think *that* is correct; and still have some doubt about which one is correct. Do not delay waiting for absolute assurance that you have the correct answer.

The testing process is sometimes known as *justification*. In this process the judge reviews the reasons for the decision. The process may be mental, oral, or written. The process may be completed rapidly or over a period of time.

If the judge intends to announce an oral decision, the justification may be accomplished initially in the judge's mind. "The plaintiff's evidence convinces me. That side should win. But there was contradictory evidence. Does the plaintiff's evidence really overcome that? Am I convinced to the required degree? And what weight do I give to the expert testimony? Maybe I am not convinced to the required degree. The other possibility is that the defendant prevails. When I retest the evidence, I think the plaintiff has not met the burden of proof."

15. *Id.*

That reasoning produces the final decision. Another part of justification is the public statement, made orally when the final decision is announced from the bench, or in writing if a written decision is required or deemed desirable. The exposition of reasons for the decision shows that the decision is not arbitrary. In appellate decisions, that justification helps indicate the rule for deciding similar cases in the future.

Step Six: Announcing the Final Decision

The last step in the decision-making process is to announce the final decision:

A trial judge in a nonjury case should always render an opinion, giving the reason for his decision. It may be delivered orally at the conclusion of the evidence and the argument, or the case may be taken under advisement and a written opinion prepared.

There is a threefold purpose in either event. First and most important is that the litigants and lawyers concerned have a right to know the basis of the trial judge's decision, what he found the facts to be, and how he has applied the law to those facts.

It is of importance that the decision be right, but it is not enough to be correct in law. It is of no less importance that the decision be given in a manner which satisfies the ordinary citizen that he has had a fair trial, that the result has been reached on the basis of reason and not on the manipulations of a ouija board. Certainly the defeated party cannot be expected to rest content with the bare conclusions of the court.

Sir Patrick Devlin, a judge of the High Court of the Queen's Bench, tells of one of his colleagues who was criticized by the members of the court of appeals for the time he took in developing very elementary propositions in his opinions, and responded:

> When I am delivering a judgment in my court I am not addressing the court of appeals. They are not in my audience. I am addressing the parties down there in front of me. And I am endeavoring to explain to them as far as I can, and so far as I can make the law clear to them, just why the facts and the law compel me to decide as I have.

After all, that is the main function of the trial judge. If he goes wrong in the law, some appellate court can correct him; if he goes wrong in the way he conducts his trial, and if he leaves an impression of being arbitrary, prejudiced, or unfair, the appellate courts have no way of correcting that impression.

. . . The second most important reason for an opinion is that the decision is more apt to be right. Where an opinion stating reasons for a decision is given, the process of determining the reasons is in itself an appeal from first impression to final wisdom. Deliberation will compel a judge to give himself reasons and to weigh their value; he recognizes that there must be adequate reasons which are a credit to the position he occupies.

The judge may by reason of the character of the case and the testimony, together with his intelligence, perceptiveness, attentiveness and other mental and emotional characteristics, have completed the process of formulating his reasons by the time the trial is ended, particularly where issues are factual. Knowing whom he has believed, he can give those reasons forthwith. To do so requires considerable skill in the analysis of evidence, and a faculty of lucid expression, not given to judges in equal degree; for that reason some will reserve judgment and write an opinion. Cases which involve numerous and close questions of law will generally require written opinions. Writing an opinion compels research which otherwise might not be so well or so thoroughly done. Research tends to produce conformity with prior decisions, which is usually but not always the equivalent of correctness in law.

. . . we have all had the experience of having determined that a case should be decided in a certain way, and after beginning to draft an opinion accordingly have found it impossible to write a logical opinion that way, and have been compelled to write one holding the opposite.

Less important, but still of great significance, is the third reason—the insight it gives the appellate court into the issues, and the trial judge's approach to them.

. . . No appeal can be properly determined unless the appellate court knows the reasons for the decision of the trial court. With increasing frequency, the trial court's opinion, in whole or in part, is adopted as the opinion of the appellate court, not because the appellate court is lazy, but because the statement of the issues and the reasoning of the trial judge are completely decisive. If the trial judge disbelieved a key witness, a statement to that effect may be of great assistance to the appellate court. It is frequently urged that the trial court erred in refusing to make a finding of fact because the testimony establishing the fact is uncontradicted, but if the trial judge says he didn't believe the witness who gave the testimony, the answer to that assignment of error becomes clear. The appellate court is entitled to the advantages of the trial judge's ability to see through the confident and plausible liar.

. . . (M)any appeals based on trial errors would not be taken if the trial judge would write an opinion after the argument on a motion for new trial, or state from the bench the issues argued on the motion and give his views with reference to them.[16]

Some judges almost never write a decision. They state the decision orally from the bench. There is merit in this position.[17] Rendering a decision in the presence of the parties allows the parties to better understand the decision. It avoids delays. There are other good reasons, which have been discussed previously in Chapter 12.[18]

Other judges feel the need to write every decision. There is a good argument for that, too.[19] Writing the decision requires written justification for it. To explain the reasons to others means that you must explain the reasons to yourself. On the other hand, in a busy court, the necessity for writing every decision can create a tremendous burden.

Unless statute requires a written opinion, which method is better will depend upon the case, the judge, and the amount of time available.

Conclusion

Whatever the process of reaching a decision and whatever the technique of the particular judge, the goal is to reach the proper decision as quickly as possible, and to state it in a way that will satisfy the parties that the trial was fair and that the case was properly decided.

Trial judges should not measure their success by the rate at which appellate courts affirm their decisions. There is no single measure of the quality of a decision. Judges must learn to compromise, to realize that no decision is perfect, to eliminate the fear of failure. A wrong decision is often better than no decision at all. Judges should cultivate decisiveness, and once they make a decision, let it go.

---

16. Hill, *The Opinion of the Trial Judge*, 11 JUDGES' J., no. 1 (1972). Reprinted with permission.

17. R. WASSERSTROM, THE JUDICIAL DECISION: TOWARD A THEORY OF LEGAL JUSTIFICATION 89 (1961).

18. *See* Chapter 12, at note 1.

19. *See* Chapter 12, at note 3.

16

JUDICIAL DISCRETION

The judge, even when he is free, is still not wholly free. He is not to innovate at pleasure. He is not a knight-errant roaming at will in pursuit of his own ideal of beauty or of goodness. He is to draw his inspiration from consecrated principles. He is not to yield to spasmodic sentiment, to vague and unregulated benevolence. He is to exercise a discretion informed by tradition, methodized by analogy, disciplined by system, and subordinated to the 'primordial necessity of order in the social life.' Wide enough in all conscience is the field of discretion that remains.[1]

What Is Discretion?

The term discretion has been defined in enough different ways that the word engenders confusion. It has a meaning for lay people as well as giving direction to legal professionals:

> In all cases courts must exercise a discretion in the sense of being discreet, circumspect, prudent and exercising cautious judgment. [Citation omitted.] But that is a duty generally laid upon all officers as well as private individuals. Judicial discretion, in its technical sense, means something more.[2]

Even used as a legal word of art, it has several meanings. It is used to describe:

- The exclusive right to decide as the court pleases—this power of free decision is an undirected choice not revisable or reviewable by the appellate tribunal. For example, "[w]hen applied to public officials 'discretion' is the power conferred upon them by law to act officially under certain circumstances according to the dictates

1. B. CARDOZO, THE NATURE OF THE JUDICIAL PROCESS (1921).
2. R. BOWERS, THE JUDICIAL DISCRETION OF TRIAL COURTS 9-10 (1931).

of their own judgment and conscience and uncontrolled by the judgment or conscience of others."[3]

- A relatively wide latitude of judgment—it is the latitude of judgment when there is an absence of a fixed or hard and fast rule. For example, "A judicial act is said to lie in discretion when there are no fixed principles by which its correctness may be determined [and] such determinations are not subject to review on appeal."[4]
- The power to make a choice from among two or more legally valid solutions. For example, " 'Discretion' in performing an act arises when it may be performed in one, two or more ways, either of which would be lawful and where it is left to the will or judgment of the performer to determine in which way it shall be performed."[5]
- The normal and usual process of decision making—in this sense, it is the process of applying legal precepts or concepts to facts. For example, "discretion . . . is the responsible exercise of official conscience on all facts of a particular situation in the light of the purpose for which the power exists."[6] The trial court's exercise of "discretion" means nothing more than the application of statutes and principles to all of the facts of a case.[7]

Why Is Discretion Granted to Judges?

Judges have discretion for several reasons. One is the superior vantage point of the trial judge.[8] Another reason is practicality; judges have discretion "where not only would it be difficult to prescribe exact and minute regulations, but where the situation itself is not easily reproduced in its original character, and cannot safely be reviewed."[9] Other purposes of discretion are to prevent erosion of the functions of the trial court[10] and to promote finality in the administration of justice. Discretion also promotes efficiency and economy in the administration of justice. Finally, it is simply necessary to have someone make a determination.

---

3. Schneider v. Hawkins, 179 Md. 21, 16 A.2d 861 (1940).
4. Palliser v. Home Tel. Co., 170 Ala. 341, 54 So. 499 (1911).
5. Texas Indem. Ins. Co. v. Arant, 171 S.W.2d 915 (Texas Civ. App. 1943).
6. Bowles v. Goebel, 151 F.2d 671, 674 (1945).
7. Shopiro v. Shopiro, 153 P.2d 62 (1944).
8. Atchison, Topeka & Santa Fe Ry. Co. v. Barrett, 246 F.2d 846 (1957).
9. Hubbard v. Hubbard, 77 Vt. 73, 58 A. 969, 970 (1904). *See also* Rosenberg, *Judicial Discretion of the Trial Court, Viewed from Above*, 22 SYRACUSE L. REV. 635 (1971) (an important article in this field); Pierce v. Underwood, 56 U.S.L.W. 4806 (June 1988) (quoting p. 638 of Rosenberg).
10. Thurmond v. Superior Court, 66 C.2d 836, 839, 59 Cal. Rptr. 273, 274, 427 P.2d 985 (1967).

When Is Judicial Discretion Used?

Judicial discretion is used in every case except where the court has no jurisdiction; [11] where the constitution demands certain action by a judge (a statute granting discretion under such circumstances is unconstitutional); [12] and where statute or rule is so clear and facts are so plain there can be only one decision.

Principles of Application of Discretion

No special words are necessary to grant discretion to the trial judge.[13] So how will a judge know when discretion has been given? Often the judge will know because no law, rule, or standard prescribes what should be done, yet the judge must make a ruling or a decision. In other cases, a statute may provide that the court, "in its discretion," may make a particular decision. Or the statutory provision could say the court "may" do *X*. What it may do, it also may not do. It has a choice. It has discretion.

When the trial judge has discretion, the judge must use it. If the trial judge states that a party is entitled to a certain result as a matter of right, and the appellate court finds the trial court had discretion, the trial court will be reversed for failure to use its discretion.[14] For example, one appellate court found that where the trial court had "broad discretion in the granting or withholding of bench paroles," it was an abuse of discretion to refuse to consider an application for bench paroles because "in all my experience on the bench I have never allowed a parole."[15] Furthermore, the record must show that the judge exercised the discretion granted. Where the exercise of discretion is shown but the reason for its exercise in a particular way is not shown, it will usually be presumed that there is a good reason for the decision.[16]

Discretion, without the existence of certain well-understood principles within which it should be exercised, cannot be used to deprive one of property or basic substantive rights.[17]

Types or Grades of Judicial Discretion

In administrative matters, the judge or judges have almost total discretion. Such matters include hiring personnel, courtroom maintenance and equipment, and the personal conduct of the judge.

11. Grant v. Corbitt, 95 So. 2d 25, 28 (1957).
12. Hubbard v. Hubbard, 58 A. 968, 970.
13. Thurmond v. Superior Court, 66 C.2d at 839.
14. Adney v. Mississippi Lime Co., 241 F.2d 43, 45 (7th Circ. 1957).
15. State v. Boston, 233 Iowa 1249, 11 N.W.2d 407, 411 (1943).
16. 24 *Corpus Juris Secundum*, Criminal Law § 1849, p. 610.
17. Hubbard v. Hubbard, 58 A. 969, at 971.

Unless the court has unusual funding provisions, personnel matters and courtroom maintenance and equipment may be better handled by good relationships with those who handle the purse. In this area the court has inherent powers. Use of those powers may be abrasive, but when patience is exhausted, the inherent power may be used.

The personal conduct of the judge is increasingly regulated by Rules of Judicial Conduct (see Chapter 18). In most procedural matters, in the absence of statute rule, the ruling of the trial judge is presumed to be correct. Such matters include:

- Rulings on motions before, during, and after trial
- Conduct of the trial
- Regulation of litigants, attorneys, and spectators

A judge should check authorities in his or her jurisdiction, because many jurisdictions have statutes or rules that limit discretion, even in the area of procedure. Discretion is very limited for substantive matters—applying law to evidence, requirements of due process, and application of laws and statutes giving rights.

Reviewability and the Standards of Review

It seems logical that the more limited the discretion, the greater the probability that a reviewing court can find an abuse of discretion. At least the appellate court has a greater opportunity for review. The converse is also logical: The greater the discretion, the narrower the review.

The basic test is whether there was an abuse of discretion.

The rulings range from, "the trial judge's denial [of an application to waive a jury trial] was a fair and proper exercise of discretion"[18] to "our review of the trial court's refusal to admit psychiatric evidence . . . is hampered by a record which does little to reveal the basis of the discretionary determination underlying that ruling. We have concluded, however, that the record as a whole is sufficient to permit our resolution of the question whether an abuse of discretion occurred, and we have resolved that question in favor of the defendant" (there was an abuse of discretion).[19]

There is a story about a California judge who never ruled in terms other than "granted," "denied," "sustained," "overruled." The story concludes that he was always affirmed because the appellate court found no wrong reason for the ruling and could find a reason why the ruling was correct.

If that was ever true in California, it appears to be true no longer.

18. People v. DiCostanzo, 296 N.Y.S.2d 576, 581 (1969).
19. People v. Russel, 70 Cal. Rptr. 210, 443 P.2d 794 (1968).

The discretionary act of a trial judge is in part predicated on the personal judgment of the judge. Consequently, unless the judge's reasons for the actions are expressed in the record, the basis for the act is unknown to the appellate court. The appellate review of a discretionary act depends in part on the record made by the trial judge:[20]

> (T)he reasoning underlying the court's conclusion as to the admission of such evidence should appear to some degree in the record in order that appellate review of that conclusion, which reaches only to abuses of the court's discretion [citation omitted], may be facilitated.[21]

The cases indicate such differing applications of the principles discussed that a judge should always check the law and rules in the judge's jurisdiction. There is discretion in varying amounts under varying circumstances. It is better to think carefully, state carefully the reasons for the rulings, and recognize that if a trial judge has discretion and exercises it properly, an appellate court usually will not substitute its judgment for that of the judge.

20. T. Lee, B. Overton, Judicial Discretion 86 (1974).
21. People v. Russel, 70 Cal. Rptr. 210, at 215.

17

COURTROOM CONTROL

The Powers of Court

The power to fine for contempt, imprison for contumacy, and enforce the observance of order within courts is said to have been "universally acknowledged" to be inherent in all courts. As stated in *In re Terry*:

> (T)here is another rule, of almost immemorial antiquity, and universally acknowledged, which is equally vital to personal liberty, and to the preservation of organized society, because upon its recognition and enforcement depend the existence and authority of the tribunals established to protect the rights of the citizen, whether of life, liberty, or property, and whether assailed by illegal acts of the government or by the lawlessness or violence of individuals.[1]

Early on it was argued and acknowledged that the power to mete out "instant punishment" was one that could be "abused and may sometimes be exercised hastily or arbitrarily," but according to the U.S. Supreme Court in *Terry*, that is not "an argument to disprove either its existence or the necessity of" such powers.

Though necessity gives rise to the powers of contempt, prudence should control the frequency of their use. The contempt powers avoid many of the guarantees of the Bill of Rights, may avoid the right to trial by jury, and may be used upon the subjective evaluation of the judge with little hope for meaningful appeal. The extent of these powers dictates careful and limited use of them.

The trial judge should keep in mind that litigants and spectators are caught up in the emotion of the case. Tension, frustration, and fear could well control their senses. An understanding of how people can lose control under stress is also vital to the just use of contempt powers. Courts have the power to lift sanctions or excuse contemptuous conduct when

1. 128 U.S. 289 (1888).

a proper and lawful mood has returned to the courtroom. A forbearance of the use of power is strong evidence of the power itself.

As stated in *Cooke v. United States*,[2] "But [the contempt power's] exercise is a delicate one, and care is needed to avoid arbitrary or oppressive conclusions. This rule of caution is more mandatory where the contempt charged has in it the element of personal criticism or attack upon the judge." The Supreme Court continued, "The judge must banish the slightest personal impulse to reprisal, but he should not bend backward, and injure the authority of the court by too great leniency."

In re Johnson[3] serves as another reason for the careful use of contempt powers. In this case, Judge Johnson was brought before the state judicial disciplinary board on charges that he abused the powers of contempt. The majority of the Pennsylvania Supreme Court upheld the judge's use of contempt powers and drew the thin line between right and wrong:

> 'Judges are supposed to be [persons] of fortitude, able to thrive in a hardy climate.' Although we have indicated our displeasure with the injudicious use of contempt authority, we have not officially reprimanded or censured a judge whose contempt order has been reversed. The authority of a judge to hold one in contempt, depriving as it does a person of liberty, is an authority that should be used rarely, and with extreme caution. Nevertheless, judges overly sensitive, or judges acting in pressure-laden situations, should not be required to fear automatic discipline because a contempt ruling might later be reversed on appeal. Judges have and will make mistakes. They are human beings and not robots woven of steel mesh.

An Attorney's Good Faith Efforts

To sustain a charge of criminal contempt, it must be shown that the contemnor's conduct was calculated to embarrass, hinder, or obstruct the court in its duties, or to derogate from the authority or dignity of the court, or to bring the administration of justice into disrepute. The intent of the contemnor may be inferred from the contemnor's actions.[4]

On the other hand, an attorney's good faith efforts on behalf of a client should not be deemed contemptuous. As stated in *People v. Miller*:[5]

> While counsel may have been overzealous or improperly sarcastic at times, we are of the opinion that his conduct in the courtroom constituted a good faith attempt to represent clients without hindering the court's functions or dignity.

The U.S. Supreme Court has overturned a contempt finding on a pro se defendant who in court told the jury that the judge was "biased and had prejudged the case," and that the defendant was a "political pris-

2. 267 U.S. 517 (1925).
3. 395 A.2d 1319 (Pa. 1978).
4. People *ex rel.* Kunce v. Hogan, 364 N.E.2d 50 (Ill. 1977).
5. 281 N.E.2d 292 (Ill. 1972).

oner." The Court stated, "The vehemence of the language used is not alone the measure of the power to punish for contempt. The fires which it kindles must constitute an imminent, not merely a likely, threat to the administration of justice."[6] The Court completed its opinion by stating:

> (T)he law of contempt is not made for the protection of judges who may be sensitive to the winds of public opinion. Judges are supposed to be men of fortitude, able to thrive in a hardy climate.[7]

The Court added that judges should not confuse "offenses to their sensibilities with obstruction to the administration of justice."[8]

An opposite situation is presented by People v. Siegel.[9] On April 28, 1980, Marie Rodriguez, charged with various criminal offenses, appeared before the circuit court. Ms. Rodriguez contended that she was a soldier and combatant fighting for Puerto Rican freedom. She contended further that she was a prisoner of war and that the circuit court had no jurisdiction over her. She waived her right to counsel for the purposes of the circuit court proceedings but asserted her "right as a prisoner of war to request legal advisers." Due to her continued disruptive conduct, the circuit court ordered that she be gagged. On April 29, 1980, the court ordered that Rodriguez be returned to the courtroom so that she could be properly advised of her right to counsel. Rodriguez, bound and gagged, was brought into the courtroom by three deputy sheriffs.

Respondent, a licensed attorney, who was seated in the spectators' section of the courtroom, approached the bench. After identifying herself by name and as legal adviser for Rodriguez, she objected to the binding and gagging of Rodriguez. She demanded that Rodriguez be treated as a prisoner of war and stated, "This is outrageous display of the United States' cruel and inhumane treatment."

The Illinois Supreme Court held this was not a case of an attorney using good faith efforts:

> The record shows that Rodriguez' prior disruptive conduct presented the possibility of disorder in the court. Clearly respondent was aware of this volatile and difficult situation. Assuming that she considered it appropriate to object to the jurisdiction of the court and to present her contention that Rodriguez was a prisoner of war, she could have done so by a limited appearance, followed by a written motion. The fact that she chose instead to make her demands in the midst of an already unstable, difficult, and conceivably dangerous setting gives rise to a reasonable inference that her con-

6. Craig v. Harney, 331 U.S. 367, 376 (1947).
7. *Id.*
8. *In re* Little, 404 U.S. 553 (1972).
9. 445 N.E.2d 762 (Ill. 1983).

duct was calculated to embarrass, hinder, or obstruct the court in its administration of justice.[10]

Intent is an essential element of contempt, and any questioned acts must demonstrate an intent to disrupt the proceedings, or embarrass the court. But it has been said that intent may be inferred.[11]

Warnings to a Potential Contemnor

Justice Brennan, concurring in *Illinois v. Allen*,[12] emphasized that basic concepts of justice include warning any potential contemnor of the jeopardy that he or she faces by unruly or improper conduct:

> Of course, no action against an unruly defendant is permissible except after he has been fully and fairly informed that his conduct is wrong and intolerable, and warned of the possible consequences of continued misbehavior.

The American Bar Association Standards for Criminal Justice[13] likewise set forth the desirability of admonition or warning. Standard 6-4.2 reads:

> No sanction other than censure should be imposed by the trial judge unless:
>
> (a) it is clear from the identity of the offender and the character of his or her acts that the disruptive conduct was willfully contemptuous; or
>
> (b) the conduct warranting the sanction was preceded by a clear warning that such conduct was impermissible and that specified sanctions might be imposed for its repetition.

As a practical matter, if a judge is dealing with an offensive courtroom outburst, the clarity of the contempt will be made by repeated improper statements. A judge could state, "I'm sorry. What did you say? I didn't hear that clearly." That pause allows cooler thinking to prevail and proves an intentional act if the improper statement is repeated.

The commentary following Standard 6-4.2 emphasizes that the use of warnings is not possible for "flagrant contempts." It goes on to caution:

> A warning may be effective in preventing further disorder and is therefore preferable to sanctions as a first step. It also assures both the court and the public that subsequent misconduct will be considered willfully contemptuous and deserving of punishment. Moreover, the practice of warning before imposing punishment reduces the risk that attorneys will be deterred by the fear of punishment from exercising zealous advocacy.[14]

Where a judge instructs a party to cease activities that are improper or contemptuous, the instruction must be clear and exact. Consider *Ram-*

10. *Id.*

11. People v. Dorris, 373 N.E.2d 77 (Ill. 1978); United States v. Marx, 553 F.2d 874 (1977).

12. 397 U.S. 337, 350 (1970).

13. American Bar Association, Standards for Criminal Justice, Ch. 6, (2d ed. 1986), Standard 6-4.2.

14. *Id.*, commentary.

sey Co. Defender's Office v. Fleming.[15] In that case, Ms. Ceisel, an attorney, was given an order by the court:

> COURT: Ms. Ceisel, I have asked you to take a seat in the courtroom. If you choose not to do so, I am going to find you in direct contempt of the Court. Do you understand that?
>
> MS. CEISEL: Yes, Your Honor, I do understand that.
>
> COURT: Please take a seat in the courtroom. (*As Ms. Ceisel is turning to leave the bench, she leans toward Mr. Aguirre [her client] and whispers something to him. The Court Reporter is unable to hear any words spoken.*)
>
> COURT: You are now found in contempt of court.

While the acts of the attorney were obviously calculated to aggravate the judge, the Minnesota Supreme Court vacated citation of contempt, holding:

> Ceisel did not directly disobey the court's order to take a seat. The court did not order her to refrain from all interaction with Aguirre. Instead the court ordered her to sit down. Therefore, when she whispered to Aguirre on her way back to take a seat, she did not directly disobey an order of the court.[16]

The Obstreperous Defendant

A judge has significant powers to deal with the disruptive, contumacious, and obstreperous defendant, but all thinking and all efforts must be toward not using them. That direction was signaled by Justice Hugo Black, who in writing *Illinois v. Allen*,[17] a decision that gave judges powers to banish a defendant from the courtroom, or even to bind and gag a defendant at his or her own trial, curiously began the decision by observing the rights protected by the Constitution:

> The Confrontation Clause of the Sixth Amendment to the United States Constitution provides that: 'In all criminal prosecutions, the accused shall enjoy the right . . . to be confronted with the witnesses against him . . .' We have held that the Fourteenth Amendment makes the guarantees of this clause obligatory upon the States. One of the most basic of the rights guaranteed by the Confrontation Clause is the accused's right to be present in the courtroom at every stage of his trial.

The *Allen* decision then went on to acknowledge that even these broad rights given by the Constitution may, in Cardozo's words, "be lost by consent or at times even by misconduct." The Court held:

> Although mindful that courts must indulge every reasonable presumption against the loss of constitutional rights, we explicitly hold today that a defendant can lose his right to be present at trial if, after he has been warned

15. 294 N.W.2d 275 (Minn. 1980).
16. *Id.*
17. 397 U.S. 337.

> by the judge that he will be removed if he continues his disruptive behavior, he nevertheless insists on conducting himself in a manner so disorderly, disruptive, and disrespectful of the court that his trial cannot be carried on with him in the courtroom.[18]

The emphasis upon the right to be present continued as the Court gave an obstreperous defendant "reentry" rights. The Court stated, "Once lost, the right to be present can, of course, be reclaimed as soon as the defendant is willing to conduct himself consistently with the decorum and respect inherent in the concepts of courts and judicial proceedings."[19]

The Right to Be Present

The right of an accused to be present during his trial was not the product of latter-day liberalism. In 1892, the U.S. Supreme Court, considering the case of *Lewis v. United States*,[20] said, "It would be contrary to the dictates of humanity to let him [the accused] waive the advantage which a view of his sad plight might give him by inclining the hearts of the jurors to listen to his defense with indulgence."

Modern-day cases have altered the inflexible position of *Lewis* insofar as waiving the right to be present, but remained true to the Confrontation Clause protections. As *Lewis* again states:

> It is the right of any one, when prosecuted on a capital or criminal charge, to be confronted with the accusers and witnesses; and it is within the scope of this right that he be present, not only when the jury are hearing his case, but at any subsequent stage when anything may be done in the prosecution by which he is to be affected.[21]

The Pro Se Defendant

When a defendant elects to exercise his or her rights to self-representation under *Faretta v. California*,[22] the court should appoint standby counsel to advise the defendant. This procedure is not only humane, but also permits an option if the pro se defendant becomes obstreperous. The American Bar Association Standards for Criminal Justice set out a standard for this contingency:

> Standard 6-3.9 Misconduct of pro se defendant
>
> If a defendant who is permitted to proceed without the assistance of counsel engages in conduct which is so disruptive that the trial cannot proceed in an orderly manner, the court should, after appropriate warnings, revoke the

18. *Id.*
19. *Id.*
20. 146 U.S. 370 (1892).
21. *Id.*
22. 422 U.S. 806 (1975).

> permission and require representation by counsel. If standby counsel has previously been appointed, the counsel should be asked to represent the defendant. In any event, the trial should be recessed only long enough for counsel to make the necessary preparations to go forward with the trial.

The commentary accompanying the standard reminds the reader that the "misconduct of a pro se defendant will frequently be a blend of ignorance, emotional involvement, and mounting recognition of the inadequacy of the defense." One might also add the element of frustration, if rules of evidence are applied technically to the pro se defendant. A judge is better advised to permit relaxed evidentiary standards and attempt substantial justice in a harmonious setting.

The facts of *United States ex rel. Boothe v. Superintendent*,[23] starkly show what binding and gagging mean. The defendant repeated a question about the procedure challenging jurors and indicated his belief that his lawyer had not correctly informed him. The judge answered that he would not speak to the defendant, ordered the jury out, and had the defendant bound. When the defendant complained that a guard was stepping on him, he was gagged, ungagged, and regagged, whereupon the jury panel was brought in. As defendant attempted to speak, the judge, before the sworn and prospective jurors, instructed the court officer to gag him "more effectively." An altercation thereupon ensued, and the gag slipped off the defendant's mouth. The trial judge rebuked a court officer for removing the gag. After sporadic interjections by the defendant complaining of his counsel, the judge ordered him gagged again. The gag loosened, and the defendant requested a challenge. When the court allowed him one peremptory challenge, the defendant indicated he wanted "to challenge the whole panel." Thereupon the trial judge ordered him regagged.

Repeated Chances to Reform

The American Bar Association Standards for Criminal Justice set out a standard for dealing justly with the obstreperous defendant:

> Standard 6-3.8 The disruptive defendant
>
> A defendant may be removed from the courtroom during trial when the defendant's conduct is so disruptive that the trial cannot proceed in an orderly manner. Removal is preferable to gagging or shackling the disruptive defendant. If removed, the defendant should be required to be present in the court building while the trial is in progress, be given the opportunity of learning of the trial proceedings through defense counsel at reasonable intervals, and be given a continuing opportunity to return to the courtroom during the trial upon assurance from the defendant of good behavior. The removed defendant should be summoned to the courtroom at appropriate

23. 506 F. Supp. 1337 (1981).

intervals and invited to remain, with the offer to remain repeated in open court each time.

The Thin Line Between Fitness for Trial and Contemptuous Acts

Illinois v. Allen[24] was treated—in the Illinois courts—as a fitness-for-trial-case, that is, one concerning whether the defendant could understand the nature of the charges. Justice Douglas, dissenting in the U.S. Supreme Court, spoke in terms of fitness or competency to stand trial: "There is more than an intimation in the present record that the defendant was a mental case." Justice Douglas went on to say that such situations do not "answer the difficult questions as to what a trial judge should do with an otherwise mentally ill defendant who creates a courtroom disturbance." He, however, considered the possibility of a mentally ill person being bound and gagged in a court of law, and determined it to be "pathetic, as well as disgusting and disgraceful."

A trial judge faced with this situation has two reasons for having psychiatric assistance close at hand. First, if the defendant is knowingly disruptive, the updated psychiatric opinion will bolster the judge's actions on appeal. The psychiatrist could make an on-the-scene evaluation and determine that the defendant is indeed fit for trial and that his or her unruly conduct is knowing. On the other hand, if the defendant is operating involuntarily, the trial could be halted on the motion of the defendant (if he or she is unfit), and the extreme measures within a judge's powers could be stayed while psychiatric attention is sought for the defendant.

Asking Another to Decide

Chief Justice Taft once stated, "[A] judge, called upon to act in a case of contempt by personal attack upon him, may, without flinching from his duty, properly ask that one of his fellow judges take his place."[25] The 1970 case of *Mayberry v. Pennsylvania*,[26] may have made Chief Justice Taft's advice into a mandatory constitutional right.

In *Mayberry*, three prison convicts were on trial in a state court for rioting and holding hostages within a prison. They chose to represent themselves. During the trial, defendant Mayberry said, inter alia, that the court was "railroading" the defendants, that the judge was a "dirty sonofabitch," that the judge was a "dirty, tyrannical old dog," that the judge was a "bum," that the judge needed "some kind of psychiatric

24. 397 U.S. 337.
25. Cooke v. United States, 267 U.S. 517 (1925).
26. 400 U.S. 455 (1971).

treatment," and that the trial was the "craziest that [he had] ever seen." The judge did not impose instant contempt penalties but deferred the matters until after trial, when the judge pronounced Mayberry guilty of eleven counts of criminal contempt.

Mr. Justice Douglas, expressing the views of seven members of the Court (with two others concurring), stated:

> Where, however, [the judge] does not act the instant the contempt is committed, but waits until the end of the trial, on balance, it is generally wise where the marks of unseemly conduct have left personal stings to ask a fellow judge to take his place.[27]

Justice Douglas then stated, "Our conclusion is that by reason of the Due Process Clause of the Fourteenth Amendment a defendant in criminal contempt proceedings should be given a public trial before a judge other than the one reviled by the contemnor."

Justice Douglas touched on what might be the most important consideration in the long run, as he held that another judge, "not bearing the sting of these slanderous remarks and having the impersonal authority of the law," should sit in judgment of the conduct of the alleged contemnor.

The *Mayberry* case also emphasized the practical. The Court made it clear that the trial judge "could, with propriety, have instantly acted, holding petitioner in contempt, or excluding him from the courtroom."[28] The Court added, "A judge cannot be driven out of a case."

Chief Justice Taft anticipated this issue too. He wrote, in *Cooke*, "where acts of contempt are palpably aggravated by a personal attack upon the judge in order to drive the judge out of the case for ulterior reasons, the scheme should not be permitted to succeed. But attempts of this kind are rare."[29]

Mayberry *Limited to Personal Attacks*

Perhaps because *Mayberry* reaches too far in the direction of fairness to the obstreperous defendant, further cases have drawn a distinction between instances of an "insulting attack upon the integrity of a judge" and a mere "disruptive, recalcitrant and disagreeable" defendant. In the first situation, a judge must follow the *Mayberry* directive and recuse himself from the contempt proceedings, but in the latter, where the judge theoretically is not "drawn into" the fray, he may sentence the contemptuous defendants.

27. *Id.*
28. *Id.*
29. 267 U.S. 517 (1925).

In re Dellinger,[30] a case from the legendary Chicago Seven trial, the court of appeals said:

> First, a distinction can and must be made between contumacious conduct generally and contumacious conduct which is 'apt to strike' at the most vulnerable and human qualities of a judge's temperament . . . Second, if the conduct of the defendant includes a personal attack on the trial judge carrying such potential for bias that he is not 'likely to maintain that calm detachment necessary for fair adjudication,' [citation omitted] the trial judge must disqualify himself if he waits to act until the conclusion of the trial.

The court in *Dellinger* went on to say that, in the latter situation, "possible prejudice to the accused as well as the diminution of the quality of justice in the public eye overrides any economy of effort that would be achieved by summary procedure."[31]

When the Contemnor Is the Trial Attorney

Where the contemnor is the trial attorney, a judge is wise to avoid instant action against the attorney in the presence of the client, if at all possible. To find the attorney guilty of contempt in the middle of the trial would likely bring a claim of prejudice by the client, who would claim that his or her right to effective assistance of counsel and a fair trial was severely impaired by the action of the trial judge.

As stated in *In re Dellinger*,[32] "the wisdom of deferring action against a lawyer has nothing to do with the requisites of due process when the trial judge does not act the instant the contempt is committed, [but] . . . the possible prejudice to the lawyer's client may counterbalance the need to preserve order in the court through immediate action."

This situation does not, of course, apply where the attorney is a witness or a defendant, and in either case the judge should consider deferring action until the end of trial, rather than making the decision to act summarily, or to refer the matter to another judge as posited in *Mayberry.*

Courtroom Spectators

Three types of behavior on the part of courtroom spectators might be contemptuous. These behaviors differ in the nature of the particular action, knowledge or intent to obstruct the work of the court.

The first situation is one in which an obviously contemptuous statement is directed toward the court or the judicial process, or actions

30. 461 F.2d 389 (1972).
31. *Id.*
32. 461 F.2d 389 (1972).

constitute an obviously obstructive act. One might call this actual obstruction.

The second situation is one in which some statement or action is likely to, or does, cause a disturbance. Appearing naked in court, as in *People v. Collins*,[33] is an example. This might be called potential obstruction.

The third situation is one in which some statement or action is going on which presents no obstruction or potential obstruction, but is behavior that cannot be permitted. Sleeping or eating in the courtroom might be examples of this type of conduct. Here the judge has the option of having the person advised that such conduct is not permitted, and then if the conduct knowingly continues, the person can be found in contempt for failing to follow the clear instruction of the court. In this type of situation, the court should give the spectator a reasonable opportunity to conform his or her conduct.[34]

Making the Record Clear

Where the judge decides to find a person in contempt of court, the judge must act skillfully to perfect a record that will sustain the judgment of contempt on appeal. To do that, the judge may make statements for the record at the time of the finding, may file a written order of contempt setting out the contemnor's conduct, may use court reporter's transcripts, and, where television is present in the court, should make the applicable videotapes a part of the record.

The judge should remember that contemptuous conduct often is not spoken, but comes in the form of unruly actions. Those actions should be described in detail for the record so that the reviewing court may appreciate the situation faced by the trial court. As stated in *United States v. Marshall*:[35]

> Much that the judge saw and heard may not be reflected in the transcript. The trial judge recognized this: he sought to incorporate in the second certificate not only the reporter's transcript but also the reporter's recordings and the audio and video tapes.

Thus the judge must unmistakably and vividly describe the conduct that he or she witnessed, and deemed contemptuous.

Criminal or Civil Contempt

The difference between criminal contempt and civil contempt lies in the nature of the relief sought. The purpose of criminal contempt is to

33. 373 N.E.2d 750 (Ill. 1978).

34. *See* People v. Watts, 384 N.E.2d 453 (Ill. 1978) (young woman came into court wearing a T-shirt with what the judge thought was an offensive message).

35. 451 F.2d 372 (1971).

vindicate the authority of the court. Where the authority of court is challenged, the court has the power to punish the offender. A civil contempt is much like any other civil action: It alleges a duty and a breach of that duty, and requests relief in the form of compensation or, more often, compliance with the court's order.

If the relief requested is future compliance with an order of court, or just compensation for a past violation of a court order, the party is seeking civil contempt. If, on the other hand, the judge is punishing the contemnor because of acts which were disrespectful to the court, then criminal contempt is involved.

The criminal contempt power has been uniformly held to be necessary to the protection of the court from insults and oppression while in the ordinary exercise of its duty, and to enable it to enforce its judgments and orders necessary to the due administration of law and protection of the rights of citizens.[36]

The civil contempt power stems from a private party alleging that through violation of a court order, injustice has occurred, asking that the court either coerce the alleged violating party into compliance or award damages because of the alleged contemnor's violation of an earlier court order.

Oftentimes, the distinction is unclear, and the same facts may give rise to both a criminal and a civil contempt petition. As stated in *United States v. United Mine Workers*,[37] "The same acts may justify a court in resorting to coercive and to punitive measures."

These hybrid situations often involve prior injunctions. At an earlier time, the court had issued an order enjoining certain practices. Then an offended party comes into court alleging that the injunction has not been honored by the defendant. This situation clearly has elements of both civil and criminal contempt: civil, to stop the offending conduct and provide damages, and criminal, to punish the party who has violated an earlier court order.[38]

In these situations it is important that the judge make an early determination of whether the matter will be treated as criminal or civil. As stated in *Richmond Black Police Officers Ass'n v. City of Richmond, Virginia*:

> (I)t is essential that a determination be made at the earliest practicable time regarding the true nature of the contempt . . . in order that the proceedings which are held thereafter are conducted in such a manner as to satisfy the appropriate rules of procedure. . . .[39]

---

36. Gompers v. Buck's Stove & Range Co., 221 U.S. 418 (1911).
37. 330 U.S. 258, 302 (1947).
38. *See* Vuitton et Fils S.A. v. Carousel Handbags, 592 F.2d 126 (1979).
39. 548 F.2d 123 (1976).

Another problem that frequently arises in contempt proceedings arising from injunctive actions is that of notice. Who has knowledge of the original court order? *United States v. Baker*[40] presents a situation where fishers in one area of the state of Washington were brought into court on contempt petitions, charging that they had violated an earlier court order from a suit to which they were not parties. The government contended that "everybody in the area knew" of the earlier injunction, asking the court to take judicial notice of that fact. The court stated that judicial notice was not designed to do that, and that knowledge of each of the parties would have to be proven satisfactorily. The Baker court stated: "One must have notice of a court order and violate it, before he can be held in criminal contempt."[41]

Civil Contempt: Defense of Inability to Comply

In a civil contempt proceeding, the defendant may assert the inability to comply with the order in question.[42] While the court is bound by the enforcement order, it need not be blind to evidence that compliance is, at the point of time in question, factually impossible. Where compliance is impossible, neither the moving party nor the court has any reason to proceed with the civil contempt action.[43] It is settled law, however, that the defendant has the burden of proof on the issue of impossibility.[44]

Direct or Indirect Contempt

Direct contempt, which may be punished summarily, takes place in the presence of the court. All elements of the offense are within the court's personal observation and knowledge. An indirect contempt, which may be punished only after charging and a trial, is one that occurs in whole or in an essential part outside the presence of the court. Elements of this offense must be proven to the judge. Direct contempts are almost always criminal in nature. Indirect contempts may be civil or criminal, depending on the relief sought or the aim of the sanction.

The unexplained absence of an attorney has been classified as indirect contempt, since the court could not be aware—by observation or knowledge—of the facts at the time the attorney was absent from court. In these cases, a rule to show cause why the attorney should not be held in contempt should issue, and the matter should be set for hearing. The

40. 641 F.2d 1311 (1981).
41. *Id.*
42. *See* Maggio v. Zeitz, 333 U.S. 56, 69 (1948).
43. United States v. Rylander, 460 U.S. 752, 757 (1983).
44. McPhaul v. United States, 364 U.S. 372 (1960).

accused attorney would have the right to counsel, and the right to call witnesses.[45]

Because direct contempts happen in the presence of the court, they may be punished summarily. After clarification of words spoken, and after a warning, the judge may simply find the offender guilty of contempt of court.

Because indirect contempt occurs outside the vision of the court, a hearing is required to determine the facts. For the hearing to be fair, there must be a charging document—a rule to show cause—to inform the offender of the nature of the accusation. Due process further requires that the offender have an opportunity to prepare a defense, a chance to testify, and a chance to call witnesses on his or her behalf. Due process also includes the right to counsel.

If an offender is charged with a "serious contempt" of a criminal nature, one where the penalty actually imposed exceeds that of a "petty offense" (i.e., six months in jail), then the offender is entitled to a jury trial.[46] Civil contempts, which are purely coercive in nature, do not require jury trials.

For example, in *People v. Edwards*,[47] a judge held a defense attorney in contempt for failing to arrive in court on time without communicating with the court. About that the court said:

> I am not holding him in contempt for being late. I am holding him in contempt because he held the orderly process of justice up by his failure to call, to have the simple courtesy to make a telephone call and say, 'I'm late.'

On appeal the defendant argued that he was convicted of indirect contempt of court and therefore entitled to his due process rights of written notice of the charges, a fair and impartial hearing with the opportunity to cross-examine witnesses, and representation by counsel.

The court found that the defendant was correct, saying direct contempt is committed in the presence of the judge or within an integral part of the court. Indirect contempt, however, occurs in whole or in essential part outside the presence of the court and depends upon evidence of some kind for its proof. Because the judge must depend upon extrinsic evidence to find the defendant guilty of indirect contempt of court, due process requires that the defendant be advised of the charges, be accorded a fair hearing, and be permitted representation of counsel.

---

45. *See* People v. McNeil, 356 N.E.2d 1073 (Ill. 1976).
46. Bloom v. Illinois, 391 U.S. 194 (1968).
47. 387 N.E.2d 969 (Ill. 1979).

Conclusion

At issue is not only the efficient and dignified administration of justice, but also the fair administration of justice. The judge should stand as a model of decorum, representing the impersonal authority of the law. The behavior of the judge, even when faced with aggravating factors, should set a mood of justice. Restraint of the contempt powers is evidence of the vast powers of the courts.

IV

The Profession of Judging

18

ETHICS FOR JUDGES

The public generally has a concept of what a judge should be. Though the public may view judges and their conduct apart from justice itself, the two are usually so bound together that the judge whose conduct is disapproved reduces public confidence that justice will be done.

One reason for formal ethical guidelines for judges is well stated in the foreword to an ethics symposium:

> What happened to cause several judges—some in high places—recently to be reprimanded for their unofficial involvements? Few would suggest that in each of these controversies, the individual judge had knowingly refused to observe clear ethical prohibitions. A few judges had engaged in activities which would be deemed unacceptable in any period. But of greater concern are those who were subjected to public criticism when their most readily identifiable failing was a lack of perception of the extent to which a shift in public sentiment had rendered unacceptable activities which formerly were presumed to be proper. While judges should perhaps be held to a level of sensitivity which perceives such a change in public sentiment, they can reasonably demand that the prevailing formal statements of ethics provide guidance for their efforts to structure their private lives.[1]

The ABA Canons of Judicial Ethics were first adopted in 1924. Despite earlier efforts, they were adopted only after a crisis:

> Despite the warm reception accorded the Canons of Professional Ethics after their adoption in 1908, resolutions presented at the ABA's 1909 and 1917 conventions calling for the appointment of a committee to draft a set of Judicial Canons were quickly forgotten. Many felt such canons were unnecessary; that the real issue was judicial competency rather than honesty. Others believed it was not the proper role of the Bar to impose standards on the judiciary, feeling that such canons would more appropriately be developed within the judiciary.

---

1. *Foreword, Judicial Ethics: A Symposium,* 35 Law and Contemporary Problems 1 (1970).

> It is likely that matters would have rested in this state of inertia for many more years had it not been for the public admission of a certain Federal District Court Judge that he was supplementing his $7,500 federal salary with $42,500 a year for legal services rendered as national commissioner of the baseball associations. Powerless to bring sanctions against him under the Professional Ethics Canons, delegates attending the 1921 ABA Convention could only vote a resolution of censure. Though this was done, it was quickly seen that dealing with each case on such an individual basis was inefficient and ineffective, as well as inequitable. An official expression of the Bar's expectations of proper judicial conduct was needed to provide fair warning against future violations of ethical standards.[2]

How do we create an effective standard for judges? Is it sufficient to simply write a standard that reflects current practice? If instead of what *is*, we talk about what *ought* to be, how do we define it? Should the standard reflect the highest expectation or a high but reasonable standard? The standards should be high enough to do four things:

1. Guide the judge to acceptable behavior.
2. Reflect and at the same time help create general public expectation.
3. Establish the judge's position in the community as a fiduciary relationship.
4. Create a standard that will aid the electorate or appointing authority to screen candidates for judicial positions.

From a pragmatic point of view, an equally important reason for having and observing the Code of Judicial Conduct is the increasing use of formal sanctions to punish aberrant behavior. The code, as adopted in each state, establishes standards, violations of which are punishable. Judges should be guided not only by their conscience but also by the code as adopted in their own jurisdictions.

Code of Judicial Conduct

The basic standard in judicial ethics is the ABA Code of Judicial Conduct.[3] Adopted by the ABA in August 1972, it was the work of a special committee of the ABA headed by retired Chief Justice Roger J. Traynor of the Supreme Court of California. The members drafted a code to establish standards that could be adopted by and applied to federal and state judges. The ABA Code of Judicial Conduct is a model to be adapted and adopted by such jurisdictions as desire to accept it.

2. Report No. 8, American Judicature Society 1969, *as quoted in Symposium: Non-Judicial Activities of Judges,* 51 CHICAGO BAR RECORDS 64 (1969).

3. *See* American Bar Association Code of Judicial Conduct, in appendix A.

To create a standard acceptable as a model requires generalization. Even generalized standards were not acceptable in some states because of circumstances unique to those jurisdictions.

From some points of view, the American Bar Association requirements will appear to be too high. In part, they may be lower than the judges in some areas of the country want to observe. They are intended as mandatory minimum standards, not maximum requirements.

Because of the Code's perceived imperfections, the American Bar Association is again being asked to take another look at it and to possibly revise it. If changes are made, they will be at least several years in gestation. Continual scrutiny is required because the formal standards should represent guidance for the present and the future, not merely reflect the past.

The current Code of Judicial Conduct consists of seven canons. Canon 1 says that judges should uphold the integrity and the independence of the judiciary. The wording of this canon is broad and general, but it affects the interpretation of each of canons 3 through 7. Canon 2 states that judges should avoid impropriety and the appearance of impropriety in all of their activities. This canon, even more specifically than canon 1, affects the interpretation of canons 3 through 7 which are far more specific.

Under canon 3, judges are to perform the duties of their offices impartially and diligently. The canon is divided into two parts. The first deals with adjudicative responsibilities and second with administrative duties. This canon exemplifies the need for a judge to examine the code or those portions of it which have been adopted in the judge's state. Many states have modified the original wording. Cases that have been decided based upon this canon deal with the practice of law, judicial education, courtroom misconduct, ex parte communication, the time by which decisions should be reached, public comment, qualification and disqualification to sit in a particular case, and remittal of disqualification.[4]

Canon 4 provides that judges may engage in activities to improve the law, the legal system, and the administration of justice. They may speak, write, lecture, teach, and participate in other activities concerning the law, the legal system, and the administration of justice. There are limitations upon appearances at public hearings before executive or legislative bodies. Judges may serve as members, officers, or directors of organizations or governmental agencies devoted to the improvement of the law, the legal system, or the administration of justice; but they may

4. *See* Fretz, Wicker, & Peeples, Ethics for Judges (1982). This NJC textbook contains annotations to each canon.

not personally participate in fund-raising activities for such organizations.

Canon 5 regulates the extrajudicial activities of judges in order to minimize the risk of conflict with their judicial duties. A judge may participate in avocational activities that do not detract from the dignity of office or interfere with the performance of judicial duties.

Suppose that a judge has been told by his or her physician that, to relieve tension, he or she ought to take up painting. Suppose our tense judge becomes expert at painting the human figure. Certainly, when it is a private matter with the paintings by the judge hanging only in the judge's home, there are no problems.

Now suppose, however, that the judge is "discovered" by a dealer who would like to show the judge's paintings in a gallery. So long as all the painting is done without interference with the performance of judicial duties, we are left only with the question as to whether it is in keeping with the dignity of the judicial office. If the paintings are as good as the dealer believes them to be, the gallery showing is not likely to subject the judge to discipline, even if the paintings are of nudes.

Now let us take our example one step further. Suppose that an attorney, recognizing the artistic value of the judge's paintings, starts buying them. While this does not detract from the dignity of the judicial office, it leads us back to canon 2, which talks about impropriety and the appearance of impropriety. Assuming that the art collector attorney is at least on some occasions in the courtroom of the artistic judge, someone on the other side of a case is likely to imagine that the art-collecting attorney has special influence over the judge. There is sufficient evidence to wonder if that is true. Thus, discipline could be imposed, or at the very least, the agency investigating the propriety of conduct could perform an investigation to the embarrassment of our artistic judge.

Canon 5b deals with civic and charitable activities.[5] It does not prevent a judge from participating in such activities unless the organization will be engaged in proceedings that would ordinarily come before the judge or will be regularly engaged in adversary proceedings in any court. Furthermore, the judge should not solicit funds for such an organization or use or permit the prestige of the office to be used for that purpose.

Again there are shades of gray. A bad example will show why the provision exists: Suppose a judge agrees to serve as a chairman of the building fund for a new hospital. For the effort to be successful, requests must be made for sizable amounts of money. Inevitably, the judge will make such requests of people over whom the judge has considerable

5. Lubet, *Participation by Judges in Civic and Charitable Activities: What Are the Limits?* 69 JUDICATURE 68 (Aug.-Sept. 1985).

influence and leverage, that is, attorneys. It is easy to imagine the reaction of an attorney who is called into the judge's chambers to be told that the attorney's pledge was considered by the judge to be about one-third of "what it should be." That is the kind of conduct which is expressly proscribed by canon 5b.

On the other hand, judges who for many years before election or appointment worked on finance campaigns for their churches are not likely to be disciplined for continuance of that conduct even though, under the wording of the canon, a judge could be so disciplined. Canon 5c deals with financial activities. Judges should refrain from financial and business dealings that tend to reflect adversely on their impartiality, interfere with the proper performance of their judicial duties, exploit their judicial positions, or involve them in frequent transactions with lawyers or persons likely to come before the court on which they serve. Subject to that basic statement a judge may hold and manage investments including real estate, but should not serve as an officer, director, manager, adviser, or employee of any business.

An alternative section 5c(2) is slightly more liberal and will allow the judge to engage in the operation of a business. This was intended to be adopted by states that do not pay their judges well. Twelve states adopted the less restrictive alternative canon 5c(2), but where the less restrictive section was adopted, usually there was added a prohibition against being involved in a business affected with the public interest. Even though an investment might otherwise be proper, if it would create a sizable number of cases in which the judge would be disqualified, the judge should dispose of the interest.

Canon 5c(4) describes certain conditions under which a judge or member of the judge's family may receive a gift. In states in which that portion of canon 5 was not adopted, a judge should be very careful to look at statutes. The reason many states did not adopt canon 5c(4) was that they have statutes regulating gifts to judges.

This subsection raises the interesting point of the judge being required to know about the business interests and investments of family members.

Judges have their own provision against insider trading. Canon 5c(7) says that information acquired by a judge in a judicial capacity should not be used or disclosed by the judge in financial dealings or for any other purposes not related to his or her judicial duty.

Canon 6 requires regular reports of compensation received for quasi-judicial and extrajudicial activities. Again, in those states which have not adopted this canon, the judge should check carefully to make sure that the matter is not regulated by statute. In many places it is.

Canon 7 deals with political activity. Canon 7a addresses political conduct in general, and canon 7b covers campaign conduct. The pattern of adoption, modification, or lack of adoption of this canon makes the country look like a checkerboard. Twelve have omitted canon 7a(2); 13 other states altered it. In some states a person must engage in intensive political activity to be elected a judge. To people in those states, proscription of political activity is tantamount to removal from office. Annotations under this section cover resignation to run for other office, the position of the judge on critical issues, and improper political conduct.

Obtaining Advice on Ethical Questions

When a judge has a question concerning a matter of ethics, he or she may see if an opinion has been rendered on the point. If no opinion has been rendered, the judge may request an opinion.

An opinion on a relevant matter may already have been rendered by a committee at the state level. Some states have committees or commissions formed by the supreme court. Others have committees of the judges or bar association. Such opinions may have been published. The most valuable opinion is that rendered within the judge's own state.

If that is not available, there are other resources. ABA opinions are contained in two volumes with supplements:

1. Opinions of the Committee on Professional Ethics are published by the American Bar Foundation in collaboration with the American Bar Association in a 1967 edition and supplements.
2. Informal Opinions, Committee on Professional Ethics, are published in a loose-leaf binder containing Informal Opinions rendered since June 1968. Such Informal Opinions are issued quarterly.

Opinions rendered by the Committee on Professional Ethics of the Association of the Bar of the City of New York and the New York County Lawyers Association are published by Columbia University Press in New York City. Annotations to the Code of Judicial Conduct for federal judges may also contain relevant information. The Committee on Ethics and Professional Responsibility of the National Conference of State Trial Judges, Judicial Administration Division, would reply to an inquiry by a judge of a trial court of general jurisdiction. The address is American Bar Association, 750 North Lake Shore Drive, Chicago, Illinois 60611.

If no opinion has been rendered, or if the judge feels a new look at the question is required, the judge may request an opinion of the appropriate ethics committee. An inquiry to the judges' association or the state bar will give the judge the necessary information as to the appropriate committee and the procedure for requesting an opinion. Or the judge may request an opinion of the Standing Committee on Ethics and Professional Responsibility of the American Bar Association. The address is Standing Committee on Ethics and Professional Responsibility,

American Bar Association, 750 North Lake Shore Drive, Chicago, Illinois 60611. The person requesting the opinion must be a member of the ABA. If not, the request for such an opinion can only be made by the state or local bar association. Note also the Jurisdiction and Rules of Procedure of the Standing Committee. See Appendix C.

The problem with formal requests for opinions is that the reply is usually long-delayed. The Committee must carefully consider the point, vote and write the opinion. A faster method is a telephone call to the chairperson of the Committee. A quick opinion will usually be given, but will not be as authoritative as a written formal or informal opinion.

> It is . . . a grave mistake to suppose that judges exercise their judicial power in a distasteful and arbitrary manner merely because they hold [office] for life or during good behavior. An arbitrary or disagreeable course of action by a judge arises principally from the fact that he is subject to no authority which can receive complaints against him and act upon those complaints by way of private or public criticism and correction of the judge. The best protection against arbitrary and disagreeable actions by judges is a duly constituted body of fellow judges who hold a position of superior power and authority and to whom complaints as to the conduct of judges may be brought and who may investigate those complaints and exercise a corrective influence.[6]

To the extent that state judges were ever "subject to no authority which can receive complaints against him and act upon those complaints," the situation has certainly changed. Fifty jurisdictions now have some mechanism for inquiring into judicial conduct.[7]

By what authority? The ABA Code of Judicial Conduct does not contain provision for sanctions. The code is an American Bar Association document and the Association would have no power to impose sanctions. The code, as adopted by the state, does not contain such authority either. The power is usually granted by a constitutional provision of which the following is illustrative:

> On recommendation of the Commission on Judicial Performance the Supreme Court may (1) retire a judge for disability that seriously interferes with the performance of the judge's duties and is or is likely to become permanent, and (2) censure or remove a judge for action . . . that constitutes wilful misconduct in office, persistent failure or inability to perform the judge's duties, habitual intemperance in the use of intoxicants or drugs, or conduct prejudicial to the administration of justice that brings the judicial office into disrepute.[8]

6. Kales, *Methods of Selecting and Retiring Judges in a Metropolitan District, Reform in Administration of Justice*, 52 ANNALS OF THE AMERICAN ACADEMY OF POLITICAL AND SOCIAL SCIENCE 1-12 (1914).

7. I. TESITOR, JUDICIAL CONDUCT ORGANIZATIONS (1978).

8. CAL. CONST. art. VI, § 18(c).

What do such commissions do? Usually they receive and consider complaints. As the accompanying table indicates, most complaints do not merit contact with the judge. Those that do merit communication frequently result in voluntary retirement or resignation. While there may be private censure, only a few complaints result in public censure or removal from office.

CASES COMING BEFORE THE CALIFORNIA COMMISSION ON JUDICIAL PERFORMANCE[9]

Five Year Summary—1983-1987

Year	Complaints Filed	Inquiries (Some kind of Investigation)	Judges Contacted	Preliminary Investigations	Cautionary/ Educational Letters	Admonish-ments	Resignations or Retirements White Under Investigation	Public Discipline
1983	351	63	56	21	*	6	3	1 censure 1 severe censure 1 removal
1984	388	62	64	17	23	3	1	1 censure
1985	317	54	47	11	20	6	2	1 censure
1986	476	113	78	22	23	3	1	1 censure
1987	547	120	75	20	32	6	5	1 censure 1 severe censure 1 removal

January 1988

*Figures not available

Reprinted with permission.

Those cases that threaten removal frequently create a great deal of publicity.[10] From the standpoint of the judge, it is a traumatic experience.

What are the legal rights of a judge called before a disciplinary commission? Disciplinary proceedings are neither civil nor criminal. Their aim is to maintain the honor and dignity of the judiciary and the proper administration of justice.[11] A judge may be removed by exercise of the supreme court's jurisdiction on commission recommendations.[12] Notice to a judge under preliminary investigation as to the nature of the com-

9. 1987 Ann. Rept., California Comm. Jud. Performance. Reprinted with permission.

10. Cameron, *The California Supreme Court Hearings—A Tragedy that Should and Could Have Been Avoided,* 8 Hastings Const. L. Rev. 11 (1980).

11. *In re* Cieminski, 270 N.W.2d 321 (N.D. 1978); *In re* Diener, 304 A.2d 587 (Md. 1973); *In re* Gillard, 271 N.W.2d 785 (Minn. 1978).

12. Small v. Guste, 383 So. 2d 1011 (La. 1980).

plaints against him or her is not compelled as a matter of due process.[13] However, the better policy is to advise the judge so that he or she can be given the opportunity to refute the allegations before formal charges are filed.[14] The commentary to standard 4.5 of the Standards Relating to Judicial Discipline and Disability Retirement[15] states in part that:

> As a matter of fact, in a great majority of the cases this notice should be given.
>
> Under standard 4.16, the commission must notify the judge after a finding of sufficient cause to proceed.

Procedural due process requires that all proceedings be conducted in a manner consistent with essential fairness.[16] In a proceeding before a Judicial Standards Commission, fundamental fairness entitles the judge to a hearing that meets the basic requirements of due process.[17]

A judge is entitled to counsel in disciplinary proceedings.[18] Further, the judge has the right to call witnesses and cross-examine adverse ones.[19] However, the judge is not entitled to be furnished with the name of the complainant if that person doesn't testify.[20]

The requirements of due process do not include pretrial discovery.[21] The determination of whether a discovery order shall issue is within the sound discretion of the judiciary commission.[22]

Due process contemplates notice that an act is a removable offense at the time it is committed. Innocent acts of today should not be declared improper and subject a judicial officer to removal tomorrow.[23] However, acts committed by a judge before the time he assumed his judicial office were considered by the Judicial Tenure Commission in Michigan in recommending his removal.[24]

The majority rule is that the standard to be applied by judicial qualification commissions or disciplinary commissions with respect to charges

---

13. *In re* Storie, 574 S.W.2d 369 (Mo. 1978); McCartney v. Commission on Judicial Qualifications, 526 P.2d 268 (Cal. 1974).

14. *In re* Storie, 574 S.W.2d 369.

15. American Bar Association Joint Committee on Professional Discipline of the Appellate Judges' Conference and the Standing Committee on Professional Discipline, Standards Relating to Judicial Discipline and Disability Retirement 23 (1978).

16. Babineux v. Judiciary Comm'n, 341 So. 2d 396 (La. 1976).

17. *In re* Nowell, 237 S.E.2d 246 (N.C. 1977).

18. *In re* Haggerty, 241 So. 2d (La. 1970); *In re* Del Rio, 256 N.W.2d 727 (Mich. 1977).

19. *In re* Haggerty, 241 So. 2d 469 (La. 1970).

20. *In re* Daniels, 340 So. 2d 301 (La. 1976); *In re* Wireman, 367 N.E.2d 1368 (Ind. 1977).

21. *In re* Wireman, 367 N.E.2d 1368 (Ind. 1977); *In re* Dupont, 322 So. 2d 180 (La. 1975); *In re* Del Rio, 256 N.W.2d, 727 (Mich. 1977).

22. *In re* Mikesell, 243 N.W.2d 86 (Mich. 1976).

23. *In re* Inquiry Concerning a Judge, J.Q.C., 357 So. 2d 172 (Fla. 1978).

24. *In re* Ryman, 232 N.W.2d 178 (Mich. 1975).

of misconduct against a judge is that of "clear and convincing evidence."[25] A minority of states require the burden of proof to be by a "preponderance of the evidence."[26] At least one state has adopted the proof "beyond a reasonable doubt" doctrine.[27]

Due process does not require that a judge be entitled to a jury trial before a disciplinary commission.[28]

Standard 4.6 on Confidentiality of the Standards Relating to Judicial Discipline and Disability Retirement provides as follows:

> All proceedings should be confidential until there has been a determination of probable cause and formal charges have been filed.[29]

Nevertheless, many states are maintaining confidentiality until the matter is filed and docketed with the supreme court of the particular state. Due process does not require a disciplinary commission to hold a public hearing.[30]

An invaluable source of information is the Center for Judicial Conduct Organizations. It has collected more than 600 decisions in judicial discipline cases, almost one-third of which are unreported; has on file nearly 1,500 advisory opinions on 60 subjects related to judicial discipline and ethics, and maintains current copies of each state's code of judicial conduct and each commission's governing provisions. In addition, the center has acquired a collection of over 400 journal and law review articles; keeps copies of annual reports from state disciplinary commissions; and gathers newspaper articles on judicial discipline from all over the country. Futhermore, it publishes a quarterly report entitled *Judicial Conduct Reporter*, which notes recent cases and developments.

The center's staff draws upon these resources to reply to requests for information, which may be directed to the Center for Judicial Conduct Organizations, (312) 558-6900.

---

25. *In re* Cieminski, 270 N.W.2d 321 (N.D. 1978); *In re* Heuermann, 240 N.W.2d 603 (S.D. 1976); McCartney v. Commission on Judicial Qualifications, 526 P.2d 268 (Cal. 1974).

26. *In re* Bonin, 378 N.E.2d 669 (Mass. 1978); *In re* Filipowicz, 388 N.Y.S.2d 920 (N.Y. App. Div. 1976); State *ex rel.* Oklahoma Bar Ass'n v. James, 463 P.2d 972 (Okla. 1969).

27. *In re* Hardt, 369 A.2d 5 (N.J. 1977).

28. *In re* Rome, 542 P.2d 676 (Kan. 1975); Schoolfield v. Tennessee Bar Ass'n, 353 S.W.2d 401 (Tenn. 1961).

29. American Bar Association, *supra* note 15, Standard 4.6.

30. Keiser v. Bell, 332 F. Supp. 608 (E.D. Pa. 1971). *But see* the dissent in *In re* Crutchfield, 223 S.E.2d 822 (N.C. 1975).

An excellent article, "Disciplining Judges for Nonofficial Conduct: A Survey and Critique of the Law,"[31] contains a comprehensive review of judicial misconduct cases.

It is to be hoped that a judge will never be involved in a disciplinary proceeding. However, it does occur, and when it does, the judge should be knowledgeable of the procedures and rights in his or her state.

31. Martineau, *Disciplining Judges for Nonofficial Conduct: A Survey and Critique of the Law,* 10 U. Baltimore L. Rev. 225-45 (1981).

19

THE JUDGE AND THE COMMUNITIES

A glance in the mirror of public opinion cannot be faulted as a mere indulgence of professional vanity, for the judiciary as an institution cannot function without the support of the people . . . And this public support, in turn, depends upon the people's confidence in the fairness and reasonableness of their judiciary.[1]

Public relations is said to be 90 percent product and 10 percent advertising. For the most part, good judges will receive good publicity. However, the headlines are made by events that are bad or that appeal to the public interest.

Fortunately, judges can do many things to combat ignorance and misunderstanding about the courts, judges, and the judicial system. Judges need only recognize the valuable opportunities and use them.

Each day, the judge has an opportunity to influence the thinking of several "communities of interest." In any given geographical community, there are many such communities. These communities often overlap. They may be within the courthouse and outside the courthouse.

In the Courthouse

Relationships Among Judges

The relationships between judges and the several communities must start with the relationships among judges themselves. Interpersonal relationships will differ depending on the number of judges on the court, their individual personalities, and the differences in their judicial ability. Judges on the same court must work as a team. Disagreements and

---

1. Kaufman, *The Courts and the Public: A Problem in Communication*, 54 ABA Journal 1192 (1968). Reprinted with permission.

personality conflicts are bound to arise among judges, who must be among the most independent of professionals. However, each court can devise discreet escape valves for resolving such disputes.

Judges' meetings, written communications, and the conscious awareness of the need to avoid cliques are important tools in establishing and maintaining the essential teamwork.

Meetings are perhaps the most important form of communication among judges. Meetings among all the judges of a very large court are nearly impossible. Such meetings are difficult enough in smaller courts. Certainly, where the size of the court is such that meetings can be held, even with some effort, they should be held because of their benefit. Where meetings of all judges would be cumbersome and unproductive, committees representing groups of judges may be used successfully.

Written communications among judges may take the simple form of interoffice memoranda. Another method is a presiding judge's newsletter. It might cover the matters of welcomes to new judges, efforts to obtain adequate staff, proceedings of interest, and relations of the court with the executive and legislative bodies.

Judges in courts of limited and general jurisdiction must nurture a relationship. For example, it would not be practical for the general trial court to attempt to restrict publicity in an appropriate criminal case if the lower court did not do so in its handling of the case. Widespread publicity would already have been given to matters that the general trial court would have restricted.

It is helpful to the judicial image if one court does not belittle the judges of another court. The relationship between state and federal judges is often cool and in need of improvement. Federal-state councils have been encouraged to create understanding, but most of them have seldom met after appointment and have done little, if anything.

Courts of general and limited jurisdiction can arrange meetings to discuss common problems. Such meetings may include only the respective presiding judges, or they may include only the court administrators of the respective courts, where such offices exist. Where numbers are smaller, meetings involving all judges should be encouraged. Such meetings can be informal or formal but may result in complementary written policies in each court.

Whatever technique is used, the goal is to prevent the clashing of gears in the judicial machinery.

Relationships with Court Personnel

No segment of the public gets a better look at the bench than do those who are in court each time the judge is there. Reporters, clerks, bailiffs—

by whatever name they may be called in a particular jurisdiction—see the court from the inside. Also closer than most people are probation officers, law clerks, secretaries, and commissioners.

Since the judge is represented in substantial part in his or her dealings with litigants, jurors, and courthouse visitors by the clerk, the bailiff, and court reporter, he or she is concerned with their actions, words, and courtesy.[2]

The bailiff deals with jurors and most other people in touch with the court. A bailiff who is gruff, grumpy, arrogant or hostile creates a bad impression of the court. If a bailiff lacks knowledge of the job or interpersonal skills, people who deal with the bailiff receive a poor impression of the court. If the judge's secretary has an offensive telephone voice or manners, the secretary creates a bad impression of the court. Other court personnel in varying degrees have a similar effect.

Judges should know what kind of impression these people give of their court. Judges can watch the bailiff deal with jurors, or they can talk to jurors about their impression of the bailiff and the court. They can listen to how the telephone is answered. If the impression is not the best, judges should consider what they can do about it.[3]

The court can create a policy manual that defines for court personnel what is expected of them. Such a manual can remind them of the importance of the impression they give. Perhaps the best of such manuals are created by interested employees themselves.[4]

A judge should be familiar with the policy manual and discuss it directly with the people involved so that they know of the judge's interest as well as the policy of the court. The judge can also pass directly to employees appropriate reading materials on the subject. Such an article would be "Etiquette in Marshal's Work" from *The Marshal's Writ.*[5]

More important than mechanics or procedure is attitude. The attitudes of employees frequently reflect the attitude of the employer. Judges should not expect the bailiff to present one face if they present another. The judge sets the example.

---

2. *See generally*, ABA Standards Relating to Trial Courts as Amended, 2.40-2.46 and commentary (1987).

3. Regional and local phone companies, upon request, will provide telemarketing classes for sizable groups.

4. *Handbook for Bailiffs*, created and revised by bailiffs of the Superior Court, King County, Washington. Distributed, when available, through the Court Administrator, King County Courthouse, Seattle, WA 98104. *See also Etiquette in Marshal's Work*, The Marshal's Writ, as cited in note 5.

5. Official publication of the Marshals Association of California, P.O. Box 1668, San Diego, CA 92112.

Whether the judge uses personal example, individual conversations with court personnel, policy guides or manuals, the judge has a duty to communicate his or her attitudes and expectations and to attempt to influence court personnel so that their words and acts reflect the degree of dignity, of warmth, and of formality or informality the judge thinks is appropriate.

Relationships with Jurors

Jurors probably have a better opportunity to view the workings of the courts objectively than do other lay persons. Moves to reduce the number of jurors coming to court may be the trend, but the result of such a trend will be to take away a potent, understanding group within the community.

For jurors to be such a force in the community, they must leave the court with an understanding of what has happened and why. It is a part of the duty of the judge to make certain they have that understanding.

How many jurors are called and why? For how long a time? How are they selected? Why must they wait? What do they do while they wait?

A well thought-out program can make excellent use of waiting time. The jury commissioner or a judge can give the jurors the answers to these questions and others. He or she can tell the jurors why cases settle "on the courthouse steps" and what courts do to encourage earlier settlement and how much jurors do to persuade people to settle. The same material can be written and furnished to waiting jurors. The annual report of the court, a juror's handbook, or other material on the legal system may not only prevent boredom but educate as well.

During the course of a trial, there are many opportunities for the judge to explain language or procedure. Some admonitions are required; others are simply desirable. The judge has some clear duties concerning the jury.

When the jury has finished its deliberations, it is appropriate for the trial judge to thank the jurors. Rules frequently provide that such comments should not include praise or criticism of the verdict. Some courts not only thank the jurors verbally but also furnish certificates of appreciation. Other courts use an exit questionnaire to obtain the criticisms of jurors about their experience.

Whatever is done should be done with the goal of letting jurors know what they are doing, or would have done, and why it is important to the administration of justice. When they understand, their sentiments ripple into the community. When they don't understand, their criticism ripples in the same way.

Relationships with Litigants and Witnesses

The courtroom needs to be a place of quiet dignity. That dignity and quiet can be very threatening to people there for the first time. The physical setting gives the first impression. The conduct of the judge and the attorneys creates another part of the impression.

Judges create an impression by what they say. They also give an impression by facial expression, body motions, and tone of voice. One of the most difficult things for a judge to do is to sound and look as well as *be* impartial throughout the whole trial.

There are methods of setting people at ease. One judge does it with opening remarks as the trial commences. Another may do it simply by tone of voice. Even though the judge in some courts will know the first names of litigants or witnesses, he or she should carefully avoid using those first names. A friendly gesture or remark to a familiar witness may take on significance if such a gesture or remark is missing when another witness takes the stand.

What goes into the record is what goes to appellate court. What is seen in the courtroom and the tone of voice do not now go to the appellate court, but they make indelible impressions upon those who are present.

Relationships with Visitors

> *I know of no safe depository of the ultimate powers of the society but the people themselves, and if we think them not enlightened enough to exercise their control with a wholesome discretion, the remedy is not to take it from them but to inform their discretion by education.*
>
> —*Thomas Jefferson*

The court is a public place. Courtroom visitors are present for many different reasons. Some are present because of an interest in a particular proceeding. Others are present because of curiosity. Some are present because they like the "drama" of criminal proceedings. Among these are some veteran courtroom spectators. Students frequently come as classes to observe. Others—such as members of the League of Women Voters—come to study the courts.

Whether people come to learn or for entertainment, whether as friends or as critics of the court, the court can do many things to educate visitors. Some courts routinely distribute material to visitors. Such material can be a simple guide to the court building (distributed at an information desk or posted on a bulletin board with a notice that copies are available in the clerk's office), an annual report, a description of the state court system, material on trial procedure, a glossary of terms, sketches of a typical courtroom and the positions of the participants, or a combination of these items. Some judges invite the public to their chambers, where they will be available at specific times.

There are all kinds of court watchers.[6] They watch for recreation. They watch in order to study court problems with the intention of finding ways to help the courts do what they cannot do alone. They watch because they believe judges are acting improperly.

The following is about a group that watches primarily for recreation.

Courtroom 'Clubhouse' for Elderly

Reprinted by Permission of Associated Press
(Date unknown)

SANTA MONICA, Calif. (AP)—The courtroom's a clubhouse for about 100 dues-paying senior citizens here. They are the Court Watchers, and their ranks include an ex-attorney and a former Ziegfeld chorine.

Judges praise the Court Watchers as "great people," have invited them into their chambers and have selected members for county grand jury service.

Court Watchers was founded three years ago by Karl Oldberg, a 73-year-old retired banker from Evanston, Ill.

"Court's a place where we can use our minds, rather than allowing someone else to do our thinking for us," said Oldberg, who is also the club's president. "It sure beats Perry Mason."

Oldberg's view of criminal justice typifies the philosophy of many of his fellow watchers.

"The courts have gone too far in protecting criminals," he said in an interview. "You know what really gets to me? When someone is caught with heroin or morphine but gets off because the search and seizure wasn't done perfectly or because the police officer didn't have his tie on straight."

But they don't all root for the prosecution.

"I probably do side with the defense. After all, they've got everything stacked against them," said T.J. Van of Los Angeles, a former psychology instructor at Wayne State University in Michigan.

Court Watchers are "model spectators and model citizens," said Superior Court Judge Charles Woodmansee. He appointed Edwin Colwell, a Court Watchers member, to the county grand jury which indicted newspaper heiress Patricia Hearst and two Symbionese Liberation Army companions on charges of kidnaping, robbery and assault.

It sometimes works the other way.

Pauline "Queenie" Sheeran, 78, a former Ziegfeld hoofer, was a grand juror when she drew the attention of the formerly all-male organization in 1972. She joined and today nearly a third of the Watchers are women.

6. For a comprehensive article, *see* Stecich, *Keeping an Eye on the Courts,* 58 JUDICATURE 468 (1975).

> The Court Watchers' ranks also include a retired dentist, a fur manufacturer, a plumber and a general contractor. They pay dues of $1 a year.
>
> "We're all different," said Oldberg. "We're not like retired farmers who used to hang around courthouse steps and spit tobacco juice."

One organization that has a court study program is the League of Women Voters. Such groups can help judges see their problems by analyzing problems from the lay point of view.

One of the criticisms of some court watchers is that the judges are not all on the bench five days a week, trying cases five or more hours a day, and handling other matters from the bench before the trial begins. Such conclusions are reached by the critic's walking the corridors to see if the courtrooms are occupied. This kind of criticism needs to be answered by explaining the work judges do in chambers. Perhaps there is also a need for signs on courtroom doors stating that judges are in chambers (but only when they are there.)

Perhaps the most important visitors are schoolchildren. Most schools send, or would like to send, students to observe the court in action. Most courts feel this is highly desirable. But it creates special problems for the courts. How can such visits be scheduled so that there are not too many visitors at the same time? Or to be sure that something appropriate for watching (not an X-rated rape or child molesting case) is going on? Who schedules the visits and how?

One way of handling this is for the presiding judge to send a letter to the superintendent of the school districts, encouraging class visits to the courts. Such a letter can outline the court's general schedule, the fact that visits should be scheduled with the court clerk or the judge's secretary or the court information officer, and the problems that may be encountered on such visits. If a courthouse tour is provided, it might be helpful to state how long the tour takes.

Depending upon circumstances, such as the size of the community, the judge may want to speak to the class during recess. If the court is not in session, the judge may be able to spend more time with the students. One thing students seem to enjoy and that makes the visit meaningful is placing students in the position occupied by court personnel during a trial. If a trial is in session, this may take too much time, but at recess counsel could be introduced. The court might also want to indicate what the students have not seen or will not see during the trial. There are many other activities the judge may feel are appropriate.

Since some trial time is lost during such visits because recesses tend to be longer than usual, some courts have assigned a deputy clerk, a bailiff, or someone else in the courthouse to the duty of escorting classes to the court and throughout the courthouse.

Another proven way of accomplishing this is through courthouse tours led by volunteers. In Los Angeles and other California counties, this is a project of Lawyers' Wives—they have a course of instruction for tour guides and a manual used by the guides.[7] Such a program saves the time of courthouse personnel and allows greater time for visits or an increased number of visitors.

Lifetime attitudes may be created by what students learn and the impressions they receive—whether good or bad. The result of such visits in some courts is that the students become so interested that they desire to participate in mock trials. It adds to the effect, then, if the judge can furnish some mock trial material prepared by the judge, the bar, or others. Such materials have frequently been prepared for Law Day exercises.

Whether court watchers come for education or recreation, to help or to find ammunition for their criticism of judges, all should receive the same information and the same courtesy. Sometimes those who would criticize come to a better understanding of why some things happen, and part of their criticism stops. No judge expects to please all of the people all of the time. Even where some critics remain unconvinced and openly critical, more is to be gained by dignity and courtesy in the courtroom than by any other treatment. Also, such groups can provide a reservoir of volunteers for court projects.

Ceremonies

Ceremonies of all kinds—from the opening of the court each day to memorial services for deceased judges and attorneys—offer an opportunity for the court to display its dignity, to show the history and the relevance of the court, and to bring the people into their courts.

Whether historical in your state or not, the opening of court should be dignified and cause people to pause for a moment.

Law Day needs more attention from judges and attorneys. The key is long-range planning. Where else is there so much planning done by others for us and the opportunity to get so many people involved?

In some areas, naturalization is handled only in federal court, but if it happens in a state court, it can be made a beautiful and meaningful ceremony for people who have worked hard to get citizenship, for school visitors, and for the court.

A retired judge dies. What should the court do? U.S. District Courts hold memorial services; they are reported in the reporter system, so a model already exists. The judge can offer the courtroom for a ceremony

7. Copies of these are on reserve at the National Judicial College Library.

that is meaningful to the judge's family, and allow public expression of appreciation for the judge's work.

A robing ceremony for a new judge is a high point in the life of the new judge and family. It is also important to the bar. It too affords a great opportunity to invite the public into court.

A swearing-in of new attorneys is another occasion in which the people can be in court on other than the sober business of litigation.

When planning any kind of ceremony, the judge will need to think about the following issues:

- Facilities—What facilities are required? How many people are likely to attend? Will newspaper reporters, TV crews, etc., require space? If so, how much?
- Participants—What people need to be involved? The judge should not overlook involving the bar association, relatives and friends of the person or persons to be honored, dignitaries from the community, and judges of other courts. It can be embarrassing to come to the time of the ceremony and recognize that a certain person or group of persons should have been invited and were not.
- Form of ceremony—Some ceremonies are easily planned. Naturalization ceremonies, for example, are outlined in a book published by the Immigration and Naturalization Service. A judge can feel free to innovate, but at least has a point of beginning. For some other ceremonies, unless the judge is familiar with those put on in other places, he or she may have some doubt. Samples of some differing kinds of ceremonies are contained in the how-to book. Is an invocation appropriate?
- Printed program—If a program will be prepared for the ceremony, it can be mimeographed, printed, or simply typed and photocopied. If it is to be printed, the printer will require time to set the type, send out the proof for review, etc. When the printer does not have enough time, the result may be very poor.

If the ceremonies are to live up to the name, they require the kind of planning and execution that will make them worthy of the court. Planning can be done by judges or others, but the judges are ultimately responsible for seeing that the planning and execution are of high quality.

Reports

An oral report may have great value to the audience that receives it, but unless it is preserved for others, its effect will be limited.[8] When

8. Sample copies of reports are available in the National Judicial College Library. The college needs four copies of your reports. Two copies go into the library files, viewed by hundreds of judges each year. Two copies will be used to form collections of reports, which

making a speech about the court (or anything else) the judge can take along a written report that can be reviewed and passed on to others. The content of a report will vary depending upon its form—oral or written. If there is a written form, an oral report could be adapted from it.

A report can contain what the judge wants it to contain. The person who writes it or authorizes it will determine what should be in it. How many cases were filed? What type? Is this a greater number than before? What is the best way to show this? How many juries were sworn last year? What is the method used in selecting prospective jurors? How expensive are the courts? What improvements in administration of the courts have been made? Are they working? What do the courts need?

Content will depend upon the intended use of the report. If it is combined with a juror's handbook, the judge may want to show a diagram that will aid people to get where they need to go. If it is to be given to courthouse visitors, the diagram would be useful. If it is a report of court business only, the diagram might not be appropriate.

Graphs, charts, and visual presentations of every kind add meaning to the report. People employed by the jurisdiction to do graphic artwork or school system people would be happy to suggest which graph is best to depict the desired information.

A report can be printed on slick paper at considerable expense. It can also be mimeographed for the cost of the stencils, the time of the typist, the one who runs the mimeograph machine, and the one who assembles and staples it. That can be very inexpensive. A printer can tell how the court can get more for its money by using different kinds of paper, etc. But if a typist and mimeograph machine are available, a written report will cost almost nothing.[9]

A written report could be placed in the hands of every person in the jurisdiction. That would be expensive and probably no more meaningful than a lot of "junk mail." But it could be presented to everyone who comes in contact with the courts—county or district employees, local legislators, attorneys, litigants, jurors. It could be distributed whenever a judge makes a speech. With such a direct tie to the court, the report will be more meaningful.

Outside the Courthouse

Relationships with Schools

We have discussed student visits to the courtroom. What about judges in the classroom? A judge who can schedule a visit will be welcomed in

---

are loaned to jurisdictions that need a starting point and would like to see how someone else does it. Mail your reports or request for a loan collection of a half-dozen reports to the The Librarian, National Judicial College, University of Nevada, Reno, NV 89557.

9. Less than five cents per report.

civics and other classes. The judge can explain court procedures, cover a prearranged subject, take other court personnel along, and answer questions. Answering questions may be more important than anything else.

Some schools have videotape equipment and can preserve a single visit for later use in other classes, with the judge's permission.

From the Chief Justice to the trial judge, there have been complaints about the ability of counsel as courtroom advocates. Judges may ethically teach at law schools if such teaching does not interfere with judicial duties. They may serve on advisory boards and the like. Surely such a relationship is a great opportunity to emphasize the need for proper trial and appellate advocacy. A single talk can have a similar effect. Talks about the court and its problems also could be beneficial to both sides.

Another possible benefit from a relationship with law schools pertains to law clerks. Many judges are still not allowed law clerks. One successful way to obtain a law clerk when there is no such position is to have the authority (sheriff, etc.) who employs the bailiff employ a part-time law student. Such students usually welcome the opportunity to clerk for a judge.

Relationships with Attorneys on the Bench

Subject to ethical restrictions, there is no reason why the judge should not maintain a cordial relationship with members of the bar. The problem of their relationship varies with circumstances. In some states (e.g., California), when a judge goes on the bench, he or she is no longer a member of the state bar association. He or she pays no dues and is rarely asked to serve on a bar committee. In many other states, judges remain members of the state bar and are appointed to committees in proportion to their numbers. Usually they cannot serve as officers, and sometimes they have no voting rights.

Where judges remain members of the bar and participate with attorneys in professional association activities, the relationship may be closer than in states where judges are not members of the bar. This has advantages and disadvantages. The closer relationship should facilitate cooperation on mutual problems. On the other hand, the appearance of propriety may be more difficult, and there can be conflicts of interest.

Relationships with Bar Associations

The bench and the bar, working together, can cause the needs of the justice system to be met. If they can reach agreement on required reforms, they can educate the people and the legislative bodies to the need for those reforms.

The judiciary frequently finds it difficult to answer criticism. Bar associations must and do defend judges against unjust criticism.

If the state or local bar association recognizes its responsibility, there is little problem except recognition of what constitutes "unjust criticism." But what can judges do if the bar does not speak up?

The foundation for cooperation must be laid long before the need for it arises. In major metropolitan areas, there may be a frequent need for such help in dealing with unjust criticism, and a tradition and working relationship must be established. In a less urban area, instances of criticism may occur so seldom that the help will need to be solicited as occasions arise. The bar association should have a committee with this duty. It may be an ethics committee or a public relations committee or a bench-bar committee. Whatever it is called, it should be ready to work with the judiciary on these issues.

Chesterfield Smith, president of the American Bar Association during 1974-75, created a Task Force on Courts and the Public. Among other things, it was asked to devise methods of encouraging bar association activity in defense of federal and state judges, when appropriate. It created a brief manual called *Meeting Criticism of Bench and Courts.*

Bar association activity is sorely needed in this area. Judges can encourage it.

Sometimes such cooperation is best begun at the state bar level. The state bar working with the judges' association establishes guidelines, or a policy, or simply encourages the idea because of the duty imposed by the Code of Professional Responsibility.

When it comes to "reforms," the difficulty in using the combined weight of bench and bar is reaching agreement on the remedy required.

Perhaps judges should have a right to expect the help of the bar, but judges need to exhibit a cooperative attitude themselves, need to take steps to reduce unjust criticism, and need to work continuously on the bench-bar relationship.

Bar associations have conducted election plebiscites for many years. Presumably such a plebiscite is an attempt to show the public whether the bar does or does not have confidence in the candidates for judicial office. A different phenomenon is the judicial evaluation poll.[10] Many places have conducted such polls.

Such polls are said to be helpful in raising the quality of the judges. The bar says the duty to appraise the qualifications of judges is imposed by canon 8 of the ABA Code of Professional Responsibility.[11]

If the bar has a responsibility for such polls, it also has a responsibility to see that they are not abused or used for improper purposes. Some judicial evaluation polls are being taken by newspapers. Attorneys should consider the propriety of their involvement in such polls.

---

10. For sample programs concentrating on the eastern states and not covering recent developments, see C. PHILIP, HOW BAR ASSOCIATIONS EVALUATE SITTING JUDGES (1976).

11. AMERICAN BAR ASSOCIATION, CODE OF PROFESSIONAL RESPONSIBILTY, EC 8-6.

Among the questions raised by judicial evaluation procedures are these:

- Who is doing the evaluating? Bar or newspaper? If the bar, are the participants only attorneys knowledgeable about why the judge asked for an evaluation, or "everyone"?
- Why is the evaluation being made?
- Are steps being taken to see that the evaluation forms are completed by the attorneys, or, as happened in one newspaper poll, does the messenger simply ask, "How many attorneys in this firm?" and, in accordance with the reply, give that many ballots to a secretary?
- Has the evaluation form been drafted carefully? Does it ask the proper questions? Is it accompanied by adequate instructions?
- What use will be made of the results?

All of these are important questions. If Gallup or Harris sampled the wrong people, the results would be wrong. In an election, that would likely be obvious. It may not even be hinted at in a nonelection survey.

Relationships with Local Legislators

In some jurisdictions, courts are funded by the state. However, in many jurisdictions, there is a local legislative body that has taxing authority and control over courts' funds or control over agencies that work with the courts.

Judges have a duty to present to the legislative body the needs of the court. Judges should certainly make every effort to obtain all of the things that are necessary for the reasonable operation of the court. On the other hand, judges must recognize other demands made upon the available funds.

At times it is necessary to push to obtain even basic facilities. At other times it is relatively easy to secure what is necessary. When facilities are clearly inadequate, or when an expenditure is essential to the operation of the court, the legislative body can usually be persuaded to supply the necessary funds. If it is not so persuaded, however, the court may be able to mandate the improvements or material. Any judge or group of judges contemplating such an action should be aware of its abrasive nature.

Much more helpful would be the education of the legislative body to an appreciation of court needs. Personal communication, written reports and courtesy may accomplish a great deal more than a demand could.

Relationships with State Legislators

In most states, the money for a portion or in some cases all of judicial salaries is appropriated by the state legislature. In some states, other personnel are furnished only by the state legislature. Retirement systems are usually creatures of the state legislature.

A common difficulty in dealing with the legislature is a lack of communication. Legislators are not given the information which would enable them to act properly upon judicial requests. This is probably more true when the percentage of lawyers in the legislature is small. Where this is true the lack of understanding is enlarged because of the lack of understanding of court vocabulary.

Communication may be improved through personal acquaintance, communication with legislative committees, or several other methods. For example, in one area, the judges annually honor their legislators with a "no politics" party and dinner. This is done when the legislature is out of session. Another example is a series of dinners throughout the state honoring "outstanding legislators."[12]

Another avenue in creating a better relationship is to raise the standard of activities of judges. If your judicial association is engaged in educational activities or in activities other than concern for salaries and retirement benefits, it may well increase the self-respect of judges and the judicial image in the eyes of the legislature. There may be other activities in individual states that will likewise enhance administration of justice.

The Case for Adequate Monetary Support

For the legislature to act, even having a generally favorable opinion of the judiciary, the judiciary must have a proposal that appeals to the legislature with convincing force. The competition for money and other support is keen in every statehouse.

What makes the case for more adequate monetary support? One important point is the need to have the best possible judges and thus to obtain the best possible attorneys for appointment or election to the bench.

Judges are under many pressures, but among these is the pressure that comes from finances. Elective and appointive authorities have not required wealth as a condition of office. But low salaries discourage from office some persons who would make excellent judges. To attract the best persons to the bench, therefore, salaries should be commensurate with the money earned by attorneys who are of the quality to be considered for the bench.

Assuming that money earned in private practice may always be reaching higher plateaus and that judges will be somewhat behind, judges will be concerned about security for the days they may no longer be on the bench. Therefore, the case needs to be made for adequate retirement benefits.

12. This may now be forbidden by revised legislation regarding lobbying.

How all of this information should be presented may depend to a large extent upon local circumstances. If legislators are primarily lawyers, one kind of job must be done. If the legislature is composed primarily of farmers or businesspeople, an entirely different approach may be required. Also significant is the foundation of friends, a history of fair dealing with the legislature, and public support obtained either for this particular presentation or generally available from past efforts or conduct.

If the timing is right and the foundation has been laid, who makes the presentation? In most places, the judicial association has a legislative committee. The duties of this committee are to analyze the problem, educate the legislature (with assistance), and obtain the favorable action of the legislature. Sometime the judicial association must oppose a bill put in by some individual judge. While it would be nice to avoid this problem, that seems impossible.

Because of the way in which the legislatures of the several states are composed and the influence that comes from numbers and the extreme importance of unanimity, the judicial association should speak for as many judges as possible. A fragmented constituency weakens the voice of the association.

How shall the presentation be made? There is no one way. Louisiana judges have been effective in their relationship with their legislature. They are well organized and have a calling arrangement whereby the association may poll its membership and communicate with judges throughout the state. The presentation may be made by the legislative committee or by the officers of the association. At the other extreme, it can be made by individual judges in their home counties. Professionals may be of assistance.

Some judges still believe that the use of professionals is anathema to the judiciary. Such an attitude indicates a lack of information as to how a professional operates. A professional can be hired as a consultant, will remain in the background, and will outline the work judges must do. The public relations person's name need not be widely known or advertised.

Professionals have greater selling expertise. They are used to dealing with news media. They can guide judges in the preparation of written material.

Long-range preparation for requests may well pay great dividends. The hastily conceived plan, quickly presented, is much more likely to be defeated than passed. Timing and advance planning are therefore of the utmost importance.

Despite the best laid plans, the request of judges will sometimes be denied. The number of such occasions can be minimized by better relationships, an attractive presentation, and proper timing.

Relationships with Law Enforcement Officers

Some of today's harsh criticism of courts comes from law enforcement people. But that should not cause judges to make such officers appear to be in a different position than others who appear before the court. The danger in creating a special relationship is that it destroys the impression of objectivity and fairness, even though the judges believe they are fair.

A judge might, if time and circumstances permit it, speak and listen at law enforcement officers' meetings.[13] Among the things the judge could talk about are why judges sentence as they do, why juveniles and adults who commit crimes are back on the street before the arresting officer is, the legal effect of an appellate court case as a trial judge sees it, and some other things that appear to irritate police.

What about a letter of commendation? If the judge observes in one or a series of cases some outstanding police work on the part of an officer, and feels strongly enough about it to write a letter, may he or she do so? A private letter would probably not damage the appearance of objectivity. A letter that becomes public might give some attorney or defendant the impression, however erroneous, that the court was not objective.

There is reason to let those who come to court, police or others, understand what the court does and why, but the consequences of speaking out must be weighed against the good to be accomplished by it.

Public Appearances and Speeches

A judge has numerous opportunities to speak. Some judges are excellent speakers and much in demand. Others, though less skilled, are asked to speak because of their position in the community. Still others feel they are not speakers and refuse speaking opportunities.

Speeches represent an opportunity to tell the community—or at least a segment of it—what goes on in court and why, what the court needs in order to function efficiently, and to reply appropriately to criticism of the court or the judicial system. The Chief Justice of the United States has such opportunities. The chief justices of the states use them. Shouldn't any responsible judge use them?

Some judges find it easy to think of speech topics. For others it is difficult. Recognizing this, the State Bar of California and the Conference of California Judges united in preparation of a *Public Affairs Manual for the Bench and Bar of California.*[14] A portion of the 108 pages was devoted to speech topics suitable for judges. Law Day always provides

13. *See* J. WAMBAUGH, THE NEW CENTURIANS (1970), which describes police attitude toward judges.

14. Now out of print. Information may be obtained from the State Bar of California, 601 McAllister Street, San Francisco, CA 94102.

a topic, and the manuals for it available from the American Bar Center[15] provide nearly ready-made speeches. *Judicature* magazine, the *American Bar Association Journal*, and other materials received by most judges furnish articles that serve as ready source material for speeches.

The subject of sentencing needs community discussion. Judges are criticized for leniency by a public that knows little about it. For one idea for a speech on this subject, see "Changing Community Opinion on Sentencing" by Donald R. Fretz, 55 *Judicature* 249 (1972).

The condition of the calendar in the judge's court is another subject of interest to people who hear a great deal about delay.

Whatever the subject of the speech, the judge should view it as an opportunity to inform the public.

Answering Criticism

The question is, should all, some, or none of the criticism be answered? The answer depends on the object, source, and nature of the criticism.

Criticism is frequently caused by emotion and usually generates more emotion. A criticized judge may attempt a personal response, but there are dangers to the individual who attempts to do battle with a newspaper. Even if the judge is right, the judge may not win the fight and runs the danger of appearing to be "scrapping in the back alley" instead of maintaining the dignity of the court.

A better way is probably to let others answer the criticism of a particular judge. An example is contained in a column from the *New York Law Journal*.[16]

Appeals Court Attacks Story in Daily News

Article on Judges Termed 'Manifestly Unfair' by Appellate Division

The justices of the Appellate Division, First Department, joined yesterday in assailing the *Daily News* for what they said was a "manifestly unfair" article critical of three judges for their handling of narcotics cases.

On Monday, District Attorney Frank S. Hogan issued a lengthy statement in defense of the three judges, all of whom sit in Supreme Court,

---

15. American Bar Association, Law Day Planning Guide and Program Manual (1983).

16. New York Law Journal, June 23, 1972, at 1, col. 6. Reprinted with permission.

New York County. The three are Justices Harry B. Frank, Gerald P. Culkin and Xavier C. Riccobono.

The *Daily News* article was based on hearings by the State Legislative Committee on Crime and was published on June 15.

Paper Not Named

In their twenty-two-line statement yesterday, the Appellate Division justices did not mention the newspaper by name and issued it over the legend "Justices. Supreme Court. Appellate Division. First Department."

The statement noted that the Supreme Court justices are at a disadvantage in replying to published charges because a "judge is constrained by ethics and custom to the extent to which he can respond to criticism of his official conduct."

The statement continued that the Appellate Division justices "deplore the ex parte criticism" of the three judges. It acknowledged that wrongdoing by a judge "should be vigorously pursued" and that the Appellate Division was prepared to do so when it is warranted.

The justices noted that District Attorney Hogan had provided a "detailed analysis which belies the innuendos" in the article. Further, they said, continuance of such articles would "seriously and adversely" affect judicial determination of criminal cases.

Appellate Court

There are eleven justices presently sitting in the Appellate Division, First Department. They are Presiding Justice Harold A. Stevens and Associate Justices George Tilzer, Louis J. Capozzoli, James B.M. McNally, Aron Steuer, Samuel W. Eager, Owen McGivren, Emilio Nunez, Arthur Markewich, Theodore B. Kupferman and Francis T. Murphy, Jr.

Following is the text of the statement:

"Articles have recently appeared in the press in which certain judges were criticized in relation to sentences meted out after pleas of guilty by certain defendants. We are prompted to issue this statement by the fact an individual judge is constrained by ethics and custom to the extent to which he can respond to criticism of his official conduct.

"It is beyond dispute that any wrongdoing by a judge should be vigorously pursued, and we are prepared to do so. We do feel, however, that it is manifestly unfair to question the integrity of a judge without full knowledge of the facts not only of the case involved but also of the necessities of proper procedure and effective administration. Consequently, we deplore the ex parte criticism of the judges and wish to call attention to our attitude in regard thereto.

"In the instance provoking this expression the District Attorney has provided a detailed analysis which belies the innuendo of the offending statements. Unfortunately, no justification can completely efface the effects of the implied accusations of this character and by this means alone incalculable harm is done. We also feel that the just and expeditious determination of the ever increasing avalanche of serious criminal cases will be seriously and adversely affected by the continuance of such statements."

When the criticism arouses public emotion, the public will often become involved. News media letters to the editor will be used to express citizen opinion on an issue.

An effective way to handle some criticism is to have the judges' association make the reply. A number of state judicial organizations have adopted a policy as to when the organization would answer criticism.[17] As a result of the policy, judges call or write to the organization, which does what is deemed appropriate under the circumstances. This may mean a letter to the editor, or a letter to the judge.

Another way of meeting the criticism, when appropriate, is for the bar association to reply.

Public Information and Public Relations

On occasion we communicate by sending a message to someone else without that party responding. Sometimes this is not very satisfactory.[18] On other occasions, communication means that *A* sends a message to *B*, and *B*, upon receiving that message, sends a message in return. The sending of a message does not necessarily mean verbal communication. It can be by body language that indicates "I understand," or eye contact, which can say many different things.

The importance of this is that when a judge is attempting to communicate, the judge needs to distinguish between these kinds of communication. While it may be highly desirable to know that that information is being received in order to know whether it is being sent in the most effective package, immediate and direct feedback may not be expected in response to public information.

On the other hand, if the judge is attempting public relations, the judge is attempting to change an attitude, belief, or action. For this purpose, the judge needs to measure whether a change has been effected.

When there is a known adverse attitude that must be changed in order for the court to get something it needs, a public relations program is usually required. If, on the other hand, the attitude is believed to be favorable, and the judge simply desires to communicate to reinforce that attitude, a release of information or a public information program may be sufficient.

17. American Bar Association Task Force on Courts and the Public, Meeting Criticism of Bench and Courts (1975).

18. If you write a letter and receive no reply, the letter may not have been received, or the receiver may be unhappy with you, or the receiver may be pleased with what you say but unable to reply. You only know you have no reply.

Planning a Public Information Program

Starting with the assumption that courts belong to the people and with the further assumption that, in any given community, a majority of people view judges and courts favorably, it is desirable to reinforce that feeling. For this purpose, the judge may want to use a public information program.

One judge acting alone can do a great deal. A judge can make speeches, watch relationships with the people who come into the courtroom, learn to communicate better with court personnel, and plan and conduct ceremonies in his or her own courtroom, just to name a few approaches.

However, some things are done better when planned by all the judges on the same court. An annual report means more if it has the approval of the several judges, even if it is prepared by only one of them or by the court administrator. School visitation programs are much more likely to be successful if a group of judges participate, rather than one judge acting alone.

A judge should not be discouraged simply because his or her colleagues do not yet go along with the idea. In such a case, the judge should attempt to accomplish a specific program without assistance. Many judges have taught their less enthusiastic colleagues the importance of public information.

One item of concern in devising a program is how to finance it. Accomplishing many of the suggested ideas requires no money. A few of the ideas, however, do require funds. Very frequently such funds are already available in one budget or another. The ideas can be put into effect in inexpensive ways at the beginning. If the results seem worth it, more money can be obtained, and the program can be expanded.

Planning a Public Relations Program

When the occasion requires modification of an attitude, the first thing to measure is that attitude. Some years ago, a proposal was made to undertake a nationwide program to modify the attitude of the public toward courts. The proposal was based upon the assumption that the public attitude toward courts was less favorable than it had been. The Public Relations Society of America suggested a nationwide poll to determine what that attitude was and the sources of concern to people generally. Cost prohibited such a study. Sometimes public relations programs are commenced on an assumption, though in a business venture or election campaign, it would be wise to verify the assumption. However, if there seems to be general adverse comment in the community about judges, a project can be undertaken without specifically defining the amount of criticism.

If legislators need to be influenced with regard to some matter pertaining to the courts (whether facilities, additional judges, court personnel, or salaries) some measurement of attitude may be possible, but a program may have to be designed without knowing exactly what the attitudes are.

It is highly desirable to recognize when a public relations program cannot be accomplished by judges acting alone. Most people when ill would employ a physician. Usually if very much money is to be spent for a building, an architect is employed. Acting upon the same assumption, it may be highly desirable for judges to employ professional public relations people to assist in the planning of a public relations campaign.

So why are judges reluctant to consult with professionals in public information or public relations? One reason is ignorance. Judges do not know what professional assistance can do, do not know how much it costs, do not know how invisible such assistance can be. What the professional can do depends upon his or her objectives and budget. The effort and cost will be different for a survey of public opinion and an extensive effort to help people see the courts in their best light than they will for a relatively brief effort to influence legislative action.

Another reason is that judges think it is unprofessional to employ public relations people. "Profit-making firms do it, but public employees should not" is the reasoning.

A third reason is money. Is public information or public relations worth a proper expenditure of public funds? Certainly, for some branches of government, it appears to be. The President of the United States has hundreds of people polishing his image. Many other governmental offices have such people in order to adequately communicate with the public, to add the specialized knowledge required, and to relieve them in part from this essential but extra work. Isn't it logical to assume that public information is a proper governmental function? The appellate opinion brief, the information concerning the workings of the court, and similar duties are properly the function of a public information officer. That person will perform better if he or she is a professional. Some kinds of PR efforts—such as influencing legislators regarding salaries—cannot be paid for at public expense. But the effort should certainly justify judges assessing themselves to pay for the required effort.

What can the professional do? The main effort will be to help influence opinion so that it will be favorable to his or her objective. Many methods may be suggested. The court need not use any that are unacceptable. A program can be tailored to the court's needs and budget.

How does one employ a public relations consultant? One way is to start in the Yellow Pages, but the odds are great that one judge on the court knows someone in PR. If not, the judge can ask some business acquaintance to recommend someone.

After identifying the name of a person or a firm, the judge should send a couple of people to talk to him or her or them—or invite them to a meeting. The first PR person may not be the right one. Ideally, that person will tell you so and refer you to a firm more suited to your needs. The judge should spell out objectives, inquire about costs, and discuss a budget.

The Judicial Public Information Committee

A public information committee offers a variety of services:

- Aiding judges by answering general criticism, or assisting the chief judge or the proper officer of the judges association to answer it
- Promoting the employment of a public relations person or seeing that someone is assigned the duties (or some of them)
- Offering suggestions for bench-media relationship to the judge involved in an attention-getting trial
- Developing a statewide public information program for the judiciary

A further divided constituency can ruin the best effort. If judges can unite in furthering a program much can be accomplished.

The News Media

The rights of the freedom of news media are continually reinforced by the courts. The courts, as public institutions under our form of government, require an informed public. News media are the primary source of the public's information about courts and other governmental bodies. Thanks in part to this interdependence, the relationship between judges and news reporters is usually a positive one. Judges do their jobs, and reporters do their jobs.

However, the relationship is complicated by what appears to be a conflict between the first and sixth amendments. While the information furnished to the public enables citizens to fulfill these duties, freedom of speech and of the press is not an unlimited right. The sixth amendment erects protections around parts of the court process in order to preserve the right of the defendant in a criminal case to a trial by an impartial jury. When vast amounts of publicity affect or could affect many potential jurors, an unfair trial may result. This conflict in responsibilities has led to misunderstandings between the bench and the media.

Bench and Media Roles

At a conference sponsored by the National Conference of Juvenile Court Judges, the judges and media representatives concluded that the most important reason for lack of understanding between bench and media was the lack of understanding of respective roles.

Judges assume everyone else understands the role of the trial judge. The judge presides over the trial, assures that it is fair and that it remains as calm as possible. Of course, that only scratches the surface, but how much of the technique of doing that is known to news people, and how much less to the general public?

News people also have pressures and problems. There is a need for accuracy, but sometimes it is sacrificed for speed. Objectivity is necessary, but so is interpretation, which is subjective. A third matter that causes problems, particularly for editors, is the matter of balance, that is, presenting both sides. And there is also the question of reliability. How credible is the news source?

Special Media Problems

Print and electronic media both have deadline problems. Each medium wants to be the first with the news. This causes problems for courts in announcing important decisions without appearing to favor one medium over the other.

Promoting Understanding

Some judges would prefer to have nothing whatever to do with news people. On the other hand, a fair and respectful relationship can be created in which the judge can help educate the news person and can release judicial rulings at times that at least do not hinder the work of the reporter. In some places the news person is on the job long enough to have a semipersonal relationship with the judge. When that happens, the judge and the news person must remember that the relationship must be at sufficient arm's length that, should occasion require it, the reporter can print something about the judge, or should the reporter come into court, the judge would not be disqualified from taking whatever action is required.

A formal way of providing assistance and information about the courts is through a public information officer. Some large courts are able to have a person who acts only in the capacity of public information officer. Smaller courts can assign this responsibility to someone with other duties. That person may be a clerk or some other employee whose duties could be adjusted to permit him or her to function as needed in this capacity.

Typical tasks of a public information officer might include the following:

- Be available to supply news people with information concerning court business that is a matter of public record
- Refer inquiries from news people to knowledgeable court employees
- Provide the media with copies of recently announced judicial decisions and opinions

- Assist in securing copies of public transcripts (at the news person's expense)
- Make necessary arrangements for electronic media to carry on their appropriate duties
- Assist news people in dealing with court employees who have been uncooperative
- Distribute a weekly schedule of court activities
- Maintain a clipping file of articles concerning the court so as to provide court personnel and news people with a useful vehicle for periodically evaluating the quality of reporting on the courts

Another way of assisting the news media is to provide physical facilities for reporters. Most courthouses built years ago have no provision for reporters. However, in many newer buildings, that was part of the architect's thinking. More modern facilities provide for electronic media. Another helpful provision is designing the courtroom so it is easier for the reporter to get in and out of the courtroom without interrupting the trial.

The judge can also visit journalism classes to foster good relations early. Journalism schools are usually glad to have judges come talk to students so that reporters can better understand judges' problems. The schools also join in bench-bar-media conferences.

Joint bench-bar-press meetings also foster communications. Some states have bench-bar-media committees. These encourage local committees, stage statewide or regional educational seminars, and aid in developing voluntary guidelines for the activities of each group. North Carolina, Washington, California and a good many other states have made extensive efforts. The California Judges Association, along with the California newspaper publishers and other organizations, holds a conference every two years.[19] Such events provide excellent opportunities to become acquainted with the problems of the other agency. Because there are new reporters and new judges each year, meetings should be held periodically. Doing it only once would certainly not lead to understanding for very long.

The judge can improve relations by acknowledging news coverage that is accurate. It is difficult for some people to accept praise, however, and the motives for giving praise are sometimes suspect. Therefore, while the rare and sincere comment may be appreciated, a judge who is frequently effusive may be suspected by the reporter, who believes that such praise is given for the purpose of obtaining a favor. The reporter

19. The text used at the Media Conference on California Courts is the California Judges Association publication, THE COURTS AND THE NEWS MEDIA, written by Professor Albert G. Pickerell, now in its fifth edition. Copies may be ordered from California Judges Association, Fox Plaza, Suite 208, 1390 Market Street, San Francisco, CA 94102.

expects to do a good job and sometimes understands from silence that the judge is approving. The news person is not attempting to please the judge by the story.

There are formal ways of giving praise that are entirely acceptable. The Gavel Award of the American Bar Association represents national praise for noteworthy reporting. Nominations are made early in the year, and nomination forms can be obtained from the American Bar Association's headquarters in Chicago,[20] or the judge can suggest to a local bar association that it do so. State bar associations also offer tributes to members of the news media who have done outstanding jobs.

Fair Trial and Free Press

"Congress shall make no law . . . abridging the freedom of speech, or of the press . . ." Freedom of the press is assumed by the public to be a clearly established right. So it is now in this country, but even here it was not always so.

In this country, John Peter Zenger was tried in New York in 1735 for seditious libel. Under the law of that day, the judge charged the jury that the truth was no defense and that the writing in question was seditious. The defense attorney argued that sedition was a question of fact and that the truth was a valid defense. The jury agreed with the attorney, not with the judge, and acquitted Zenger. The unpopularity of the law that so infringed upon freedom of expression was clear. In 1776 and thereafter, the rights to freedom of speech and press were established. But considering the good sense of the framers of the Constitution, it is surprising that it was not until the Bill of Rights was proposed and passed that the right to trial by jury was guaranteed in the federal Constitution.

These rights, as spelled out in the first and sixth amendments, usually exist together harmoniously, but at times the judge encounters a conflict between them.

One problem in the debate about fair trial and free press is to define a "fair trial."

To the legal profession, the definition of fair trial is much more complicated than mere entitlement to an impartial jury. But the problems between news media and courts arise primarily because of the right to a "trial by impartial jury."

What state of mind is required for one to be an impartial juror? How is the state of mind affected by pretrial publicity?

There is a considerable history to the definition that is now accepted. In *Irvin v. Dowd*, [21] the U.S. Supreme Court stated:

20. American Bar Association, 750 N. Lake Shore Drive, Chicago, IL 60611.
21. 366 U.S. 717, 81 S. Ct. 1639, 6 L. Ed. 2d 589 (1961).

> To hold that the mere existence of any preconceived notion as to the guilt or innocence of an accused, without more, is sufficient to rebut the presumption of a prospective juror's impartiality would be to establish an impossible standard. It is sufficient if the juror can lay aside his impression or opinion and render a verdict based on the evidence presented in court.

In *Murphy v. Florida*, the Supreme Court added:

> At the same time, the juror's assurances that he is equal to his task cannot be dispositive of the accused's rights, and it remains open to the defendant to demonstrate 'the actual existence of such an opinion in the mind of the juror as will raise the presumption of partiality'[22] (quoting *Irvin v. Dowd).*

The Court stated also in *Murphy v. Florida*, that "[e]ven these indicia of impartiality might be disregarded in a case where the general atmosphere in the community or courtroom is sufficiently inflammatory."[23]

The general rule appears to be that there is no presumption of prejudice where jurors say they will not be influenced by publicity or outside matters, that they can decide the case upon the evidence received in court, and that they feel no prejudice against the defendant. The burden is then upon the defendant to demonstrate the existence of an opinion in the minds of jurors that raises the presumption of partiality. While this defines the U.S. Constitutional standard, a judge will want to check other law that may apply in the judge's jurisdiction. Of course, the application of the test to determine the fairness of the juror's mind comes during voir dire examination of prospective jurors.

If the trial reaches this stage, how will the trial judge know when to declare a mistrial? How many jurors must have minds that do not meet the standard before the judge grants the defendant's motion? Again, we look to *Irvin v. Dowd* and *Murphy v. Florida.* The judge should pay close attention to the circumstances of *Irvin v. Dowd*, where 90 percent of those examined were inclined to believe in the defendant's guilt and the court excused 268 of the 430 veniremen.

How to Preserve the Fairness of the Trial

It is unlikely that the judge will have to initiate the proceedings to attempt to keep the trial fair. Counsel for the defendant usually raise the issue.

One common method is by requesting that the court issue an order restraining pretrial publicity. Such orders, regardless of their form, are referred to by the news media as "gag orders." Judges believe that the only "gag order" is an order of prior restraint. Such an order is one that

---

22. 421 U.S. 794, 95 S. Ct. 2031, 44 L. Ed. 2d 589 (1975).
23. *Id.*

tells the news media that they may not publish a story they already have. Such an order would almost always be improper.[24]

The second kind of order, and one that courts have been told may be appropriate in some cases, is a so-called restrictive order. Such an order might restrict law enforcement and prosecuting authorities, defense counsel, parties, witnesses, and court attaches from releasing certain kinds of information.

Prior restraints and restrictive orders, as here defined, are different in effect and different in proof required. A judge, more than anyone else, must know and respect the difference. The test for the issuance of an order of prior restraint is the "clear and present danger" test. This test has strong historical implication for cases of free speech and free press.[25] The test for making a restrictive order is said to be the "reasonable likelihood" test. The question is, whether there is a reasonable likelihood of prejudicial news that would make it impossible to impanel an impartial jury and thus tend to prevent a fair trial.[26]

Any judge who can see a multiple homicide case, or any other case likely to attract large amounts of publicity, headed toward his or her court should obtain a quick education with regard to the pitfalls of entering an order, whether it be prior restraint or restrictive order. A list of books and articles that might help to give such an education is set forth at the end of this chapter.

One of the problems with the making of such an order is that a violation requires that the court determine whether someone is in contempt. If a reporter is in contempt, the contempt must then be punished. The judge should be knowledgeable and deliberate before entering this thicket. One other warning: Such orders are frequently requested. A judge requested to issue such an order should remember that the media are entitled to due process and promptly set the matter for hearing.

The U.S. Supreme Court in *Sheppard v. Maxwell*[27] suggested methods by which the fairness of the trial could be preserved:

- Restrictive orders
- Exclusion of the public and news media personnel
- Change of venue
- Carefully worded jury instructions
- Sequestration of the jury
- Contempt for violation of a proper court order
- New trial

---

24. Nebraska Press Ass'n v. Stuart, 427 U.S. 539, 96 S. Ct. 2791, 49 L. Ed. 2d 683 (1976).

25. *See* Bridges v. California, 314 U.S. 252, 62 S. Ct. 190, 86 L. Ed. 192 (1941).

26. *See* Sheppard v. Maxwell, 384 U.S. 333, 352, 86 S. Ct. 1507, 1517, 16 L. Ed. 2d 600 (1966); United States v. Tijerina, 412 F.2d 661 (10th Cir. 1969), 5 A.L.R. Fed. 935.

27. *See* Sheppard v. Maxwell, 384 U.S. 333.

Change of venue is a commonly used method of avoiding the effect of prejudicial pretrial publicity. News media, if they are to continue to follow the trial, must travel along with the prosecutor, defense counsel, witnesses and other personnel connected with the trial. The logistics are cumbersome for all. One method of conducting a trial before an impartial jury is to select the jury from another county and transport those jurors to the county in which the offense occurred. While this avoids the logistical problems, the imported jury may have to be sequestered in order that it will not be affected by publicity during the course of the trial.

Of course, one method of avoiding such trial publicity is to advise jurors not to read anything about the case. The difficulty with this is that the jurors must also be shut off from electronic media. The results of such an admonition can be difficult to monitor.

A new trial is not only expensive but usually must be held in another jurisdiction in order to avoid the problem that caused the granting of the new trial.

Sequestration of the jury may be a valuable tool for avoiding the effect of publicity during the course of the trial. However, it does not avoid the prejudicial effect of pretrial publicity.

Access to Courts

The U.S. Supreme Court has indicated that excluding the public and news media might be an appropriate method of protecting the fairness of the trial. Later, in *Richmond Newspapers v. Virginia*,[28] the Supreme Court said that, throughout its evolution, the trial has been open to all who care to observe; both civil and criminal trials have been presumptively open.

The suggestion made by the Supreme Court in *Sheppard v. Maxwell*, along with its admonition that trial judges have the duty of ensuring the fairness of the trial, caused an increase in the use of orders closing hearings, prohibiting out-of-court statements by participants, and sealing evidence and transcripts. In two Supreme Court opinions—*Cox Broadcasting Corp. v. Cohn*[29] and *Oklahoma Publishing Co. v. District Court*[30]—the Court held that the state could not regulate the publication of information seen in open court or in open judicial records, but suggested that the state could have denied access altogether consistently with the Constitution. In other words, there could not be prior restraint, but there could be a restrictive order.

---

28. 448 U.S. 555, 65 L. Ed. 2d 973, 100 S. Ct. 2814 (1980).
29. 420 U.S. 469, 43 L. Ed. 2d 328, 95 S. Ct. 1029 (1975).
30. 430 U.S. 308, 51 L. Ed. 2d 355, 97 S. Ct. 1045 (1977).

Over a period of years, with changing fact situations presented to the court, the right of access became a constitutional issue. The first Supreme Court case testing the right of access to pretrial proceedings was *Gannett v. DePasquale.*[31] A number of opinions were written in that case. The gist of all of them is that seven justices reserved the question as to whether there is a first amendment right of access. The ruling upon the sixth amendment and the rights of the defendant upheld the exclusion of the press and the public.

Though *Gannett* involved a *pretrial* hearing, Justice Stewart's majority opinion stated that members of the public and press have no sixth or fourteenth amendment right of access to criminal *trials*. The broad language of the decision was used by lower courts as a basis for closure, not only of pretrial hearings, but of all criminal proceedings when the parties and the court agreed. The result was many more closed proceedings.

The landmark case in the field is *Richmond Newspapers v. Virginia.*[32] The case arose when the defendant was brought to trial for the fourth time on the same murder charge. He moved to close the courtroom, the prosecutor acquiesced, and the motion was granted. Richmond Newspapers had two reporters covering the case, both of whom were ejected from the courtroom. The trial was closed, and the defendant was acquitted. The Virginia Supreme Court denied the various petitions of Richmond Newspapers.

When the case came to the Supreme Court, seven members of the court recognized the first amendment right of access to trials. While there were seven opinions, none of which commanded a majority, the order closing the criminal trial was held to be invalid under the first and fourteenth amendments. The court did leave a tiny crack in the door by stating that if the trial court found an "overriding interest" supporting closure, the trial might be closed. The court did not say what facts might show such an overriding interest.

After finding that trials had traditionally been open, the court turned to the question of whether the function of the trial was enhanced by openness. Four benefits were found in keeping trials open:

1. Public trials enhance public confidence in the trial process.
2. Public attendance operates as a check on abuses of the judicial system.
3. Public knowledge of the process promotes the truth-finding function.
4. Publicity helps achieve a community cleansing effect following serious crimes.

31. 443 U.S. 368, 61 L. Ed. 2d 608, 99 S. Ct. 2898 (1979).
32. 448 U.S. 555, 65 L. Ed. 2d 973, 100 S. Ct. 2814 (1980).

Closure was prohibited unless the trial court made findings on the record that there would be immediate and irreparable damage to the defendant's fair trial right, that there were no alternative methods to protect such rights, such as change of venue, and that the closure would be effective.

The Supreme Court followed *Richmond Newspapers* with a narrow holding in *Globe Newspaper Co. v. Superior Court.*[33] The Court held that, in individual cases and under appropriate circumstances, the first amendment does not necessarily bar excluding the press and general public from the courtroom during the testimony of minor sex-offense victims. But a mandatory rule, requiring no particularized determination in individual cases, is unconstitutional.

In a Riverside Press Enterprise case,[34] the Court found that there was a qualified public and press right to attend voir dire, and found closure of voir dire and sealing of transcripts to be impermissible in the absence of the express findings called for in Richmond Newspapers. In a second case involving Riverside Press Enterprises,[35] the Court held that there was a right of access to the California preliminary hearing which is a part of the pretrial process. Thus, *Gannett* is no longer a viable precedent for closure. In the second Riverside Press Enterprise case, the Supreme Court said that the proponent must show a "substantial probability" of prejudice. This is a higher standard than the "reasonable likelihood" standard required in other situations.

Contempt and the Reporter's Privilege

Another of the remedies proposed by the Supreme Court in *Sheppard v. Maxwell*[36] was contempt for violation of a proper court order. While the probability of making a successful order of prior restraint is nil, the making of restrictive orders in appropriate circumstances has commonly been upheld.

A serious problem arises for judges, however, when the news reporter obtains information that appears to have been given to the reporter in violation of a proper order. How does the court find out who leaked the information? Such a situation usually results in the subpoenaing of the reporter with a demand by the court that the journalist reveal the source of the information.

The reason for the request seems proper. The problem is that journalists fear that information would less likely come to them if sources

---

33. 457 U.S. 596, 73 L. Ed. 2d 248, 102 S. Ct. 2613 (1982).

34. Press-Enter. Co. v. Superior Court of Cal., 464 U.S. 501, 78 L. Ed. 2d 629, 104 S. Ct. 819 (1984).

35. Press-Enter. Co. v. Superior Court of Cal., 478 U.S. 1, 92 L. Ed. 2d 1, 106 S. Ct. 2735 (1986).

36. 384 U.S. 333.

know that, at least in some cases, the reporter may be required to reveal the source of the information.

In addition to protecting an order properly made by the court, there may be other reasons for the subpoena to the reporter and the revelation of the information. Thus there are competing interests: the litigant's right of access to evidence relevant to the case versus the journalist's free press right to gather information safe from compulsory disclosure.

The first case on this subject to reach the Supreme Court was *Branzburg v. Hayes*.[37] The court's opinion, of four judges, declined to recognize the reporter's privilege at all. Four dissenters argued strenuously for acknowledgment of a constitutional privilege. Justice Powell broke the deadlock by concurring with Justice White's majority opinion but adding his own concurring opinion stressing the limited nature of the majority opinion. He went on to say that such a claim to privilege should be judged on its fact by striking of a proper balance between freedom of the press and the obligation of all citizens to give relevant testimony with respect to criminal conduct.

While *Branzburg* seems a somewhat poorly constructed precedent, many but not all courts have recognized the qualified first amendment privilege against compelled testimony and the production of reporter's materials in response to subpoenas. Note that *Branzburg*, in its way, seems to have established a constitutional privilege.

In addition to the constitutional privilege, however, many states have passed shield laws that expressly protect defined categories of reporters. Such shield laws invoke mixed emotions. Some reporters would rather stand on the constitutional protection; others are willing to accept that which the legislature gives, even while recognizing that what the legislature gives it can also take away. Most such shield laws withhold from the court the power to hold a reporter in contempt for violating an order to disclose information.

When asked to make some kind of an order that involves the rights of news reporters, a judge should carefully consider the alternatives available. If any of them are likely to be effective and are less invasive of the rights of reporters, the requested order should probably be refused. It is at least an area in which judges need to be very alert.

As a San Francisco judge said after making an overbroad order, "If I had known at the time that I made the order what I learned when the parties went to the Court of Appeals, I would never have made the order in the first place."

37. 408 U.S. 665, 92 S. Ct. 2646, 33 L. Ed. 2d 626 (1972).

Television in the Courtroom

For a number of years, the electronic media and the courts were in sharp conflict about television in the courtroom. That battle is now over in the state courts. Most state trial courts now permit televised coverage of courtroom proceedings under supervision of the trial judge and subject to certain restrictions. A judge should consult the rule in his or her jurisdiction to know the extent of the judge's control.

Some of the original objections to cameras in the courtroom were their disruptive influence and the possibility that they would affect the deliberations of jurors and their actions during the course of the trial. There have now been many trials with television in the courtroom. Perhaps no one can say with certainty that the results of a trial covered by television are not changed, but if they are changed, the new result seems to be accepted. The Supreme Court has declared that television in the courtroom is not inherently prejudicial, that cameras in the courtroom are constitutionally permissible, not that they are constitutionally required.

While there are still occasional skirmishes, the major battles in the war between the first and sixth amendments seem to have been fought. It is hoped that the relationship between courts and the news media will be respectful, knowledgeable, and as accommodating as the law and good sense will allow.

Bibliography: Fair Trial v. Free Press

Books

1. American Bar Association. *Standards for Criminal Justice,* ch. 8, "Standards Relating to Fair Trial and Free Press," 2d ed. 1980.

2. New York Bar Foundation. Law and the Press, 1975.

3. Winters. *Selected Readings: Fair Trial—Free Press,* 1971.

Articles

Burton. "Prejudicial Pretrial and Trial Publicity," 45 *Tulane Law Review* 1043 (June 1971).

"Cameras in the Criminal Courtroom: A Sixth Amendment Analysis," 85 *Columbia Law Review* 1546-72 (Nov. 1985).

Carter. "Mass Media: How Responsible, How Free?" 39 *Arkansas Law Review* 297-309 (1985).

"Confusion in the Courthouse: The Legacy of the *Gannett and Richmond Newspapers* Public Right of Access Cases," 59 *Southern California Law Review* 603-39 (Mar. 1986).

"Constitutional Law—Judicial Restraint of the Press," 9 *Creighton Law Review* 693 (1976).

Cullen. "Circumventing *Branzburg*: Absolute Protection for Confidential News Sources," 18 *Suffolk University Law Review* 615-39 (Winter 1984).

Kaplan. "Free Press/Fair Trial: Rights in Conflict: Freedom of the Press and the Rights of the Individual," 29 *Oklahoma Law Review* 361 (Spring 1976).

Larson. "Free Press v. Fair Trial in Nebraska: A Position Paper," 55 *Nebraska Law Review* 543 (1976).

Lewis. "Cantankerous, Obstinate, Ubiquitous: The Press," 1975 *Utah Law Review* 75 (Spring 1975).

Monk. "Evidentiary Privilege for Journalists' Sources: Theory and Statutory Protection," 51 *Missouri Law Review* 1-62 (Winter 1986).

"The Newsgatherer's Shield—Why Waste Space in the California Constitution?" 15 *Southwestern California Law Review* 527-73 (1985).

Schatz. "Gagging the Press in Criminal Trials," 10 *Harvard Civil Rights Law Review* 608 (Summer 1975).

Stern. "Free Press/Fair Trial: The Role of the News Media in Developing and Advancing Constitutional Processes," 29 *Oklahoma Law Review* 349 (Spring 1976).

Warren and Abell. "Free Press—Fair Trial: The 'Gag Order,' a California Aberration," 45 *Southern California Law Review* 51 (Winter 1972).

20

SATISFACTIONS OF JUDGING: A JUDGE'S LEGACY

Judges are volunteers. The primary reason judges take office[1] is a desire to serve the community. Judicial service is very rewarding, although it often involves considerable personal stress as well as financial sacrifice.

The stressors are more readily apparent than the satisfactions. The judge works under the pressure of constant conflicts over freedom, wealth, and even life itself. The court's day-to-day work is usually not understood by the public being served, so there are few congratulations for jobs well done. Yet a judgeship is, for those imbued with love of the law, the culmination of a professional lifetime of training and experience. It can provide a unique sense of accomplishment.

Judges, as do other celebrities, understand the strange status of life in a fishbowl. The community is rightfully demanding of those who would judge others. Judges are held to the highest standards of personal conduct because if one slips, the reputation of justice itself suffers.

Justice is, after all, the judge's chief concern. He or she has both the duty to articulate society's values and the duty to use the power of the state to enforce them.

For many, the attraction of judicial service is the opportunity to uphold society's most basic values and the opportunity to work for what is right. A lawyer takes clients as they come, and is duty bound to advance their cause, but a judge is bound to no side, except the cause of justice.

The judge, however, cannot impose personal preferences. Rights and duties are found in statutes, case law, and regulations. We are guided by constitutions and the common law, theoretical standards of behavior

1. J. Martin, The Effects of Compensation on the Career Satisfaction Experienced by Federal Judges (1988).

and actual social norms. From this the judge not only determines the values that apply to a set of facts, but is usually bound to state why that decision was made. The law springs from the collective body of those individual decisions.

The trial judge's jurisprudential legacy to the community is developed case by case. It is seldom expressed in single judicial opinions that change the course of the law. Few judges can write in large letters on a clean slate. When a case of lasting historical importance does appear, the trial judge must make the decisions that shape events, but it is usually the appellate judge whose ruling is recorded in the annals of the law.

While developing and implementing the law, the fair, just, and impartial judge inspires the next generation of its stewards. Many of today's finest lawyers and judges were shaped by role models who saw the bench and bar as a high calling, or were motivated by the ideal of justice to improve a court that was wanting. This raises an important series of questions. What part of the legacy left by our predecessors has most inspired us? What have we resolved to change and improve? Do we understand what litigants and the community feel is most important?

Litigants tell us that the best legacy a judge can leave the public, the court, and those to follow is a reputation for fairness, for considering all sides of an issue before reaching a decision.

The trial judge must demonstrate ability to withhold judgment until the facts are in. This may be difficult when there are pretrial hearings, motions, and orders as well as numerous rulings during the trial itself.

Lawyers, judges, and litigants all place great importance on an open judicial mind.

A survey of criminal case defendants showed that often their satisfaction with their court experience depended not upon whether they won or lost and not upon the sentence imposed, but upon whether they felt that the judge heard what they had to say. Similarly, experiments in traffic courts find that entering a plea of guilty or not guilty is often less meaningful to many defendants than the opportunity to explain to the court why they did what they did.

The concern for open mindedness is also strong in civil cases. In a study of the settlement process for civil suits in the federal courts, lawyers were very uneasy about having the same judge try a case who had attempted to settle it.[2] They feared that the judge may have adopted a position during the prior negotiations. In view of its central importance to justice, possessing a hard-won reputation for fairness is therefore perhaps the major satisfaction of a trial judge.

2. W. Brazil, Settling Civil Suits (1985).

The judge, like the lawyer, is concerned with resolution of conflicts. Both deal with ambiguity. Conflicts reach court even where both sides tell the truth in good faith. Many disputes arise out of misunderstanding, missed meeting of the minds, half memories and misinterpretations.

The judge develops ways of resolving not only the legal contentions between the parties, but, where possible, the underlying problems that caused the dispute to boil. On a good day a judge may preserve family relationships strained by an ambiguous will, find a way that neighbors can peacefully coexist, point a young life in a more fruitful direction, intercede between the general power of the government and the special needs of the individual or make another of innumerable possible contributions to domestic peace and tranquility. Routine cases are very important to the parties involved, and resolving them brings the trial judge quiet satisfaction. The sum of all the court's cases is peace in the community, the reason for our laws.

The modern court requires the judge to go well beyond hearing individual cases. Duties off the bench require many skills. Management of the court, public relations, teaching, and more are part of the office.

There are as many personal styles as there are judges. This book contains the contributions of many judges, each with his or her own viewpoints and concerns. As the book demonstrates, a judge's legacy to the community can range widely, based upon individual abilities and interests.

Many judges develop particular strengths and talents. Each large courthouse has a judicial scholar—a judge to whom colleagues can turn for advice on difficult points of law and procedure. In rural areas, judges consult by telephone and even have informal "hotlines" on particular subjects. As judicial scholars become more widely known to their colleagues, they appear on state and national judicial education programs, serving other judges as well as the public.

Some judges are innovators. They have devised applications of technology and procedures to make courts better and more efficient. They have adapted computers, telephones, video recorders, audio tape players and other technology in new ways that have been spread around the country to the benefit of all litigants.

Some judges have improved the judicial environment. They have developed intervention programs to help fellow judges face alcohol or drug problems. They serve on judicial selection panels, work for needed pay raises, develop judicial self-evaluation programs and respond to concerns about maintaining the independence of the judiciary.

Some judges improve the administration of the courts. They revise rules and procedures, finding new ways to reduce backlogs and delay and make justice more accessible.

Some judges improve the public understanding of the courts. They work to educate the public about the Constitution, the courts and the judiciary. They speak to community groups, invite the public into their courts and reach out to the schools.

Each of these activities outside the courtroom is both an additional contribution to the community and an additional source of satisfaction.

In as many ways as there are judges, each can make her or his own contribution toward supporting and building the fundamental commitment to equal justice for all.

The judge who leaves his or her community an enduring set of values, a reputation for integrity, and a commitment for the improvement of justice has earned the true satisfaction of genuine service to the common good and has made the community a better place for all.

21

THE JUDGE OF THE FUTURE

Although speculations about "the judge of the future" bring visions of robotic truth-assessing machines, law-dispensing computers, and chemical-test-determined dispositions, human beings, rather than mechanical marvels, will continue to exercise the fine art of judgment for any foreseeable future.

The judge's calling is one of the most solitary. Yet it is profoundly affected by changes in the legal profession, changes in the public service generally, and eventually by major developments in the society at large. Incremental extensions of current trends point toward the judge of the future.

Who Is the Judge?

The most visible recent change in the judiciary has been the growing diversity of judges themselves. The stereotypical elderly white male has given way to a bench with age, racial, ethnic, and gender diversity. Although Perry Mason appeared before female judges in televised fiction of the late 1950s and early 1960s, it was not until the late 1980s that women judges would no longer be considered pioneers.

The changes in the demographics of the bench mirror changes in the law schools of 20 years ago. Movements for rights and equality, the baby boom, and the changing American work force are all being reflected in the courts. To predict who will be the judge of the future, look at the law schools of today. The judiciary of the future will be half female and probably one-quarter minority.

Among the court reforms proposed in the 1930s and 1940s that gained wide acceptance and adoption in the 1970s and 1980s, merit selection of judges continues to make headway across the nation. It is propelled by public dissatisfaction with a partisan political process tainted with proven corruption in some places, suspicion of ethical problems elsewhere, and unmanageable financial burdens for judicial election campaigns almost everywhere they occur. We can expect to see a continued movement toward using a nominating commission approach or, at least, the palliative of nonpartisan elections.

Since studies have shown that more women and minorities become judges under appointive than under elective processes, and since merit selection has been shown to draw candidates from a wider pool than does the traditional elective process, the trend toward merit selection will accelerate the diversification of the judiciary.

As retention ballots replace the partisan process, fewer judges will lose office through contested elections. It will no longer be possible to defer issues of judicial propriety to the give-and-take of contested elections. Judicial conduct commissions can therefore be expected to play a more important role in judicial discipline and removal. Since their adoption by all states in the 1970s and 1980s, discipline commissions have often been underfunded, understaffed, and reactive. The commissions will be strengthened to keep courts free of impropriety and corruption. We should expect them to become more active in investigating on their own initiative.

An anticipated revised Code of Judicial Conduct and the commissions' experience will lead to clearer definition of prohibited conduct, leaving disciplinary authorities to concentrate on serious breaches of law, ethics, and decorum. These efforts will gain increasing support from the judiciary, which may gain more latitude for investment and postretirement activities.

Sound evaluation processes conducted within the court system will encourage judicial self-improvement and correct minor lapses before they can become issues for the conduct commission.

Reflecting the makeup of the legal profession and the population generally, the bench will become younger and less experienced. A new boom in judicial education can be expected. State-level courses and national programs will be supplemented by law school offerings at the graduate level, as the pioneering efforts at the University of Nevada–Reno/National Judicial College and University of Virginia expand and are emulated. Previously ignored needs for career development and renewal, as through judicial sabbaticals, will gain favor.

The judge of the future will likely do postgraduate legal study in the profession of judging, will comfortably consider ethical questions, and will periodically turn to outside interests as a respite from official routine.

The Role of the Judge

The judge, today and in the future, appears to be gaining visibility while losing identity. In years past, many communities had a local, often part-time, judge handling limited disputes or charges within the community, while a relatively autonomous jurist in the county seat presided over grave matters at an individualized pace.

The citizen voters were presumed to have known their judges well enough to vote upon their futures, although this knowledge was much more likely to be gained at community functions in a social setting than by observance of the court in action.

As court reforms accelerated in the 1970s, courts were unified, part-time judges were eliminated, jurisdiction was broadened, and the practice of sitting by assignment in distant counties became widespread. As reforms and improved management continued to respond to growing caseloads, single-judge districts were consolidated to provide flexibility of assignment. The number of judges grew, although more modestly than the caseload or the population. Thus, where there once had been a judge for each court who could be called the community's own, there is now a court with a panel of judges, some of whom inevitably are considered strangers.

If there is less opportunity to know the individual judge, there is now a much greater likelihood of observing the judge at work. A variety of citizens groups have become interested in monitoring the courts. Organized court watchers, ranging from the impartial proponents of good government to single-issue pressure groups, have developed techniques for observing judges, recording and evaluating their findings, and sharing their analyses with a wider membership. The courts have also been opened to television reporting, ranging from snippets to full trial coverage.

Thus, if a judge is presiding over a momentous or controversial case, it is now much more likely that the public will learn something useful about it. Although community leaders may have less personal acquaintanceship with the judge, the public at large is much more likely to know of the judge's work. This trend will continue as cable outlets for local television proliferate, courthouse reporting continues to improve, and judicial evaluations by the court and others grow more sophisticated.

Consolidation of judicial districts is leading to a collegiality previously unknown on the trial bench. Where judges once held court as solo authorities, they are now much more likely to take a team approach to accelerating the docket, sharing the caseload, and developing management procedures.

The teamwork concept is spreading to the employment of court staff. Trained administrators, working with chief judges, are freeing most judges from time-consuming operational details. Information systems and management techniques allow the judges to set court policy affirmatively, rather than being swept along in the tide of cases.

Years ago there was spirited debate over the extent to which a judge should intervene in a poorly tried case. Now the center of controversy has turned from the extent of permissible judicial participation in a particular trial to the degree of control judges should exercise over the significant time points of all trials. There seems little doubt that the philosophy of judicial control and case management will prevail, with judges becoming ever more responsible for affirmatively moving cases through the courts. The judge of the future will be a provider of judicial services rather than a passive umpire.

Technology is also changing the role of the judge. Innovations are allowing traditional tasks to be done more efficiently. Not only do computers facilitate docket control and case management, but word-processing applications also allow ready production of orders, opinions, jury instructions, and the myriad of judicial documents featured in the modern lawsuit. Telephones with inexpensive speaker and conferencing devices let judges hear routine matters telephonically, with impressive savings in time and cost. Similarly extending the reach of the courtroom, videotaped depositions of busy expert witnesses are finding wide usage, although the showing of prerecorded trials to jurors has not caught on.

Varied technological solutions are being applied to the problem of how to produce transcripts rapidly. These include computer-aided transcription of the court reporter's notes, use of an automatically produced videotape as the transcript for appeal, and various adaptations of sound-recording technology.

Many of these technologies point in the direction of limiting a judge's personal staff while increasing the number of higher-paid technical specialists available to the court as a whole. This shift of staff resources can be expected to increase productivity while making more services available to many judges who had been hindered by lack of administrative support.

The technology most directly affecting the judge, however, will be the communications and research capability of the personal computer network. Far beyond word processing, the computer gives the judge research access to cases and statutes until now available only in the largest law libraries. Computers can be expected to put new emphasis on judicial scholarship.

The computer also provides instant communication with law offices throughout the country and, ultimately, will allow electronic filing, service, and notice of court documents. All of these uses are now available to a few state courts.

Collegiality and automation are contributing to a growing nationalization of the state judiciary. Other centralizing factors are increased legislative reliance upon national uniform and model laws, a return to federally funded demonstration projects, regional and national judicial education programs, and, most importantly, a growing national consensus about the law. These will make the judge of the future much more like his or her counterparts in other states than had been thought possible. It has even been suggested that exchange judges could go across state lines to sit temporarily in other general jurisdiction courts to broaden their judicial experience. The judge of the future will have a national perspective.

The Judge's Work

If the judge of the future will hear more cases in less time, taking advantage of improved case management and technology, what types of cases will those be?

With the aging of the U.S. population, it seems safe to predict that the docket will have fewer criminal cases, which are generally the province of the young. We can expect more will contests and more family disputes over support of aged relatives as well as the children of long-dissolved marriages. There will be an influx of cases formerly heard in federal courts as diversity jurisdiction is restricted and as state constitutions are increasingly viewed as sources of fundamental rights.

We can assume a continuing flow of legislation leading to an undiminished need for definitive interpretation of murky statutory language and enforcement of new rights and duties.

We may anticipate a rising level of contentiousness as the political pendulum inevitably swings from the current era of conservative consensus to a new time of testing and controversy over issues as yet unarticulated.

Although courts, as relatively conservative institutions, are comfortable with precedent, we can look forward to a degree of intellectual ferment not seen for several decades.

Recent trends toward limiting class actions suggest that there will be more repetitive lawsuits over substantial claims and less litigation of claims that are substantial in the aggregate but uneconomic individually.

Accompanying the increased use of different forms of alternative dispute resolution such as arbitration and mediation, we can expect the judge to spend less time on case settlement, a function served by ADR. Judges will be called upon to rule on challenges to the informal adjudications, however.

Paralleling the increasing importance of paralegals and other law firm specialists, we can expect growing use of judicial or quasi-judicial officers other than judges. In fact, service as commissioner, magistrate, hearing officer, special master, or such other parajudicial may constitute an important new career path toward the judiciary.

The Judge's Career Path

In years past, a judgeship was usually a final destination in the legal profession. Lawyers were reluctant to give up a practice only to assemble it anew after a term in office. Ethical and financial constraints substantially circumscribed the retired judge's options.

The profession's movement toward larger aggregations of lawyers and new opportunities for retired judges in government, academia, and private dispute resolution, together with the increased youthfulness of the bench and healthier life-styles, suggests that many judges in years to come will undertake third careers. These may be commenced either after leaving the bench or concurrently with judicial service through sabbaticals, leaves of absence, or adjunct status. These increased opportunities will add to the stimulation and challenge of the judicial career while providing additional outlets for our most talented and widely experienced public servants.

Conclusion

Ahead lies an optimistic future where a diverse group of highly capable trial judges will undertake important challenges in a collegial atmosphere. They will be freed of routine drudgery to deal with a series of new issues while progressing toward a wide variety of opportunities in middle or later life.

These predictions are extensions of present trends and will not come into being by themselves. Either the nation's judges will work together to shape the judicial environment toward their own vision of the future, or all will be carried by events to an uncharted destination.

22

JUDICIAL EDUCATION

When the judicial history of this century is written, one of the significant chapters will deal with the development of programs for the continuing education of judges. As recently as fifteen years ago, the thought of judges going back to school would have seemed ludicrous to most members of the legal profession. Now it is accepted as a matter of course.[1]

Before the advent of schools for judges, the only training available to American judges was on-the-job. When the first small steps of judicial education were taken, the common attitude was that if an attorney did not know how to be a judge when he or she went on the bench, he or she should never have been elected or appointed.[2] That point of view has nearly disappeared.

The first formal judicial educational programs were those of the National Council of Juvenile and Family Court Judges, then called the National Council of Juvenile Court Judges, held in 1937; the course conducted in 1946 by the Committee on the Traffic Court Program of the Section of Judicial Administration of the ABA; and the appellate judges seminar at New York University Law School which was first held in 1956.[3] All three of these programs are alive and well today and are

---

1. Karlen, *Judicial Education,* 52 ABA JOURNAL 1049 (1966).

2. Chief Justice Earl Warren in 1967 at the opening session of the California College of Trial Judges said, "If during my term as Governor of the State of California anyone had suggested that my judicial appointees required education, that person would have been laughed out of the room."

3. For some of the flavor of the Appellate Judges Seminars, see Burger, *School for Judges,* 33 F.R.D. 139 (1963); Leflar, *The Appellate Judges Seminar at New York University,* 9 J. OF LEGAL EDUC. 359 (1957).

the respected ancestors of all formal judicial education in America.

The state judicial organizations in a number of states commenced educational efforts at their annual meetings in the early 1960s. Many of these efforts were aided by the National Conference of State Trial Judges, which had available as seminar leaders a number of distinguished judges throughout the country.

Beginning in 1961, the Joint Committee for the Effective Administration of Justice was organized. Justice Tom C. Clark of the United States Supreme Court was its chairman. Over a period of several years, the committee planned and organized seminars for state trial judges throughout the United States. The seminars, frequently held at the same time as the annual meeting of the judges, divided those judges into relatively small groups with discussion leaders moving from one group to another. During a general meeting, summaries of the discussions would be presented to all those present.

The National Judicial College

This effort by the Joint Committee resulted in the formation of the National College of State Trial Judges. With grant money from the W.K. Kellogg Foundation, the American Bar Association, acting primarily through the Joint Committee and the National Conference of State Trial Judges, created the college.

The first session was held at Boulder, Colorado, in 1964. Ninety-six judges formed that first class. They came from all but three states, and one judge was from the Navajo tribe of Native Americans. The first session was four weeks long. During the four weeks, the student judges lived in dormitories, and ate, attended school, and socialized together.

Most of the student judges had been recently appointed or elected. The faculty was drawn in most cases from judges who had been discussion leaders at the seminars held during the several preceding years.

While the classroom sessions were the core of the program, it soon became apparent that one of the most informative parts of the program was the evening seminars—groups of 10 to 12 of the participating judges led by more experienced faculty advisers (translated by one adviser, Judge Robert Gardner, into "den mothers"). Judges not only reviewed the work already completed and had a preview of what was to come, but they were also able to participate in the discussions to a much greater extent than during the daytime classroom sessions.

One of the textbooks at that first session was *A Handbook for State Trial Judges*, the original predecessor of this book.

After the first session was held at Boulder, Colorado, the following year one session was held at Boulder and another at the University of Nevada–Reno. In subsequent years, the four-week sessions were held at the main site of the college, Reno, but additional sessions were conducted at the University of Pennsylvania and the University of North Carolina.

The length of the basic session at the National College—now called the National Judicial College—is four weeks. However, there are a variety of special and innovative programs of shorter lengths, designed primarily for students who have attended the basic session.

In those early days of judicial education, money was difficult to obtain. But when the Fleischmann Foundation, then headquartered in Reno, offered a grant of $3 million, lingering doubts about whether the University of Nevada would be a good home for the college were dispelled. Now nearly 2,000 student judges attend the National Judicial College each year. Often, several different educational programs are under way at the same time. The annual budget is now $4.2 million.

State Efforts

After the success of the National Judicial College, several of the larger states became interested in having their own programs. For example, in 1966 the California judges attending the National College held a meeting and felt that California, which then had 800 state trial judges, should make some effort to provide such a program for the 80 to 90 new judges appointed or elected in California each year.

One judge, Donald R. Fretz, the spokesperson for the judges in attendance, spoke to the president of the Conference of California Judges. He was asked for an estimate of the cost. The best computations by the group were $40,000 per year. The purpose of this $40,000 was to provide transportation, room and board, books, and all of the expenses of the college, so that those costs would not become an obstacle preventing the judge from attending. Because the Conference of California Judges had an annual income between $10,000 and $12,000, it was obvious that the money could not come from that source.

The conference did grant a small budget, appointed a committee, and made an effort to obtain grant funds. Everyone to whom the committee talked pointed to the Ford Foundation as the most likely source of funds. However, Justice Clark felt that there was no use talking to Ford because he had already tried that when the grant was obtained from the Kellogg Foundation. Despite this, two California judges traveled to New York, spoke to several foundations, and the Ford Foundation made a grant of $135,000 to fund California College for three years.

The notification of receipt of the grant came in December 1966. Those connected with the effort intended to put together the college session for the summer of 1967. Judge Fretz was appointed the first dean. One of the very important questions was where the college should be located. After considering two potential locations in Southern California and two in Northern California, the organizers selected the new Earl Warren Legal Center, connected with the Boalt Hall School of Law at the University of California, Berkeley.

The faculty of the law school was initially apprehensive about a program that would be taught by judges, composed of judges, and for judges. However, once it was established that the college was going to be a hardworking group of judges who would be living in the dormitory, eating meals together, and sharing evening discussions with a relatively minimal amount of time for extracurricular activity, the faculty gave warm acceptance.

The California College progressed from funding by the Ford Foundation to funding by the Law Enforcement Assistance Agency and then to funding by the State of California through the Judicial Council.

The programs of the California College are now only one facet of the California Center for Judicial Education. Indoctrination sessions for new judges, the two-week college session, and graduate programs constitute much of the work of the center.

This is but one example of what has happened in many jurisdictions at the state level. Those connected with the National Judicial College initially had doubts as to whether they should encourage state efforts. Justice Clark and the administration of the National Judicial College were encouraging and helpful.

Some states have persisted in the field of judicial education, while others have ceded the effort to the National Judicial College.

For jurisdictions with many state trial judges and the financing to accomplish it, there is merit in state judicial educational programs. Such programs can be tailored more specifically to the law of the particular jurisdiction. On the other hand, jurisdictions that do not participate in the National Judicial College do not obtain the cross-fertilization of ideas that comes from hearing the methods and procedures from each of the other jurisdictions in the United States. That opportunity to learn what others do that is more efficient, easier, or more economical is just one of the many benefits of the National Judicial College.

Other Programs

Another organization providing education for judges on the national level is the American Academy of Judicial Education.[4] Originally founded by the American Judges Association, it is now an independent not-for-profit corporation. It provides national educational conferences for judges and also contracts to provide state judicial institutes in which the acad-

4. For further information, contact the academy at 510 Park Lane Building, 2028 Eye Street, N.W., Washington, DC 20006.

emy will provide the entire program or will provide faculty for programs devised at the state level. It is particularly active in providing training at the state level for judges before they begin their service on the bench and for other judges within their first year on the bench.

Other programs are provided by the National Council of Juvenile and Family Court Judges, the Institute of Judicial Administration Seminars for Appellate Judges, the American Bar Association Appellate Judges Seminars, the National College of State Trial Judges and American Academy of Judicial Education, and the National Center for State Courts.

Conclusion

Now judicial education is accepted as the norm in the United States. This is due in substantial part to the initial efforts of the joint committee, the continuing efforts of the American Bar Association, the National Conference of State Trial Judges, and the several other organizations within the American Bar Association that form the Judicial Administration Division. The judicial educational effort now is made available not only to appellate judges and state trial judges, but also to judges of every kind.

The unique opportunity of a lawyer in the United States to become a judge makes the education of judges imperative. In Great Britain, judges are chosen only from those who are experienced litigators. In other countries, judges are chosen at the time they are in law school and given special training. They may never practice law except on the bench. In the United States, judges are either appointed, whether by the governor or by the legislature, or are elected. Through either process, it is possible for a person to be an attorney one day and a judge the next.

Happily for the judge newly appointed these days, there are bench books, desk books, indoctrination courses, basic courses, and graduate courses available to help. They not only help the judge, but they help the public as well by enabling the judge to more quickly and with fewer errors handle the mass of litigation that pours into, and in some cases inundates, trial courts.

V

Help and Resources for Judges

APPENDIX A

CODE OF JUDICIAL CONDUCT

Table of Contents

CANON 1
A Judge Should Uphold the Integrity and Independence of the Judiciary

An independent and honorable judiciary is indispensable to justice in our society. A judge should participate in establishing, maintaining, and enforcing, and should himself observe, high standards of conduct so that the integrity and independence of the judiciary may be preserved. The provisions of this Code should be construed and applied to further that objective.

CANON 2
A Judge Should Avoid Impropriety and the Appearance of Impropriety in All His Activities

A. A judge should respect and comply with the law and should conduct himself at all times in a manner that promotes public confidence in the integrity and impartiality of the judiciary.
B. A judge should not allow his family, social, or other relationships to influence his judicial conduct or judgment. He should not lend the prestige of his office to advance the private interests of others; nor should he convey or permit others to convey the impression that they are in a special position to influence him. He should not testify voluntarily as a character witness.

Commentary: Public confidence in the judiciary is eroded by irresponsible or improper conduct by judges. A judge must avoid all impropriety and appearance of impropriety. He must expect to be the subject of constant public scrutiny. He must therefore accept restrictions on his conduct that might be viewed as burdensome by the ordinary citizen and should do so freely and willingly.

It is inappropriate for a judge to hold membership in any organization that practices invidious discrimination on the basis of race, sex, religion or national origin. Membership of a judge in an organization that practices invidious discrimination may give rise to perceptions by minorities, women, and others, that the judge's impartiality is impaired. Whether an organization practices invidious discrimination is often a complex question to which judges should be sensitive. The answer cannot be determined from a mere examination of an organization's current membership rolls but rather depends on the history of the organization's selection of members and other relevant factors. Ultimately, each judge must determine in the judge's own conscience whether an organization of which the judge is a member practices invidious discrimination.[1]

The testimony of a judge as a character witness injects the prestige of his office into the proceeding in which he testifies and may be misunderstood to be an official testimonial. This Canon, however, does not afford him a privilege against testifying in response to an official summons.

CANON 3
A Judge Should Perform the Duties of His Office Impartially and Diligently

The judicial duties of a judge take precedence over all his other activities. His judicial duties include all the duties of his office prescribed by law. In the performance of these duties, the following standards apply:

A. ADJUDICATIVE RESPONSIBILITIES

(1) A judge should be faithful to the law and maintain professional competence in it. He should be unswayed by partisan interests, public clamor, or fear of criticism.

(2) A judge should maintain order and decorum in proceedings before him.

(3) A judge should be patient, dignified, and courteous to litigants, jurors, witnesses, lawyers, and others with whom he deals in his official capacity, and should require similar conduct of lawyers, and of his staff, court officials, and others subject to his direction and control.

Commentary: The duty to hear all proceedings fairly and with patience is not inconsistent with the duty to dispose promptly of the business of the court. Courts can be efficient and business-like while being patient and deliberate.

(4) A judge should accord to every person who is legally interested in a proceeding, or his lawyer, full right to be heard according to law, and, except as authorized by law, neither initiate nor consider *ex parte* or other communications concerning a pending or impending proceeding. A judge, however, may obtain the advice of a disinterested expert

---

1. As amended August 8, 1984, American Bar Association House of Delegates, Chicago, Illinois, per Report 120.

on the law applicable to a proceeding before him if he gives notice to the parties of the person consulted and the substance of the advice, and affords the parties reasonable opportunity to respond.

Commentary: The proscription against communications concerning a proceeding includes communications from lawyers, law teachers, and other persons who are not participants in the proceeding, except to the limited extent permitted. It does not preclude a judge from consulting with other judges, or with court personnel whose function is to aid the judge in carrying out his adjudicative responsibilities.

An appropriate and often desirable procedure for a court to obtain the advice of a disinterested expert on legal issues is to invite him to file a brief *amicus curiae.*

(5) A judge should dispose promptly of the business of the court.

Commentary: Prompt disposition of the court's business requires a judge to devote adequate time to his duties, to be punctual in attending court and expeditious in determining matters under submission, and to insist that court officials, litigants and their lawyers cooperate with him to that end.

(6) A judge should abstain from public comment about a pending or impending proceeding in any court, and should require similar abstention on the part of court personnel subject to his direction and control. This subsection does not prohibit judges from making public statements in the course of their official duties or from explaining for public information the procedures of the court.

Commentary: "Court personnel" does not include the lawyers in a proceeding before a judge. The conduct of lawyers is governed by DR 7-107 of the *Model Code of Professional Responsibility* and by Rule 3.6 of the Model Rules of Professional Conduct.

(7) A judge should prohibit broadcasting, televising, recording or photographing in courtrooms and areas immediately adjacent thereto during sessions of court, or recesses between sessions, except that under rules prescribed by a supervising appellate court or other appropriate authority, a judge may authorize broadcasting, televising, recording and photographing of judicial proceedings in courtrooms and areas immediately adjacent thereto consistent with the right of the parties to a fair trial and subject to express conditions, limitations, and guidelines which allow such coverage in a manner that will be unobtrusive, will not distract the trial participants, and will not otherwise interfere with the administration of justice.[2]

B. ADMINISTRATIVE RESPONSIBILITIES

(1) A judge should diligently discharge his administrative responsibilities, maintain professional competence in judicial administration,

2. As amended August 11, 1982, American Bar Association House of Delegates, San Francisco, per Report 107.

and facilitate the performance of the administrative responsibilities of other judges and court officials.

(2) A judge should require his staff and court officials subject to his direction and control to observe the standards of fidelity and diligence that apply to him.

(3) A judge should take or initiate appropriate disciplinary measures against a judge or lawyer for unprofessional conduct of which the judge may become aware.

Commentary: Disciplinary measures may include reporting a lawyer's misconduct to an appropriate disciplinary body.

(4) A judge should not make unnecessary appointments. He should exercise his power of appointment only on the basis of merit, avoiding nepotism and favoritism. He should not approve compensation of appointees beyond the fair value of services rendered.

Commentary: Appointees of the judge include officials such as referees, commissioners, special masters, receivers, guardians, and personnel such as clerks, secretaries, and bailiffs. Consent by the parties to an appointment or an award of compensation does not relieve the judge of the obligation prescribed by this subsection.

C. DISQUALIFICATION

(1) A judge should disqualify himself in a proceeding in which his impartiality might reasonably be questioned, including but not limited to instances where:

(a) he has a personal bias or prejudice concerning a party, or personal knowledge of disputed evidentiary facts concerning the proceeding;

(b) he served as lawyer in the matter in controversy, or a lawyer with whom he previously practiced law served during such association as a lawyer concerning the matter, or the judge or such lawyer has been a material witness concerning it;

Commentary: A lawyer in a governmental agency does not necessarily have an association with other lawyers employed by that agency within the meaning of this subsection; a judge formerly employed by a governmental agency, however, should disqualify himself in a proceeding if his impartiality might reasonably be questioned because of such association.

(c) he knows that he, individually or as a fiduciary, or his spouse or minor child residing in his household, has a financial interest in the subject matter in controversy or in a party to the proceeding, or any other interest that could be substantially affected by the outcome of the proceeding;

(d) he or his spouse, or a person within the third degree of relationship to either of them, or the spouse of such person:

(i) is a party to the proceeding, or an officer, director, or trustee of a party;

(ii) is acting as a lawyer in the proceeding;

Commentary: The fact that a lawyer in a proceeding is affiliated with a law firm with which a lawyer-relative of the judge is affiliated does not of itself disqualify the judge. Under appropriate circumstances, the fact that "his impartiality might reasonably be questioned" under Canon 3C(1), or that the lawyer-relative is known by the judge to have an interest in the law firm that could be "substantially affected by the outcome of the proceeding" under Canon 3C(1) (d) (iii) may require his disqualification.

(iii) is known by the judge to have an interest that could be substantially affected by the outcome of the proceeding;

(iv) is to the judge's knowledge likely to be a material witness in the proceeding.

(2) A judge should inform himself about his personal and fiduciary financial interests, and make a reasonable effort to inform himself about the personal financial interests of his spouse and minor children residing in his household.

(3) For the purposes of this section:

(a) the degree of relationship is calculated according to the civil law system;

Commentary: According to the civil law system, the third degree of relationship test would, for example, disqualify the judge if his or his spouse's father, grandfather, uncle, brother, or niece's husband were a party or lawyer in the proceeding, but would not disqualify him if a cousin were a party or lawyer in the proceeding.

(b) "fiduciary" includes such relationships as executor, administrator, trustee, and guardian;

(c) "financial interest" means ownership of a legal or equitable interest, however small, or a relationship as director, advisor, or other active participant in the affairs of a party, except that:

(i) ownership in a mutual or common investment fund that holds securities is not a "financial interest" in such securities unless the judge participates in the management of the fund;

(ii) an office in an educational, religious, charitable, fraternal, or civic organization is not a "financial interest" in securities held by the organization;

(iii) the proprietary interest of a policy holder in a mutual insurance company, of a depositor in a mutual savings association, or a similar proprietary interest, is a "financial interest" in the organization only if the outcome of the proceeding could substantially affect the value of the interest;

(iv) ownership of government securities is a "financial interest" in the issuer only if the outcome of the proceeding could substantially affect the value of the securities.

D. REMITTAL OF DISQUALIFICATION

A judge disqualified by the terms of Canon 3C(1) (c) or Canon 3C(1) (d) may, instead of withdrawing from the proceeding, disclose on the record the basis of his disqualification. If, based on such disclosure, the parties and lawyers, independently of the judge's participation, all agree in writing that the judge's relationship is immaterial or that his financial interest is insubstantial, the judge is no longer disqualified, and may participate in the proceeding. The agreement, signed by all parties and lawyers, shall be incorporated in the record of the proceeding.

Commentary: This procedure is designed to minimize the chance that a party or lawyer will feel coerced into an agreement. When a party is not immediately available, the judge without violating this section may proceed on the written assurance of the lawyer that his party's consent will be subsequently filed.

CANON 4
A Judge May Engage in Activities to Improve the Law, the Legal System, and the Administration of Justice

A judge, subject to the proper performance of his judicial duties, may engage in the following quasi-judicial activities, if in doing so he does not cast doubt on his capacity to decide impartially any issue that may come before him.

A. He may speak, write, lecture, teach, and participate in other activities concerning the law, the legal system, and the administration of justice.

B. He may appear at a public hearing before an executive or legislative body or official on matters concerning the law, the legal system, and the administration of justice, and he may otherwise consult with an executive or legislative body or official, but only on matters concerning the administration of justice.

C. He may serve as a member, officer, or director of an organization or governmental agency devoted to the improvement of the law, the legal system, or the administration of justice. He may assist such an organization in raising funds and may participate in their management and investment, but should not personally participate in public fund-raising activities. He may make recommendations to public and private fund-granting agencies on projects and programs concerning the law, the legal system, and the administration of justice.

Commentary: As a judicial officer and person specially learned in the law, a judge is in a unique position to contribute to the improvement of the law, the legal system, and the administration of justice, including revision of substantive and procedural law and improvement of criminal and juvenile justice. To the extent that his time permits, he is encouraged to do so, either independently or through a bar association, judicial conference, or other organization dedicated to the improvement of the law.

Extra-judicial activities are governed by Canon 5.

CANON 5
A Judge Should Regulate His Extra-Judicial Activities to Minimize the Risk of Conflict with His Judicial Duties

A. AVOCATIONAL ACTIVITIES

A judge may write, lecture, teach, and speak on non-legal subjects, and engage in the arts, sports, and other social and recreational activities, if such avocational activities do not detract from the dignity of his office or interfere with the performance of his judicial duties.

Commentary: Complete separation of a judge from extra-judicial activities is neither possible nor wise; he should not become isolated from the society in which he lives.

B. CIVIC AND CHARITABLE ACTIVITIES

A judge may participate in civic and charitable activities that do not reflect adversely upon his impartiality or interfere with the performance of his judicial duties. A judge may serve as an officer, director, trustee, or non-legal advisor of an educational, religious, charitable, fraternal, or civic organization not conducted for the economic or political advantage of its members, subject to the following limitations:

(1) A judge should not serve if it is likely that the organization will be engaged in proceedings that would ordinarily come before him or will be regularly engaged in adversary proceedings in any court.

Commentary: The changing nature of some organizations and of their relationship to the law makes it necessary for a judge regularly to reexamine the activities of each organization with which he is affiliated to determine if it is proper for him to continue his relationship with it. For example, in many jurisdictions charitable hospitals are now more frequently in court than in the past. Similarly, the boards of some legal aid organizations now make policy decisions that may have political significance or imply commitment to causes that may come before the courts for adjudication.

(2) A judge should not solicit funds for any educational, religious, charitable, fraternal, or civic organization, or use or permit the use of the prestige of his office for that purpose, but he may be listed as an officer, director, or trustee of such an organization. He should not be a speaker or the guest of honor at an organization's fund-raising events, but he may attend such events.

(3) A judge should not give investment advice to such an organization, but he may serve on its board of directors or trustees even though it has the responsibility for approving investment decisions.

Commentary: A judge's participation in an organization devoted to quasi-judicial activities is governed by Canon 4.

C. FINANCIAL ACTIVITIES

(1) A judge should refrain from financial and business dealings that tend to reflect adversely on his impartiality, interfere with the proper performance of his judicial duties, exploit his judicial position, or involve him in frequent transactions with lawyers or persons likely to come before the court on which he serves.

*(2) Subject to the requirements of subsection (1), a judge may hold and manage investments, including real estate, and engage in other remunerative activity, but should not serve as an officer, director, manager, advisor, or employee of any business.

Commentary: The Effective Date of Compliance provision of this Code qualifies this subsection with regard to a judge engaged in a family business at the time this Code becomes effective.

Canon 5 may cause temporary hardship in jurisdictions where judicial salaries are inadequate and judges are presently supplementing their income through commercial activities. The remedy, however, is to secure adequate judicial salaries.

*[Canon 5C(2) sets the minimum standard to which a full-time judge should adhere. Jurisdictions that do not provide adequate judicial salaries but are willing to allow full-time judges to supplement their incomes through commercial activities may adopt the following substitute until such time as adequate salaries are provided:

(2) Subject to the requirement of subsection (1), a judge may hold and manage investments, including real estate, and engage in other remunerative activity including the operation of a business.

Jurisdictions adopting the foregoing substitute may also wish to prohibit a judge from engaging in certain types of businesses such as that of banks, public utilities, insurance companies, and other businesses affected with a public interest.]

(3) A judge should manage his investments and other financial

interests to minimize the number of cases in which he is disqualified. As soon as he can do so without serious financial detriment, he should divest himself of investments and other financial interests that might require frequent disqualification.

(4) Neither a judge nor a member of his family residing in his household should accept a gift, bequest, favor, or loan from anyone except as follows:

(a) a judge may accept a gift incident to public testimonial to him; books supplied by publishers on a complimentary basis for official use; or an invitation to the judge and his spouse to attend a bar-related function or activity devoted to the improvement of the law, the legal system, or the administration of justice;

(b) a judge or a member of his family residing in his household may accept ordinary social hospitality; a gift, bequest, favor, or loan from a relative; a wedding or engagement gift; a loan from a lending institution in its regular course of business on the same terms generally available to persons who are not judges; or a scholarship or fellowship awarded on the same terms applied to other applicants;

(c) a judge or a member of his family residing in his household may accept any other gift, bequest, favor, or loan only if the donor is not a party or other person whose interests have come or are likely to come before him, and, if its value exceeds $100, the judge reports it in the same manner as he reports compensation in Canon 6C.

Commentary: This subsection does not apply to contributions to a judge's campaign for judicial office, a matter governed by Canon 7.

(5) For the purposes of this section "member of his family residing in his household" means any relative of a judge by blood or marriage, or a person treated by a judge as a member of his family, who resides in his household.

(6) A judge is not required by this Code to disclose his income, debts, or investments, except as provided in this Canon and Canons 3 and 6.

Commentary: Canon 3 requires a judge to disqualify himself in any proceeding in which he has a financial interest, however small; Canon 5 requires a judge to refrain from engaging in business and from financial activities that might interfere with the impartial performance of his judicial duties; Canon 6 requires him to report all compensation he receives for activities outside his judicial office. A judge has the rights of an ordinary citizen, including the right to privacy of his financial affairs, except to the extent that limitations thereon are required to safeguard the proper performance of his duties. Owning and receiving income from investments do not as such affect the performance of a judge's duties.

(7) Information acquired by a judge in his judicial capacity should not be used or disclosed by him in financial dealings or for any other purpose not related to his judicial duties.

D. FIDUCIARY ACTIVITIES

A judge should not serve as the executor, administrator, trustee, guardian, or other fiduciary, except for the estate, trust, or person of a member of his family, and then only if such service will not interfere with the proper performance of his judicial duties. "Member of his family" includes a spouse, child, grandchild, parent, grandparent, or other relative or person with whom the judge maintains a close familial relationship. As a family fiduciary a judge is subject to the following restrictions:

(1) He should not serve if it is likely that as a fiduciary he will be engaged in proceedings that would ordinarily come before him, or if the estate, trust, or ward becomes involved in adversary proceedings in the court on which he serves or one under its appellate jurisdiction.

Commentary: The Effective Date of Compliance provision of this Code qualifies this subsection with regard to a judge who is an executor, administrator, trustee, or other fiduciary at the time this Code becomes effective.

(2) While acting as a fiduciary a judge is subject to the same restrictions on financial activities that apply to him in his personal capacity.

Commentary: A judge's obligation under this Canon and his obligation as a fiduciary may come into conflict. For example, a judge should resign as trustee if it would result in detriment to the trust to divest it of holdings whose retention would place the judge in violation of Canon 5C(3).

E. ARBITRATION

A judge should not act as an arbitrator or mediator.

F. PRACTICE OF LAW

A judge should not practice law.

G. EXTRA-JUDICIAL APPOINTMENTS

A judge should not accept appointment to a governmental committee, commission, or other position that is concerned with issues of fact or policy on matters other than the improvement of the law, the legal system, or the administration of justice. A judge, however, may represent his country, state, or locality on ceremonial occasions or in connection with historical, educational, and cultural activities.

Commentary: Valuable services have been rendered in the past to the states and the nation by judges appointed by the executive to undertake important extra-judicial assignments. The appropriateness of conferring these assignments on judges must be reassessed, however, in light of the demands on judicial manpower created by today's crowded dockets and the need to protect the courts from involvement in extra-judicial matters that may prove to be controversial. Judges should not be expected or permitted to accept governmental appointments that could interfere with the effectiveness and independence of the judiciary.

CANON 6
A Judge Should Regularly File Reports of Compensation Received for Quasi-Judicial and Extra-Judicial Activities

A judge may receive compensation and reimbursement of expenses for the quasi-judicial and extra-judicial activities permitted by this Code, if the source of such payments does not give the appearance of influencing the judge in his judicial duties or otherwise give the appearance of impropriety, subject to the following restrictions:

A. COMPENSATION

Compensation should not exceed a reasonable amount nor should it exceed what a person who is not a judge would receive for the same activity.

B. EXPENSE REIMBURSEMENT

Expense reimbursement should be limited to the actual cost of travel, food, and lodging reasonably incurred by the judge and, where appropriate to the occasion, by his spouse. Any payment in excess of such an amount is compensation.

C. PUBLIC REPORTS

A judge should report the date, place, and nature of any activity for which he received compensation, and the name of the payor and the amount of compensation so received. Compensation or income of a spouse attributed to the judge by operation of a community property law is not extra-judicial compensation to the judge. His report should be made at least annually and should be filed as a public document in the office of the clerk of the court on which he serves or other office designated by rule of court.

CANON 7
A Judge Should Refrain from Political Activity Inappropriate to His Judicial Office

A. Political Conduct in General

(1) A judge or a candidate for election to judicial office should not:

(a) act as a leader or hold any office in a political organization;

(b) make speeches for a political organization or candidate or publicly endorse a candidate for public office;

Commentary: A candidate does not publicly endorse another candidate for public office by having his name on the same ticket.

(c) solicit funds for or pay an assessment or make a contribution to a political organization or candidate, attend political gatherings, or purchase tickets for political party dinners, or other functions, except as authorized in subsection A(2).

(2) A judge holding an office filled by public election between competing candidates, or a candidate for such office, may, only insofar as permitted by law, attend political gatherings, speak to such gatherings on his own behalf when he is a candidate for election or re-election, identify himself as a member of a political party, and contribute to a political party or organization.

(3) A judge should resign his office when he becomes a candidate either in a party primary or in a general election for a non-judicial office, except that he may continue to hold his judicial office while being a candidate for election to or serving as a delegate in a state constitutional convention, if he is otherwise permitted by law to do so.

(4) A judge should not engage in any other political activity except on behalf of measures to improve the law, the legal system, or the administration of justice.

B. Campaign Conduct

(1) A candidate, including an incumbent judge, for a judicial office that is filled either by public election between competing candidates or on the basis of a merit system election:

(a) should maintain the dignity appropriate to judicial office, and should encourage members of his family to adhere to the same standards of political conduct that apply to him;

(b) should prohibit public officials or employees subject to his direction or control from doing for him what he is prohibited from doing under this Canon; and except to the extent authorized under subsection B(2) or B(3), he should not allow any other person to do for him what he is prohibited from doing under this Canon;

(c) should not make pledges or promises of conduct in office other than the faithful and impartial performance of the duties of the office; announce his views on disputed legal or political issues; or misrepresent his identity, qualifications, present position, or other fact.

(2) A candidate, including an incumbent judge, for a judicial office that is filled by public election between competing candidates should not himself solicit or accept campaign funds, or solicit publicly stated support, but he may establish committees of responsible persons to secure and manage the expenditure of funds for his campaign and to obtain public statements of support for his candidacy. Such committees are not prohibited from soliciting campaign contributions and public support from lawyers. A candidate's committees may solicit funds for his campaign no earlier than [90] days before a primary election and no later than [90] days after the last election in which he participates during the election year. A candidate should not use or permit the use of campaign contributions for the private benefit of himself or members of his family.

Commentary: Unless the candidate is required by law to file a list of his campaign contributors, their names should not be revealed to the candidate.

[Each jurisdiction adopting this Code should prescribe a time limit on soliciting campaign funds that is appropriate to the elective process therein.]

(3) An incumbent judge who is a candidate for retention in or re-election to office without a competing candidate, and whose candidacy has drawn active opposition, may campaign in response thereto and may obtain publicly stated support and campaign funds in the manner provided in subsection B(2).

Compliance with the Code of Judicial Conduct

Anyone, whether or not a lawyer, who is an officer of a judicial system performing judicial functions, including an officer such as a referee in bankruptcy, special master, court commissioner, or magistrate, is a judge for the purpose of this Code. All judges should comply with this Code except as provided below.

A. PART-TIME JUDGE

A part-time judge is a judge who serves on a continuing or periodic basis, but is permitted by law to devote time to some other profession or occupation and whose compensation for that reason is less than that of a full-time judge. A part-time judge:

(1) is not required to comply with Canon 5C(2), D, E, F, and G, and Canon 6C;

(2) should not practice law in the court on which he serves or in any court subject to the appellate jurisdiction of the court on which he serves, or act as a lawyer in a proceeding in which he has served as a judge or in any other proceeding related thereto.

B. JUDGE PRO TEMPORE

A judge *pro tempore* is a person who is appointed to act temporarily as a judge.

(1) While acting as such, a judge *pro tempore* is not required to comply with Canon 5C(2), (3), D, E, F, and G, and Canon 6C.

(2) A person who has been a judge *pro tempore* should not act as a lawyer in a proceeding in which he has served as a judge or in any other proceeding related thereto.

C. RETIRED JUDGE

A retired judge who receives the same compensation as a full-time judge on the court from which he retired and is eligible for recall to judicial service should comply with all the provisions of this Code except Canon 5G, but he should refrain from judicial service during the period of an extra-judicial appointment not sanctioned by Canon 5G. All other retired judges eligible for recall to judicial service should comply with the provisions of this Code governing part-time judges.

Effective Date of Compliance

A person to whom this Code becomes applicable should arrange his affairs as soon as reasonably possible to comply with it. If, however, the demands on his time and the possibility of conflicts of interest are not substantial, a person who holds judicial office on the date this Code becomes effective may:

(a) continue to act as an officer, director, or non-legal advisor of a family business;

(b) continue to act as an executor, administrator, trustee, or other fiduciary for the estate or person of one who is not a member of his family.

APPENDIX B

NATIONAL COURT ORGANIZATIONS

Administrative Office of the U.S. Courts L. Ralph Mecham, Director Washington, DC 20544	202/633-6097
American Academy of Judicial Education Douglas Lanford, Executive Director 510 Park Lane Building 2028 Eye Street, N.W. Washington, DC 20006	202/775-0083
American Bar Association 750 N. Lake Shore Drive Chicago, IL 60611	312/988-5000
Division for Judicial Services Wantland L. Sandel, Jr., Director	312/988-5685
Judicial Administration Division Ernest S. Zavodnyik, Staff Director	312/988-5688
Secretariat for:	*Staff Director*
Appellate Judges Conference	Mary Ellen Donaghy
National Conference of Administrative Law Judges	Diane Livingston
National Conference of Federal Trial Judges	Ernest S. Zavodnyik
National Conference of Special Court Judges	Myra S. Moglowsky
National Conference of State Trial Judges	Stephen Goldspiel
JAD Lawyers Conference	Stephen Goldspiel

Lawyers Conference Task Force on Reduction of Litigation Cost and Delay — Douglas K. Somerlot

Committee on Traffic Court Program — Stephen Goldspiel

National Judicial College — 702/784-6747
University of Nevada
Reno, NV 89557

American Judicature Society — 312/558-6900
Frances K. Zemans, Executive Vice President
25 E. Washington
Suite 1600
Chicago, IL 60602

Federal Court Clerks Association — 202/535-3515
Mr. James F. Davey, Clerk of Court
U.S. District Court for D.C.
Third & Constitution Avenue, N.W.
Washington, DC 20001

Federal Judicial Center — 202/633-6311
A. Leo Levin, Director
1510 H Street, N.W.
Washington, DC 20005

Division for Inter-Judicial Affairs & Information Services — 202/633-6359
Alice L. O'Donnell, Director

Institute of Judicial Administration — 212/598-7721
Margaret L. Shaw, Executive Director
One Washington Square Village
New York, NY 10012-1699

Judicial Conference of the United States — 202/479-3000
Chief Justice William H. Rehnquist, Chairman
U.S. Supreme Court
Washington, DC 20543

L. Ralph Mecham, Secretary — 202/633-6097

National Association of Administrative Law Judges — 212/488-7391
David Agatstein, Director
Two World Trade Center, Room 52C12
New York, NY 10047

National Association of Judicial Educators 612/296-6508
William P. Westphal, Jr., Director
40 N. Milton Street
St. Paul, MN 20036

National Center for State Courts 804/253-2000
Edward B. McConnell, Executive Director
300 Newport Avenue
Williamsburg, VA 23185-8798

Secretariat for:	*Liaison*
American Judges Association	Shelley Rockwell
Conference of Chief Justices	Brenda Williams
Conference of State Court Administrators	Marilyn Roberts
Coordinating Council of National Court Organizations	Florence Leonard
National Association for Court Management	Linda Perkins
National Association of Women Judges	Susan Kiletz
National College of Probate Judges	Mary Hogan
National Conference of Appellate Court Clerks	Shelley Rockwell
National Council of Judicial Planning	Mary Hogan

Center for Jury Studies of the NCSC 703/841-0200
G. Thomas Munsterman, Executive Director
Washington Project Office
4001 N. 9th Street, Suite 218
Arlington, VA 22203

Institute for Court Management of the NCSC 303/293-3063
Harvey E. Solomon, Executive Director
1331 Seventeenth Street, Suite 402
Denver, CO 80202

National Clearinghouse for Criminal Justice Planning and Architecture 217/333-0312
James Brown, Director
505 E. Green Street, Suite 200
Champaign, IL 61820

National Conference of Metropolitan Courts 313/259-7777
Hon. Joseph A. Sullivan, Executive Director
Bodman, Longley & Dahling
100 Renaissance Center, 34th Floor
Detroit, MI 48243

National Conference of State Criminal Justice Planning Administrators 202/347-4900
R. Thomas Parket, Executive Director
1909 K Street, N.W., Suite 204
Washington, DC 20006

National Criminal Justice Reference Service 301/251-5500
Harvey Byrd, Director
Box 6000
Rockville, MD 20850

National Institute for Dispute Resolution 202/466-4764
Madeleine Crohn, President
901 L Street, N.W., Suite 600
Washington, DC 20036

National Institute of Justice 202/724-2942
James K. Stewart, Director
633 Indiana Avenue, N.W.
Washington, DC 20530

National Shorthand Reporters Association 703/281-4677
Charles G. Hagee, Executive Director
118 Park Street, S.E.
Vienna, VA 22180

Rand Corporation 213/393-0411
Gustave H. Shubert, Director
1700 Main Street
P.O. Box 2138
Santa Monica, CA 90406-2138

State Justice Institute 703/684-6100
David I. Tevelin, Executive Director
120 S. Fairfax Street
Alexandria, VA 22314

APPENDIX C

STANDING COMMITTEE ON ETHICS AND PROFESSIONAL RESPONSIBILITY

Composition and Jurisdiction

The Standing Committee on Ethics and Professional Responsibility, which consists of eight members, shall:

(1) by the concurrence of a majority of its members, express its opinion on proper professional or judicial conduct, either on its own initiative or when requested to do so by a member of the bar or by an officer or a committee of a state or local bar association, except that an opinion may not be issued on a question that is pending before a court;

(2) periodically publish its issued opinions to the legal profession in summary or complete form and, on request, provide copies of opinions to members of the bar;

(3) on request, advise or otherwise help state or local bar associations in their activities relating to the interpretation of the Model Code of Professional Responsibility and the Code of Judicial Conduct;

(4) recommend appropriate amendments to or clarifications of the Model Code of Professional Responsibility or the Code of Judicial Conduct, if it considers them advisable; and

(5) adopt such rules as it considers appropriate relating to the procedures to be used in expressing opinions, effective when approved by the Board of Governors.

Rules of Procedure

1. The Committee may express its opinion on proper professional and judicial conduct. The Model Rules of Professional Conduct, and the Code of Judicial Conduct, as those Codes may be amended or superseded, contain the standards to be applied. For as long as a significant number

of jurisdictions continue to base their professional standards on the predecessor Model Code of Professional Responsibility, the Committee will continue to refer to the Model Code in its opinions.

2. The Committee may issue an opinion on its own initiative or upon a request from a member of the bar or the judiciary individually or on behalf of a professional organization or a court.

3. The Committee may issue opinions of two kinds: Formal Opinions and Informal Opinions. Formal Opinions are those upon subjects determined by the Committee to be of widespread interest or unusual importance. Other opinions are Informal Opinions. The Committee shall assign to each opinion a non-duplicative identifying number, with distinction between Formal Opinions and Informal Opinions.

4. The Committee will not usually issue an opinion on a question that is pending before a court. The Committee is not obliged to issue an opinion as to completed conduct or as to the proposed conduct of someone other than the person requesting the opinion, but may do so upon request of a professional organization or a court having jurisdiction over the conduct which is the subject of the request. The Committee will not issue an opinion on a question of law.

5. As a condition of issuing an opinion, the Committee may require that the request be submitted in writing, with information sufficiently specific to enable adequate consideration.

6. The Committee shall not issue an opinion with respect to judicial conduct until the proposed opinion has been submitted to the Judges' Advisory Committee and the Committee has considered any objection or comment from the Judges' Advisory Committee and any member of it. The Committee may assume that the Judges' Advisory Committee has no objection or comment if none is received by the Committee within 30 days after the submission.

7. If the Committee decides not to issue a requested opinion, the requestor shall be promptly notified.

8. The Committee shall issue an opinion only with the concurrence of five members at a meeting or with the concurrence of six members other than at a meeting. If a member specifically so requests, the Committee shall not issue an opinion unless approved at a meeting. A member may express a dissent or a special concurrence, which shall be appended to an opinion if the member specifically so directs.

9. The chair may assign to one or more members the responsibility of preparing a proposed opinion for consideration and action by the Committee. The Committee shall issue a requested opinion without undue delay after sufficient information is received.

10. A Formal Opinion overrules an earlier Formal Opinion or Informal Opinion to the extent of conflict. An Informal Opinion overrules

an earlier Informal Opinion to the extent of conflict but does not overrule an earlier Formal Opinion.

11. Opinions of the Committee issued before the effective dates of the Model Rules of Professional Conduct, the predecessor Model Code of Professional Responsibility and of the Code of Judicial Conduct continue in effect to the extent not inconsistent with those standards and not overruled by a later opinion.

12. The Committee shall make opinions available for publication in the American Bar Association Journal, with Formal Opinions for publication in full and with Informal Opinions for publication in summary. The Committee shall cause Formal Opinions and Informal Opinions to be published in loose-leaf form. Before publication of opinions, the Committee shall remove information identifying the person who requested or was the subject of the opinion.

13. The Committee may through its staff arrange to provide informal responses to ethics inquiries the answers to which are substantially governed by applicable ethical codes and existing written opinions. The staff shall maintain a log of such inquiries which shall periodically be reviewed by the Committee.

14. Information contained in Committee files relating to requests for opinions which would disclose the identity of the inquirer or the person whose conduct is the subject of the opinion will not voluntarily be disclosed by the Association without the consent of the affected persons.